Religion and Healing in Native America

Recent Titles in
Religion, Health, and Healing

Among the Healers: Stories of Spiritual and Ritual Healing around the World
Edith Turner

Kabbalah and the Spiritual Quest: The Kabbalah Centre in America
Jody Myers

Religion and Healing in
Native America

Pathways for Renewal

✠

Edited by Suzanne J. Crawford O'Brien

Foreword by Inés Talamantez

RELIGION, HEALTH, AND HEALING
Susan Starr Sered and Linda L. Barnes, Series Editors

Westport, Connecticut
London

Library of Congress Cataloging-in-Publication Data

Religion and healing in Native America : pathways for renewal /
Suzanne J. Crawford O'Brien, editor.
    p. cm. — (Religion, health, and healing, ISSN 1556–262X)
  Includes bibliographical references and index.
  ISBN-13: 978–0–275–99013–8 (alk. paper)
  1. Indians of North America—Medicine. 2. Indians of North America—
Religion.   3. Indians of North America—Health and hygiene.
4. Traditional medicine—United States   I. Crawford, Suzanne J.
  E98.M4.R45   2008
  615.8'5208997—dc22   2008002460

British Library Cataloguing in Publication Data is available.

Library of Congress Catalog Card Number: 2008002460
ISBN: 978–0–275–99013–8
ISSN: 1556–262X

First published in 2008

Praeger Publishers, 88 Post Road West, Westport, CT 06881
An imprint of Greenwood Publishing Group, Inc.
www.praeger.com

Printed in the United States of America

The paper used in this book complies with the
Permanent Paper Standard issued by the National
Information Standards Organization (Z39.48–1984).

10 9 8 7 6 5 4 3 2 1

Contents

Series Foreword

The Religion, Health, and Healing series brings together authors from a variety of academic disciplines and cultural settings in order to foster understandings of the ways in which religious traditions, concepts, and practices frame health and healing experiences in diverse historical and social contexts. The present volume provides insight into contemporary approaches to healing in Native American communities around the United States.

In this volume, as in other books in this series, we see that the word "healing" in and of itself is multi-dimensional and multi-functional, especially in religious settings. It can mean the direct, unequivocal and scientifically measurable cure of physical illnesses. It can mean the alleviation of pain or other symptoms. It can also mean coping, coming to terms with, or learning to live with that which one cannot change (including physical illness and emotional trauma). Healing can mean integration and connection among all the elements of one's being, reestablishment of self-worth, connection with one's tradition, or personal empowerment. It can also involve the pursuit of justice and equity, as a process of resisting the forces that generate social ills. Healing can be about repairing one's relationships with friends, relations, ancestors, the community, the world, the Earth, and/or God. It can refer to developing a sense of well-being or wholeness, whether emotional, social, spiritual, physical, or in relation to other aspects of being that are valued by a particular group. Healing can be about purification, repenting from sin, the cleaning up of one's negative karma, entry into a path of "purer," abstinent, or more moral daily living, eternal salvation, or submission to God's will.

Perhaps the most common theme in religious accounts of healing is the enactment of change, whether understood as restoration to an earlier state or as transformation to a new one.[1] The transformation that comes about in the healing process implies movement from one, less desirable state, to another, more desirable state. Thus, the study of religion and healing includes looking at how individuals, communities, and religious traditions diagnose and interpret causes of illness and misfortune, as well as practices aimed at addressing affliction both ideally and pragmatically. In the case of Native American communities this theme is developed both in relationship to the individual in terms of healing from physical and spiritual illness, and more broadly to healing the world of Native communities in relation to larger social challenges.

We hope that through facilitating the publication of studies of diverse healers, healing communities, and healing practices we will offer readers tools to uncover both the common and the uncommon, the traditional and the innovative, and the individual and the communal ways in which Americans engage with, find meaning in, and seek to embrace, transcend, or overcome affliction and suffering.

Susan Starr Sered and Linda L. Barnes

NOTE

1. For more on this, see Linda Barnes and Susan Sered, eds., *Religion and Healing in America* (New York: Oxford University Press, 2005).

Foreword

Inés Talamantez

In America today, Native and non-Native communities alike face enormous challenges: global warming, the breakdown of communities and families, and the trauma of war. These crises reveal the deep need for healing, for individuals, for communities, and for the ecosystems within which we live. This timely book challenges this contemporary ethos marked by the imbalance of human society from the natural world, and breathes new life into a moral philosophy of being, a way of incorporating indigenous wisdom in the creation of a new paradigm. An Apache example of healing, which goes back to mythological times, serves as an exemplar of what this book works to achieve.

It was Isánaklèsh, the Apache female deity, who instructed her son, Child of the Water, on healing and the use of medicine, and how to use the many herbs and minerals that will cure diseases. From her teachings contemporary Apache people have been taught how to work alongside the natural world. For instance, if a plant's root is used, then there are explicit instructions on what to do with the other parts of the plant. They are not to be left behind in a careless way. Even today, the rocks used to crush herbs and the various minerals are to be used in a sacred manner, so that nothing is wasted.

Isánaklèsh went on to speak of the herbs, trees, and mineral substances vital to the people's well-being, all of the things necessary to sustain life and cure humankind so that people could live in a peaceful, harmonious way. She taught the people that cattail pollen, known as the pollen of the earth, is the symbol for the generative life-giving powers of the earth as they go out to the four directions through chants and prayers. If anything is mixed with pollen, then Isánaklèsh will give it the power to heal. Herbal medicines, she instructed, will cure if they are breathed four times in a ceremonial way. In Apache tradition, things of a ritual nature are usually repeated four times and in a prescribed directional manner, starting with the place where the sun rises in the east, then recognizing the way the sun moves over the southern sky, then where it sets in the west, and finally the direction in which it does not appear at all (the north) until it again rises in the east.

To *live in the pollen way* means to live in balance and harmony. This symmetry is learned by observing the balance and harmony that we see in nature. Nature teaches in the most perfect way what it is that we as people need to learn to live in an aesthetic, sustainable manner. In the creation myth, Isánaklèsh gave to the Mescaleros the ceremonies for counteracting the diseases and imbalances that provoke disharmony. Through continued use of these ceremonial practices, the women and men of the tribe make it clear that they still see Isánaklèsh as the model for appropriate behavior. This Apache example provides an Indigenous American paradigm, one that is reflected in the essays of this book: healing through living in balance. The traditions explored in this book contribute to this indigenous paradigm, teaching ways of living appropriately both in and with our ecosystem that can lead to good health.

Preface

Suzanne J. Crawford O'Brien

In the summer of 2001, I stood on the shore of Panhandle Lake in southwest Washington. I was at a three-day intertribal women and girls' gathering, the result of months of planning by the women of five local Native communities, who had come together to promote women's health and wellness. I came as a volunteer, having been told that this was a gathering where Native women and girls could explore their culture, affirm community and family ties, and experience traditional approaches to health and wellness. And indeed, as I walked through the camp that day, I saw a sweat lodge, women teaching classes in basketry and beadwork, a talking circle, and later, an elder teaching about traditional plants and herbal remedies. But I had also paused when I saw a tipi (a structure not indigenous to the Coastal Northwest), and later, during the sweat lodge itself, I had noticed that it followed the northern Plains style of ceremony—including the use of Lakota language—a form relatively new to the region. This I could easily rationalize: Since the 1970s northern Plains styles of ritual, ceremony, and prayer have become nationally prolific, part of a pan-Indian identity and political sensibility. And, indeed, given the wide migration of Native people throughout the country, it was not surprising that northern Plains women had moved or married into these communities bringing their traditions with them. But I had found it harder to rationalize when, later, I learned that the tipi would provide space for a Reiki practitioner and massage therapist, or when I strolled down to the lake to find a Tai Q'i class in progress. This had me stumped. Was this "traditional"? What did "traditional" mean for these Native Northwest women and girls, and how did they understand what it meant to be healthy?

It is my hope that this book contributes to many ongoing conversations surrounding these very questions. How are indigenous communities defining what it means to be well? How are they drawing upon traditional practices to create culturally congruent modes of health care? The chapters that follow have rich possibilities for reflection, offering new perspectives on the ways in which religion and culture contribute to individual and collective healing. They offer comparative examples of the intersection of religion and healing for scholars studying religious approaches to healing in other traditions and cultures. These chapters also offer valuable insights for people working on-the-ground with Native tribes and communities, seeking to develop programs that are culturally relevant and effective at addressing indigenous concerns.

I extend my deep gratitude to the authors who contributed to this volume, offering their diverse, insightful, and often very personal experiences with these traditions. Their essays are a great gift, and I thank them. Thanks as well to the series editors, Linda Barnes and Susan Sered, the editorial staff at Praeger, the anonymous external reviewers, and my colleagues at Pacific Lutheran University who offered valuable critique and insight to these pieces. I also thank my former graduate advisor Inés Talamantez, who graciously agreed to write a forward for this project. Talamantez's own interest in religion and healing initially inspired my own. I am privileged to consider her a friend and mentor. Great thanks are due to my parents Timothy and Jeanne Crawford for their ongoing love, support, and encouragement. This project could not have been completed without my sounding board and "third half," Tanya Marcovna Barnett, nor without the patience, strength and endless optimism of my husband and dearest friend, Michael Timothy O'Brien, whose faith and presence continues to make these impossible tasks somehow possible.

CHAPTER I

———— ✠ ————

Introduction

Suzanne J. Crawford O'Brien

The chapters that follow take a nuanced look at religion and healing in Native America, emphasizing the lived experience of indigenous religious practices. This book works to challenge stereotypical images of Native people that would leave them locked in nineteenth-century daguerreotypes. Rather, the case studies in this volume introduce readers to a variety of practices that are steeped in indigenous traditions and philosophies even as they respond and adapt to the present context. In contrast to previous studies, these are not descriptions of traditions isolated from their historical, cultural, and so-cial contexts, but are located within the lives of the individuals and com-munities from which they come. The stories told here draw from first-hand experiences, ethnographic accounts, narratives, and current scholarship on Native practices, to present a richly textured portrait of the intersection of tradition, cultural renewal, ceremony, and healing. These portraits range from discussions of precolonial healing traditions to reflections on contemporary indigenous approaches that exist in a complex mélange with other cultural traditions—both Native and non-Native.

At the heart of all the chapters contained herein, there is a concern for the ways in which diverse Native communities understand what it means to be healthy, to achieve wellness through spirituality and traditional culture, and how to make sense of and engage with the realities of living in a neoco-lonial society. The chapters here also share a commitment to participatory knowledge—knowledge that goes beyond analytical knowledge—that is supposedly detached from experience. They also share a (at times unspoken) commitment to the importance of embodied, lived experience as a means of knowing and healing.

HISTORICAL POSITIONING

Within contemporary Native America, the current moment is particularly important for learning how Native nations can heal the bodies, minds, and spirits of their communities. Since the 1970s, the federal government has transformed its relationship with American Indians, and for the first time in centuries Native communities have increasing access to sovereignty, self-determination, and control over local health care. This is a dramatic shift. Since its founding, the U.S. government had sought to curtail Native spiritual and medical practices through legal suppression, missionaries, and boarding schools. These efforts became more systematic with the establishment of reservations in the mid to late nineteenth century, where government officials and missionaries would work to limit Native approaches to health and well-ness, seeing them as obstacles to assimilation. As long as their traditional healers remained, it was argued, Native people would resist conversion to Christianity and full assimilation into white society.

But today after more than two hundred years of efforts to suppress and eradicate indigenous cultures, spirituality, languages, and medicine, govern-mental policies have shifted, granting Native nations the rights (and some-times the resources) to govern themselves, to organize their communities, and to address their own needs. President Richard Nixon's 1970 Indian Policy Statement, wherein he called for Native self-determination and tribal control of federal programs, was one of the first marks of this policy shift.[1] In 1975, the Indian Self-Determination and Education Assistance Act followed, di-recting "the BIA [Bureau of Indian Affairs] and IHS [Indian Health Service] to turn over to the tribes management of most of the services administered by these agencies upon formal request by the various tribes."[2] Slowly at first, but increasingly within recent years, tribal governments have moved to take control of social and medical services. As Everett Rhoades put it, "The move-ment toward tribal management has accelerated in the last two decades. As of October 11, 1996, tribes were operating 12 of 40 hospitals and 379 of 492 ambulatory facilities, including 134 health centers, 4 school health centers, 73 health stations, and 168 Alaska Village clinics"[3] and these numbers have only increased in the last decade. In recent years Native health care has trans-formed from a consolidated "single national, directly operated federal program to one under the control and direction of the local Indian community."[4]

During this same era, federal policies toward Native American religious freedom have also changed. Throughout most of its history, the federal gov-ernment had outlawed Native religious practices, enacting legislation that suppressed Native traditions through imprisonment, restriction of rations, and military might. These included the Indian Civilization Fund Act (1819), the Rules for Indian Courts (1882), the Indian Religious Crimes Code (1883), and Circular 1665 (1922). These policies were not overturned until the Wheeler Howard Act of 1934 (which did so in part), and the American

Indian Religious Freedom Act of 1978 (which did so in essence). In the current era, as local Native communities are taking control of their resources and social services, they are embracing the opportunity to do so in ways that address pressing issues by drawing upon traditional cultures, oral traditions, symbol systems, and relational networks. The ways in which contemporary Native individuals, communities, families, and tribal nations are making sense of illness and constructing approaches to healing are vastly important: it points toward these peoples' fundamental value systems, worldviews, and spiritual beliefs. Health and wellness concerns are the most pressing issues facing Native communities today, issues arising directly from the experience of colonialism, racism, and systemic oppression. The ways in which these issues are being addressed reflect the indigenous understandings of body and self that inspire them: they are relational and adaptable, and they draw upon indigenous religious traditions to reflect local notions of what it means to be a healthy self-in-community. The revival of indigenous religious traditions in the late twentieth and early twenty-first centuries has been accompanied by a revival of traditional approaches to wellness, albeit in a modified form, as they respond to new needs in a new context.

BUILDING BRIDGES BETWEEN THEORY
AND COMMUNITY ENGAGEMENT

This book locates itself at a particular junction within current thinking about indigenous traditions in North America. In many ways, this is exemplified by the voices that bookend this volume. Inés Talamantez, who has written our foreword, has been a central voice for the development of American Indian religious studies. She has called for work that draws upon participatory knowledge, in which Native communities—and Native elders in particular—are returned to positions of authority. She argues that the task of scholars, particularly in this neocolonial context, is to learn to listen to these voices and to give them space for speech. Talamantez's own work with her Mescalero Apache community exemplifies this ethos of careful scholarship that defers to Native voices and experiences. This is in contrast to previous generations of work by non-Native academicians who often overlooked emic (or insider) perspectives in the interest of fitting Native traditions into preexisting Euro-American frameworks. If Dr. Talamantez's voice begins this volume, it concludes with an afterword by Thomas Csordas. Csordas's contributions to the study of religion and healing have also been hugely influential within Native American studies today. While likewise engaging with participatory knowledge, Csordas wrestles with central theoretical questions and approaches, particularly concerning the nature of embodied experience and what it means to be a *self*. Drawing on such issues, this book hopes to contribute to a larger philosophical conversation that crosses disciplinary and area studies boundaries. Framed by these two voices, this collection of works seeks to link community-engaged scholarship that privileges Native voices and authorities while working toward the practical improvement of Native health and wellness, with theoretically informed reflections upon the nature of embodiment and subjectivity. Put more succinctly—it is my hope that this book bridges participatory and theoretical knowledge.

HEALING AND SELF-MAKING

Before reading the chapters that follow, it is helpful for readers to have a better understanding of several key terms and ideas. For example, it is important to consider what is meant by *illness, healing,* and *self*. Many of this book's authors are guided by notions set forth by medical anthropologist Arthur Kleinman, who has argued that *healing illness* should be placed in contrast with *curing disease.* If, as Kleinman suggests, *disease* is the diagnosis of a particular ailment, *illness* has to do with the actual experience that plays itself out in one's life. Illness encompasses not only the disease itself, but also its symptoms, the side effects associated with treatment, and the impact on one's sense of self. It involves one's ability to fulfill one's obligations, to care for others, *and* the ways in which one's illness impacts those around one. If the disease is breast cancer, the illness might include the effects of chemotherapy, the compromised sense of identity as a woman following a mastectomy, the impact of sickness on one's children and spouse, or the impact it may have upon professional, emotional, or spiritual life. If disease can be reduced to a single cause and a single concern, illness is the impact of that ailment on a person's entire sense of self, their family, and their community. In such an instance, healing illness for a cancer patient may have more to do with addressing the challenges posed in relation to identity, fear, and anxiety than with removing the cancer itself. For Kleinman, healing includes the ways in which terminally or chronically ill patients are able to renegotiate their sense of self, and make meaning within their suffering. From such a perspective, healing is fundamentally about meaning making, and is often a deeply spiritual process.

THE SOUL OF SICKNESS: THE COMPROMISED SELF

If we shift the conversation from disease to illness, we are concerned with whatever compromises one's ability to *be oneself.* For Robert Hahn, illness is "an unwanted condition in one's person or self,"[5] and healing activities are fundamentally about the maintenance and re-creation of that self. But this is not an easy notion to grasp. What *is* this self that needs to be restored? For Kleinman and Hahn, understandings of illness and healing are manifestations of culturally specific notions of selfhood. Ideas about illness and healing reflect the relationship between a person's self and body: what one might call *embodied subjectivity,* or the sense of self one has as one lives in one's body.

As Kleinman explains, to understand what symptoms and illness mean to people, we must know what is thought to be a normal state of being. He notes, "local social systems inform how we feel, how we perceive mundane bodily processes, and how we interpret those feelings and processes... Illness takes on meaning as suffering because of the way this relationship between body and self is mediated by cultural symbols of a religious, moral, or spiritual kind."[6] The experience of illness will differ from culture to culture. How people think about themselves, their bodies, and what it means to be healthy will differ as well. This is not to suggest that illness is purely a product of culture. We do, after all, inhabit material bodies. Selfhood—what it means to be *me*—depends on a complex interplay of embodied experience and cultural experience.

As Csordas reminds us, both our lived experience from *within* the body, *and* what our culture teaches us to think about it frames how we see the world. This means different cultures will define illness in different ways. As Hahn explains: "For example, disturbances in the capacity for independence may be regarded as pathological in the West, whereas disturbances in the capacity for interdependence may be regarded as pathological elsewhere." As he concludes: "the soul of sickness is closer to the self than the cell."[7] This is illustrated in Jerome Levi's notion of healing as the restoration of a "working identity." If illness is seen within indigenous communities as a compromised self, then healing must entail the restoration of the person to a self identity that functions appropriately, that works within one's social context: honoring obligations, embodying cultural identity, and existing in proper relationship within spiritual, human, and ecological communities.[8] In this book, healing is thus conceived as the place where culturally specific ideas about the body and self are brought to light, expressed, and reconciled with lived, embodied experience.

THINKING ABOUT HEALING: BEGINNING WITH EMBODIED EXPERIENCE

For Csordas (1994), the body (and our bodily experience) is a source of culture. We experience the world from a body—and that lived experience shapes how we see and interact with the world. This is particularly relevant when considering communities still suffering from the on-going consequences of colonialism. Native communities embody the colonial process: their loss of land, resources, personal and tribal control, and centuries of cultural suppression and oppression manifest today within physical, spiritual, and mental illnesses. Csordas suggests we begin from the body—its illness and its healing—to gain a better understanding of indigenous cultures and peoples, and the impact of colonialism upon them. Csordas calls us to consider how individuals experience "being-in-the-world" rather than the ways in which they may simply be *acted upon* by history and culture.[9] We should, he suggests, start "*from embodiment* as the preobjective condition of social life."[10] Such an approach is "the difference between understanding culture in terms of objectified abstraction, and existential immediacy."[11] We start from where we live.

WHY RELIGION AND HEALING?

This approach to healing might help to explain why this book is about *religion* and healing—we are after the "lived immediacy" of religious experience as it translates into healing for people and communities. This is a complicated issue, not the least because the notion of religion as a separate category of human existence is not part of indigenous cultural worldviews and experience. Prior to the arrival of Euro-Americans, Native Americans had rituals, ceremonies, sacred stories, ritual restrictions, morals, ethics, spiritual leaders, and charismatic healers. There were prophets and visionaries, spiritual beings and remarkable occurrences. But such things were integrated into the fabric of life. "Religion" was not likely to be set apart from the mundane, but rather to be integrated into the daily experiences of hunting, fishing, farming, gathering, raising children, leading communities, mourning the dead, and healing the sick. If words existed for "religion," they were something akin to *living right*, or living a long, healthy life in balanced and harmonious relationships with the cosmos. In the contemporary era, what we think of as Native religious practices and beliefs continue to be found throughout many areas of life. Reflecting this, the authors in this book look for religion in unexpected places, seeking spiritual approaches to health and wellness in tribal gatherings, family celebrations, storytelling, and tribal health clinics.

Further, if we understand healing to be fundamentally about meaning-making, about identity formation, and about orientation of the self in relation to the cosmos, it ought to be clear that we are talking about the fundamental work of what scholars think of as *religion*. Within this book, authors think about religion as activities that locate the self in relation to the world, and that construct identity, ethics, values, and meaning. Religious activities—collective rituals, storytelling, symbol systems—work to locate the self within a web of relations and meanings.

Scholars who study religion are concerned with interpreting cultural symbols that reveal what Clifford Geertz described as a peoples' ethos (how they ought to live), and their worldview (a general order of existence).[12] Symbols manifest throughout cultural life. They shape and reflect particular views of the embodied self and its relationship to the cosmos. They reveal what theologian Paul Tillich has described as "the dimension of depth" in human culture, the places where individuals and communities are "grasped by an ultimate concern," a state which cannot be restricted to a special realm within society.

Tillich argues that, "religion as ultimate concern is the meaning-giving substance of culture, and culture is the totality of forms in which the basic concern of religion expresses itself." From such a perspective, religion is not restricted to overtly religious events, but can be located wherever ultimate concerns are expressed and engaged. As Tillich argues, "He who can read the style of a culture can discover its ultimate concern, its religious substance."[13] Sorting out what it means to be whole and healthy is essentially a *religious* activity. When we work to make meaning out of our illness and suffering, we are engaging those aspects of *depth* and *ultimate concern*, where relationships between self and cosmos are negotiated.

And finally, considering religion in relation to healing is particularly relevant because it is in times of illness and healing that religious sensibilities are most powerfully expressed, and that our deepest concerns are most profoundly experienced. What this suggests is that we *ought* to be concerned with the ways in which cultures understand what it means to be a self in a body, an *embodied subject*. Without this foundation for understanding, we cannot begin to grasp the significance of practices such as rituals and ceremonies, or embodied symbols found within oral traditions, dance, and sacred art. Without understanding culturally specific ideas about the embodied subject, we cannot begin to grasp the full significance and lived-body-experience of colonialism, missionization, and resistance.[14]

POSTCOLONIALISM, LIVING TRADITIONS, AND EMIC PERSPECTIVES

Before reading the case studies provided in this book, it is also important that readers understand the significance of colonialism for Native communities, and the impact that postcolonial scholarship has had on the ways in which Native cultures are studied. As suggested here, Native communities define illness, wellness, and means of healing in ways that draw upon culturally specific understandings of the self and the body. Such understandings are shaped by indigenous cultural and spiritual traditions, and the experience of colonialism. This neocolonial context in which we live (for indeed, Native Americans are still being colonized on a daily basis—there's nothing "post" about it) has brought new challenges for researchers working with Native communities. After decades of scholarship that prioritized European and Euro-American ways of seeing the world—often in ways that resulted in biased misinterpretations of Native life and culture—contemporary research has shifted toward the *emic* perspective. That is, toward seeking to first understand how Native people perceive and experience their own cultural traditions, and only then to think about external categories for comparison.

Dale Stover has offered a framework for what this kind of respectful listening might entail, which he describes as "four modes of respect."[15] The first involves seeing Native religious life as a *living tradition*, that is, a tradition animated and inspired by genuine spiritual entities—as real to adherents as God is to Christians. Since living spiritual beings are involved, traditions are adaptive and creative. They can be inspired to transform to meet new spiritual challenges, even as they draw upon a continuous heritage of symbol, spirit, and meaning. Secondly, Stover argues that we must consider the importance of *place* for Native cultures—particularly given that most non-Native people come from cultures where spirituality has been largely detached from place. He reminds us to consider the role of both human-created ritual space and creator-created ecological space as central to indigenous religious life. Third, Stover reminds us to consider the importance of communally determined meanings in Native religious life. That is to say, how people decide what is traditional and how they understand it, how legitimacy is assigned to it, and how to find meaning within it. This all comes about through consensus, arrived at by the community as a whole (though with the direction of respected elders). This is a "ground-up," rather than a "top-down" spirituality. Finally, Stover describes a central indigenous ethos or worldview, which he calls *cosmic kinship*. This notion of kinship reminds researchers considering post and neocolonial communities that ideas of selfhood are often fundamentally different in these contexts. Here, self is determined by relationships, through which one fits within a profoundly complex interconnected cosmos. This, he suggests, is a fundamentally radical thing—to affirm a worldview that is in many ways diametrically opposed to that put forth by the colonizing culture.

The authors in this volume explore these issues that Stover has identified. Many have found that an ethnographic approach can be very helpful toward gaining an understanding of embodied, culturally specific notions of the self and the meaning-making activity of healing. As Kleinman has argued, such an understanding of the culturally distinct definitions of self and healing requires careful reflection upon illness narratives, life stories, and critical readings of signs, symbols, and language. Such approaches allow individuals to express "culturally salient illness meanings" within their cultural and political contexts.[16] Many of the authors here engage such a method, seeking to allow individuals and communities to voice their experiences of illness, healing, and the meaning-making processes that shape them.

The chapters that follow examine these experiences, reflecting upon contemporary approaches to health and healing within Native communities of North America. Practices are seen not as static, ahistorical endeavors, but as part of the ongoing negotiation of identities, meanings, and significances that comprise the heart of religious and cultural life. They do so by considering issues of religion and healing within a wide variety of indigenous communities throughout Native America. These chapters address individual as well as communal responses to illness. They explore the role of ceremony, oral traditions, traditional healing practices, and community-led wellness programs.

All engage with some kind of ethnographic fieldwork, from formal recorded interviews to participant observations, and they all consider the historical context of the group in question. Finally, they all share commitments to both the conceptual issues raised within their pieces *and* to the material, practical improvement of indigenous health and wellness.

HEALING THE SOUL WOUNDS OF COLONIALISM: WELLNESS AS RESISTANCE

In the chapters that follow, several key themes emerge that are worth highlighting here. One such theme is the central impact of colonialism on indigenous well being. Those ailments that most gravely affect Native people today stem from the consequences of colonialism (including changes in diet and lifestyle), which have led to high rates of diabetes, cancer, obesity, and heart disease. Likewise, the despair and alienation wrought by colonialism, the resultant poverty, and the loss of social and political power have contributed to high rates of drug and alcohol abuse, domestic violence, and suicide.

When ailments stem from colonialism and the ill-effects it has wrought on Native people, then healing itself becomes an act of resistance. Choosing traditional lifestyles and medicines are an affirmation of indigenous cultures and identities, and a rejection of Euro-American dominance. In many ways, choosing to be *well* is to take an active stance against assimilation and colonial control. Several chapters of this book emphasize locally directed health care geared toward healing the soul wounds of colonialism. These wounds can manifest in physical ways (such as type II diabetes) and in spiritual and emotional ways, like those left by the traumas of sexual and emotional abuse.

In her chapter, "'Lightning Followed Me': Contemporary Navajo Therapeutic Strategies for Cancer," Maureen Trudelle Schwarz explores how Navajo (Diné) people describe their experiences with cancer, how they view traditional Diné healing techniques for cancer, and how they experience biomedical approaches to cancer. Her collaborators express a general preference for indigenous approaches to healing over *biomedicine*—a term used to describe the kind of medical care provided by most physicians in the western world. In this piece they describe the ways in which they both resist and accommodate biomedicine. Through strategic practical and symbolic negotiations of these differing medical systems, Diné people are able to maintain a sense of identity and pride in their culture, even within a context of religious and medical pluralism. Pointing out the power of the spoken word in Navajo culture, Schwarz explains why many Navajo reject biomedicine's negative prognoses in favor of prayer language that affirms healing and wholeness. Schwarz explains further that the ways in which Navajo people make sense of cancer and seek healing reveals how they negotiate power dynamics and tensions between biomedical and indigenous worldviews.

Or consider Michelle M. Jacob's chapter, "'This Path Will Heal Our People': Healing the Soul Wound of Diabetes." Her piece explores one reservation community's response to diabetes. Based on extensive ethnographic and lived experience with this Columbia Plateau community, Jacob suggests that illnesses such as diabetes can be seen as the external sign of damages done to indigenous people's spiritual well-being. While Euro-American medical specialists have tended to construe diabetes as an ailment dependent upon individual behavior, she suggests we consider diabetes within the larger collective context of Native America. A direct result of the effects of colonialism, diabetes is perhaps the quintessential postcolonial disease, the result of a loss of land, and the foods and activities that accompanied that land. Her work illustrates the importance of "collective identity and experiential knowledge" for Native people as they make sense of the diabetes epidemic and seek to combat it. Jacob skillfully points to the spiritual significance of traditional food resources such as salmon—for both spiritual and physical well-being and survival. She also explores the ways in which exercise is promoted and perceived by members of the reservation community, where the ceremonial dedication of a new walking path takes on profound spiritual significance as a sign of collective healing and restoration in the face of colonization. Throughout, people's narratives reveal their sense that indigenous approaches to healing engage the spirit and are generally more effective than biomedicine. In doing so, these approaches affirm indigenous identity and culture, symbolically and materially resisting the on-going experience of colonialism.

HEALING AND CULTURAL REPRISE: (RE)DISCOVERING IDENTITY AND TRADITION

A second key theme is the relationship between *healing and identity*. If, as has been discussed above, healing has to do with the construction of a working identity, it is particularly true within post or neocolonial communities where indigenous identities have been systematically decimated by forces of religious, economic, political, and medical assimilation. Indeed, if healing is about defining identity—determining who one is—it is also about determining who one is *not*. As Deborah Lupton has noted, "Health has become a way of defining the boundaries between self and other, constructing moral and social categories and binary oppositions around gender, social class, sexuality, race, and ethnicity."[17] In the chapters that follow, contemporary Native American definitions of health and wholeness often hinge upon what it means to be Native (or Diné, or Coast Salish, or Lakota), and where lines of ethnicity, community, and family have been drawn.

This importance of identity within healing is addressed in the chapter by Dennis F. Kelley, "Alcohol Abuse Recovery and Prevention as Spiritual Practice." Kelley explores the growth of pan-tribal programs promoting sobriety, or *wellbriety*, among American Indian people. He traces the history of these programs, and argues that they illustrate a cultural reprise occurring within Native America today. He emphasizes that this is not a cultural revival (for something must first be dead to be revived), but a *reprise*—the reemergence of traditions that have not ceased to exist, but that had simply gone underground for a season of time. Kelley points to the importance of cultural reprise within American Indian programs promoting sobriety. For, as he argues, sobriety depends upon the restoration of a whole self, with a clear sense of identity, continuity with tradition, and purpose in life. This necessitates a return to tradition, to the symbols, rituals, and ceremonies found therein. As Kelley explains, identity is a complicated issue in contemporary Native America, raising a host of competing concerns and complications. However, it is also the linchpin upon which successful healing and restoration depends. Just as the introduction of alcohol was paired with the decimation of Native cultures, Kelley demonstrates that historical movements and contemporary programs promoting sobriety were and are necessarily built upon a restorative return to traditional identity and culture.

The complex nature of identity and the revival of tradition in the contemporary context leads to a related question: if for many Native people reclaiming identity has to do with a return to tradition, what does it mean to be "traditional"? In many of the chapters that follow, *traditional* has become synonymous with a way of life viewed as intrinsically healthier. Traditional spirituality, cultural practices and notions of self are seen as pathways for wellness. But, as our authors demonstrate, notions of what it means to be traditional are not static, rigid structures. Rather they are inherently fluid. Traditional identities and practices are malleable and responsive to pressing social concerns. As Stover has pointed out, if we are to view Native American religions as living traditions we must also recognize them as *dynamic* entities, able to respond, adjust, and adapt to changing spiritual and social needs. Further, as Stover has argued, we need to be aware that Native traditions emerge from "communally determined meanings." That is, what it means to be *traditional* is worked out through collective consensus.

In Larissa Petrillo's chapter "Figuring It Out: Sundancing and Storytelling in the Lakota Tradition," she explores this question of tradition. As Petrillo explains, if healing necessitates the renewal of culture and identity, then how people come to determine authenticity and tradition is a centrally important concern. As she asserts, both identity and tradition are dynamic processes. Healing communities and individuals requires this accommodation to change as Lakota people contend with modernity and religious pluralism. As Petrillo demonstrates, tradition is defined among Lakota individuals and communities through an on-going dialogical process, expressed within conversation, storytelling, and ceremony. As she describes peoples' journeys toward the Sundance, she explains that tradition works as a dynamic and regenerative process, restoring people and families to wholeness. Ceremony works to renew identity, and to locate individuals within the web of relationships that makes them who they are. As a dynamic regenerative process, tradition is constantly changing, being worked on, maintained, and negotiated through dialogue and lived experience.

COSMIC KINSHIP: AN INTERRELATIONAL SELF

A third theme has to do with the nature of the embodied self as it is seen within these communities: *self* here is inherently relational, defined by its relationships with others (both human and other-than-human). When those relationships are strong and in balance, wellness results. But because they are living things, relationships are also flexible. In his 1995 work, Csordas reflects upon such a view of the embodied self, when he defines selfhood as an "indeterminate capacity to engage or become oriented in the world, characterized by effort and reflexivity."[18] If this notion of the self seems elusive it is because, "there is no such 'thing' as the self. There are only self processes, and these are orientational processes."[19] The embodied self resides at the center of a web of dynamic relationships. It is a place of orientation, a center from which one shapes one's relationships with the world around it. The self, itself, is continually in-process.

Within the chapters that follow, one gains a sense of embodied subjects that are neither unitary nor contained, that are without absolute boundaries, that are inherently permeable, and that are defined not by their borders but by their interrelatedness. The authors point to a mode of healing that restores a sense of self, not to a rigid dogmatic notion of identity, but toward a sense of self that is a process of meaning making within an open system of possibilities.[20] One can express "creativity in the production of one's identity."[21] Healing is about restoring relationships and "linkages," it is about "transformations" and "becomings."[22] These are chapters about reorienting the self, about placing individuals and communities on paths toward making meaning, toward restoring identity, and toward securing collective survival.

This notion of an interdependent self can be found in the chapter, "Restoring Sacred Connection with Native Women in the Inner City." In this chapter Denise Nadeau and Alannah Young explore their experience as facilitators of a program for urban aboriginal women in Vancouver, British Columbia. The program combats the disabling effects of colonialism that many Native women have experienced in the form of emotional, physical, and mental abuse, and have manifested as profound alienation. This diverse group of women varies widely in their religious commitments, cultural backgrounds, and tribal affiliations. Nadeau and Young suggest a framework for healing based upon foundational principles and approaches with which all the women can engage: the value of restoring a body-spirit connection; the importance of renewing a sense of community and interconnectedness with one another; and the necessity of healing the spirit wounds of colonialism.

In a similar way, my chapter, "Healing Generations in the South Puget Sound," explores contemporary community-directed health care programs in an attempt to articulate an intertribal vision of health and wellness—a shared vision informed by a sense of self that is intrinsically interconnected with human, spiritual, and ecological communities. Drawing upon participant observation, conversations, and interviews, this chapter argues that tradition has been gradually redefined to suit contemporary needs, but that despite changes in its outward form, modes of healing in the South Puget Sound remain consistent at their core, maintaining a view of a healthy self as one that is inherently relational and reciprocal, existing in a cosmos of kinship. Tradition as it is understood today affirms this sense of self, through strengthening connections to heritage, ancestors, sacred symbols, activities, and landscape. Through their innovative attempts to create culturally relevant and spiritually empowered approaches to health and wellness, these women honor tradition, even as they integrate biomedical and alternative health-care providers.

WALKING WITH STORIES: MAKING MEANING IN ILLNESS

A final theme found throughout the chapters that follow involves healing as meaning-making. An essential task of the religious life—whatever practice or faith may be involved—is to discover or create meaning within one's life. For those suffering from illness, this need—and the opportunities to meet it—becomes all the greater. This point is perhaps illustrated most powerfully in the chapters that address the role of storytelling, oral traditions, and mythology in the art of meaning making. Eva Marie Garroutte and Kathleen Delores Westcott's chapter "The Stories Are Very Powerful: A Native American Perspective on Health, Illness, and Narrative," begins by recalling Arthur Kleinman's call for physicians to consider their patients' illness narratives to better understand the ways in which patients give meaning to suffering through their stories and illness. Garroutte and Westcott present what they prefer to call a *wellness narrative:* one patient's experience of illness and healing. The chapter explores the ways in which traditional stories—told, re-told, heard, and re-heard—provide means of healing and renewal. This process of resolving illness, they argue, requires active engagement by the entire community and with the natural world. It becomes clear, that this mode of healing is a gradual, incremental process.

Rodney Frey's chapter, "If All These Great Stories Were Told, Great Stories Will Come!," coauthored with elders Tom Yellowtail (Crow) and Cliff SiJohn (Coeur d'Alene), reflects on his own experience with illness through the lens of a Crow story, *Burnt Face*. Just weeks after agreeing to write a chapter for this volume, Frey was diagnosed with Hodgkin's lymphoma, an experience that radically changed his approach to the piece. Drawing upon 30 years of ethnographic fieldwork, personal experience, and close personal relationships, Frey provides a deeply moving narrative of his own journey with this illness. As members of his adopted communities bring him into ceremony and offer their blessings, Frey reflects upon how traditional Crow and Coeur d'Alene religious practices and oral traditions provide means of renewal and support for those facing their own mortality. Joyfully, as Frey concluded the chapter, he also received a clear bill of health from his physician. His chapter reflects upon this remarkable experience, and the ways in which these religious traditions enable individuals to retell one's own, to give meaning to their experience, to discover their working identity, and to bring that knowledge back to the community.

Throughout these various chapters, important themes emerge. These are useful for reflecting further upon the essays themselves, but they also offer spaces for others to reflect on the intersections of religion and healing in post and neocolonial contexts. All of the chapters address, to some degree, the renewal of indigenous traditions in the contemporary context. While authors use different terms for reflecting on this process (reprise, regeneration, or retraditionalization) they all shed light on the ways in which Native communities are returning to tradition, and reshaping it in light of contemporary needs.

These chapters also remind us of the necessity of listening to peoples' stories, of considering the culturally distinct ways in which indigenous people understand illness and what it means to be a healthy self. Whether through ceremony, ritual, or oral narrative, the telling of stories enables patients and their communities to make meaning out of their experience, and to frame it in the context of their sacred narratives and cultural memories. Frequently, this return to tradition and a clear sense of identity occurs through the restoration of relationships—with their community, with their natural world, and with their ancestors. Healing becomes a restoration of an embodied self that is relational and interconnected.

All of these chapters show us the remarkable complexity of contemporary Native American life, where individuals and communities negotiate complex hybrid identities, moving gracefully between one culture and another, between indigenous medicine and biomedicine, and where tradition is renewed and refashioned to fit changing needs. And finally, the chapters also demonstrate that the work of healing can be seen as an act of resistance. Determining to be well, to have a working identity that engages with community is, in many ways, a rejection of colonialism and assimilation. It is a determination to live, and to live fully.

NOTES

1. Everett R. Rhoades, ed., *American Indian Health: Innovations in Heath Care, Promotion and Policy* (Baltimore, MD: The Johns Hopkins University Press, 2000), 69.

2. Rhoades, *American Indian Health*, 70.

3. Rhoades, *American Indian Health*, 79.

4. Rhoades, *American Indian Health*, 89.

5. Robert A. Hahn, *Sickness and Healing: An Anthropological Perspective* (New Haven, Conn.: Yale University Press), 5.

6. Arthur Kleinman, *The Illness Narratives* (New York: Basic Books, 1988), 13, 27.

7. Hahn, *Sickness and Healing*, 5, 39.

8. Jerome Levi, "The Embodiment of a Working Identity: Power and Process in Raramuri Ritual Healing," *American Indian Culture and Research Journal* 23, no. 3 (1998): 13–46.

9. Thomas Csordas, *Embodiment and Experience: The Existential Ground of Culture and the Self* (Cambridge, UK: Cambridge University Press, 1995), 9.

10. Thomas Csordas, *Sacred Self: A Cultural Phenomenology of Charismatic Healing* (Berkeley: University of California Press, 1997), 278.

11. Csordas, *Embodiment and Experience*, 10.

12. Clifford Geertz, *Interpretation of Cultures* (New York: Basic Books, 2000).

13. Paul Tillich, *Theology of Culture* (Oxford: Oxford University Press, 1959), 41–42.

14. See for example Csordas, *Sacred Self*; Jane Marie Law, ed., *Religious Reflections on the Human Body* (Bloomington: Indiana University Press, 1995); and Elizabeth L. Lewton and Victoria Bydone, "Identity Healing in Three Navajo Religious Traditions: Sa'ah Naaghai Bik'eh Hozho," *Medical Anthropology Quarterly* 14, no. 4 (2000): 476–97.

15. Dale Stover, "Postcolonial Sun Dancing at Wakpamni Lake," *Journal of the American Academy of Religion* 69, no. 4 (2001).

16. Kleinman, *The Illness Narratives*, 23.

17. Deborah Lupton, *The Imperative of Health and the Regulated Body* (London: Sage Publications, 1995), 69.

18. Csordas, *Sacred Self*, 276.

19. Ibid.

20. Jana Sawicki, "Feminism, Foucault, and 'Subjects' of Power and Freedom," in *Feminist Interpretations of Michel Foucault*, ed. Susan Hekman (University Park: Pennsylvania State University Press, 1996), 159–78.

21. Mona Lloyd, "A Feminist Mapping of Foucauldian Politics," in *Feminist Interpretations of Michel Foucault*, ed. Susan Hekman (University Park: Pennsylvania State University Press, 1996), 247.

22. Elizabeth Grosz, *Volatile Bodies: Toward a Corporeal Feminism* (Bloomington: Indiana University Press, 1994), 165.

BIBLIOGRAPHY

Csordas, Thomas. *Embodiment and Experience: The Existential Ground of Culture and the Self*. Cambridge: Cambridge University Press, 1995.

Csordas, Thomas. *Sacred Self: A Cultural Phenomenology of Charismatic Healing*. Berkeley: University of California Press, 1997.

Geertz, Clifford. *Interpretation of Cultures*. New York: Basic Books, 2000.

Grosz, Elizabeth. *Volatile Bodies: Toward a Corporeal Feminism*. Bloomington: Indiana University Press, 1994.

Hahn, Robert A. *Sickness and Healing: An Anthropological Perspective*. New Haven, Conn.: Yale University Press, 1984.

Kleinman, Arthur. *The Illness Narratives*. New York: Basic Books, 1988.

Law, Jane Marie, ed. *Religious Reflections on the Human Body*. Bloomington: Indiana University Press, 1995.

Levi, Jerome. The Embodiment of a Working Identity: Power and Process in Raramuri Ritual Healing. *American Indian Culture and Research Journal* 23, no. 3 (1998): 13–46.

Lewton, Elizabeth L., and Victoria Bydone. Identity Healing in Three Navajo Religious Traditions: Sa'ah Naaghai Bik'eh Hozho. *Medical Anthropology Quarterly* 14, no. 4 (2000): 476–97.

Lloyd, Mona. "A Feminist Mapping of Foucauldian Politics." In *Feminist Interpretations of Michel Foucault*, edited by Susan Hekman. University Park: Pennsylvania State University Press, 1996: 241–64.

Lupton, Deborah. *The Imperative of Health and the Regulated Body*. London: Sage Publications, 1995.

Rhoades, Everett R., ed. *American Indian Health: Innovations in Heath Care, Promotion and Policy*. Baltimore, MD: The Johns Hopkins University Press, 2000.

Sawicki, Jane. "Feminism, Foucault, and 'Subjects' of Power and Freedom." In *Feminist Interpretations of Michel Foucault*, edited by Susan Hekman. University Park: Pennsylvania State University Press, 1996: 159–78.

Stover, Dale. Postcolonial Sun Dancing at Wakpamni Lake. *Journal of the American Academy of Religion* 69, no. 4 (2001): 817–36.

Tillich, Paul. *Theology of Culture*. Oxford: Oxford University Press, 1959.

PART I

——— ✠ ———

Healing the Soul Wounds of Colonialism

CHAPTER 2

———— ✠ ————

"Lightning Followed Me": Contemporary Navajo Therapeutic Strategies for Cancer

Maureen Trudelle Schwarz

We went to the doctor first. And then he told us that she had cancer. But not right away. They went through all kinds of examinations with the lab tests.... We got a test from California, that is when [we learned] that she really had it—had cancer. And that is when I knew that cancer is nothing that—(pause.)... My husband's family told us that if it is cancer, it is one of those Lightning Way that could be done on her. So that is what we did on her. But then one of the medicine man told me that, "If she didn't have the operation first, then it would have worked." But this time the medicine man that I talked with told me that, "She had an operation so that the doctor touched her on the sore that she has and then it is just spreading now. If the doctor didn't bother [the cancer], if we found out before; if this [the Lightning Way] was done it would have helped. It would be safe. It would have cured [her] if we [had] done [it] in an early stage." But we went to the doctor first so she was operated [on] trying to cut out the sores that she had on the cancer, but we try and do that and see what happens. But she died anyway.
—*Amelda Sandoval Shay, Lukachukai, Arizona*[1]

Understandings of health, illness, and healing are not neutral in the Navajo world and the sources to which people attribute the cause of diseases—especially ones many consider to be of recent origin like cancer—and the power of cures, offer important clues about how they comprehend the contemporary moral and political landscape.[2] Information drawn from consultations with traditional herbalists, practitioners, Native American Church roadmen, Navajo Christians, traditionalists, mothers, grandparents, sons, and daughters reveals talk about health and illness to be a key aspect of the cultural positioning by which contemporary Navajo people define both themselves and the colonizing "other." Navajo testimonies reveal that adoption of allopathic health-care practices is a global phenomenon but it is not monolithic. More correctly, it is shaped and reflected by local meanings and practices. Collectively these narratives clearly indicate how the local informs the global.

Three critical narrative strands having to do with language, power dynamics, and pluralistic therapeutic practices are most evident in the account shared by Amelda Sandoval Shay, a respected grandmother in her late sixties from Lukachukai, Arizona, in this chapter's epigraph and in the following narrative about her teenaged daughter's battle with cancer.

MS: Can you tell me where the cancer was?

AS: It was in her womb, in her womb inside. At first they say it was cysts. In where her, [she] gets her period, in there.

MS: In her uterus?

AS: Yes.

MS: How old was she?

AS: She was 18. I don't know how long she was complaining when she had her period. I tried to ask her, "Let's go have it checked." She won't do it.... She said, "I don't want to go Mom. They might tell me I only have a few months to live."...Finally when she got really sick, we took her. [Pause while Amelda collects herself.]

MS: OK, so after the surgery then when [your husband] Kee's family decided, now did they take her to a diagnostician?...

AS: It was by hand trembling. Somebody did a hand trembling right here, it was Mae's brother Paul....He did all that and that is when he found it out that is what the lightning is from.

MS: Did he say how she was affected by lightning?

AS: I don't know. That is what I wondered about it. I always had that question. How did she get it? How did this happen? So I ask her did she have sex with someone? She said, "No Mom you should know me better." So that was the question. Maybe she was lying to me or she was[n't], but it was too late. I didn't have to pressure her; she was in pain.[3]

These integrating themes of language, power dynamics, and pluralistic therapeutic practices are articulated and echoed in many testimonies offered by other consultants.

As noted, Mrs. Shay's daughter initially refused to go to the Indian Health Service clinic to be checked by an allopathic physician despite her mother's persistent urging because she feared being given a negative prognosis. She is not alone in being apprehensive about visiting a biomedical doctor at the first sign of a health problem. Fear of such a negative prognosis contributes to the reservation-wide pattern whereby Navajo people do not seek help for cancer until it is too far advanced to respond well to available biomedical treatments, which is a contributory factor in rising mortality rates associated with cancer.[4]

A two-step explanation for the cause of cancer is offered in this account. First, while Mrs. Shay does not explicitly state it, the fact that Lightning Way is recommended indicates that contact with lightning is deemed the causative factor. In our conversations, other cancer patients such as Beverlianna Hale were far more explicit about the direct connection drawn between these elements. Mrs. Hale stated:

> They told me that lightning and cancer go together. That if the lightning bothers you that is where the cancer comes from. So I prayed, and I remember when I was a little girl, we were herding sheep and the lightning went right in between me and my uncle, and struck the tree in front of us, and we go [leans backward quickly]—pass out. So I said, "I know that is where I first got into contact with lightning."[5]

As Beverlianna Hale makes clear in her narrative, the carcinogenic agents from lighting strikes can be fumes inhaled through the respiratory system. Other consultants concur on this point.[6]

Importantly, however, the traditional singer who counseled Mrs. Shay told her that if her daughter "didn't have the operation first, then it [the Lightning Way] would have worked." Furthermore, the ceremonial practitioner lends the surgeon's actions instigating power when he tells Mrs. Shay, "the doctor touch[ed] her on the sore that she has and then it is just spreading now. If the doctor didn't bother [the cancer], if we found out before; if this [the Lightning Way] was done it would have helped. It would be safe. It would have cured [her]."[7] These statements disclose crucial ongoing tensions between traditional practitioners and biomedical providers. Numerous forms of this particular dissention are illustrated by vignettes from other patients seeking treatment through traditional ceremonials or herbal remedies as well as the Native American Church. In fact, the way in which this practitioner described the situation implies that the illness was in fact latent and would have remained so if not for the allopathic provider's action—in this particular case, his touch but in other instances a physician's words. This is a powerful political statement whereby dominance—over life and death—is granted to the colonizer.

Yes, I said *the colonizer*. Whether it is comfortable to accept or not, America in the twenty-first century continues to be a colonial country and the Navajo colonized people. Given changing and emerging Federal Indian policies, scholars and politicians suggest the use of the term neocolonialism: the term postcolonialism does not apply to the current American situation because Native Americans remain a conquered people. As will be shown, this type of friction, which can be said to derive from sociopolitical changes since contact are vital to understanding pluralistic treatment strategies as described by patients as well as power dynamics between extant systems. As a result, Navajo people experience cancer and other such diseases within the entanglement of power dynamics inherent to the colonial context.

While a small percentage of the Navajo people with whom I consulted consider themselves to be living only according to the Holy Laws established by Changing Woman, a *Diyin Dine'e*, or "Navajo supernatural," who created them here on the earth's surface, most do not. Thousands of Navajo people—part of the largest Native American Nation and currently numbering over 290,000, the majority of whom occupy a 13 million acre reservation that spans parts of Arizona, New Mexico, and Utah—today celebrate spirituality through introduced Christian denominations or the Native American Church. None of the people with whom I conferred limit themselves to the use of one health system such as traditional Navajo diagnosticians, herbalists, or ceremonial practitioners, Native American Church roadmen and women, Christian pastors and congregations, or the care provided at Indian Health Service hospitals and clinics. Like the Shay family, the majority of those consulted choose to mix health beliefs and behaviors from two or more of those available to treat a single ailment. For example, the latter group draws on parallel and seemingly distinct structures causing the health-seeking, decision-making process to at times become quite complex and compelling.

The context of medical and religious pluralism is essential to understanding how contemporary Navajo people such as Mrs. Shay perceive cancer, its nature and progress as an illness, or the potential treatments and remedies available to them within the colonial context. How Navajo individuals and families make sense of cancer and seek healing demonstrates the means by which they negotiate power dynamics and tensions between biomedical, syncretic, and indigenous worldviews.

Throughout this chapter the voices of Navajo consultants of various religious persuasions are highlighted in order to reveal a sense of how indigenous approaches to healing engage the spiritual and are generally understood to be more effective than biomedicine alone. These Navajo accounts characterize biomedicine as potentially beneficial, but aggressive, painful, and spiritually bereft. According to Navajo people, biomedicine can, at best, work on the material body, but at worst it can actually aggravate the illness and entirely miss the spiritual components of the person.

Consultants demonstrate a general eagerness to engage in a variety of spiritual practices. Their personal testimonies avow that their seeking is not necessarily about one particular spirituality, however, it is about making use of all available spiritual power to combat illness, as well as seeking community support and encouragement; things biomedicine does not do for them. Although many report involvement in various forms of Christianity, when diagnosed with cancer consultants give priority to indigenous approaches to healing—both Native American Church and traditional Navajo ceremonies and herbal remedies.

Importantly, herbs, ceremony, and Native American Church ceremonies are only understood to be *efficacious*—if they are tried before the allopathic physician touches the patient! By positing that indigenous approaches to healing are primarily effective—in many cases as the only means to a cure and contrasting them with the rather brutal and purely physical approach of biomedicine—such narratives serve to affirm indigenous identity and culture, and empower the disempowered.

HISTORY OF PREVIOUS STUDY

While cancer has been documented amongst the Navajo since at least the 1930s, to date relatively little research has been done on it amongst the *Nihookáá Dine'é,* or Earth Surface People.[8] Gladys Reichard wrote about the care of two patients sickened prior to the late 1940s.[9] The treatment selected in one of these cases, a Shooting Way—often referred to as the Lightning Way—parallels that mentioned in this chapter's opening epigraph and by most of the other Navajo people who shared their cancer experiences with me. The overall prevalence rate of cancer in the Navajo population has remained low (approximately 0.63 percent), although a gradual increase was evident among Native Americans throughout the twentieth century with cancer mortality on the rise amongst the Navajo during the last quarter century.[10] To date, the canonical anthropological study of cancer among the Navajo is Thomas Csordas's (1989) essay entitled "The Sore That Does Not Heal: Cause and Concept in Navajo Experience of Cancer."

Recent research on how Navajo people accommodate invasive biomedical technologies afforded me the opportunity to converse with several Navajo people who are either currently battling the disease, have battled the disease, or had their lives touched by the disease. Their testimonies offer insights into Navajo perspectives on cancer a decade and a half after Csordas's seminal work. Whereas Csordas was interested in how Navajo people conceptualize cancer—as a growth or as a sore—I am most concerned with how Navajo people accommodate the biomedical technologies currently available to them within the context of religious and medical pluralism. This analysis reveals how consultants use traditional and Native American Church healing practices as powerful tools within colonial power plays.

VIEWS OF BIOMEDICINE

"Well a long time ago we don't really, our grandparents they never talk about illness. They say that if you talk about illness, then it is going to come to you. So our grandparents never talk about illness."[11]

Most of the Navajo people with whom I consulted have secured treatment at Indian Health Service hospitals or clinics at one time or another. Testimonies indicate that many consider this form of care to be potentially effective, yet others express distrust of biomedicine. The critical narrative strands that most frequently come to the fore in consultants' testimonies about allopathic treatment have to do with language and unequal power dynamics. The latter is evidenced by varying degrees of resistance to biomedical coercion and control.

In part, Navajo reluctance to allopathic providers can be traced to age-old cultural beliefs about language. Larry Todachinee, a crystal gazer from just north of Jeddito, Arizona, notes an inherent inappropriateness to asking about illness, due to beliefs held by Navajo people about the power of language to call things into being.[12] This view parallels that of scholars who, recognizing what people can literally *do* with words, have come to regard language as a form of social action, a cultural resource, and a set of sociocultural practices.[13] Whether spoken or written, linguistic anthropologists currently hold language to be inextricably integrated into every aspect of sociocultural life.[14]

As Mikhail Bakhtin reminds us neutral words do not exist; rather, "Each word tastes of the context and contexts in which it has lived its socially charged life."[15] In an effort to be explicit and direct in discussions of negative information with their patients, allopathic providers unintentionally conflict with Navajo values and ways of thinking, thereby generating tension between themselves and their patients. Informed consent requires disclosing the risks of medical treatment or treatment refusal. Truth-telling requires disclosure of bad news, or the truth of a patient's condition.[16] Given these specific Navajo understandings about the power of language, what physicians see as "truth-telling" Navajo patients see as "calling into being." Hence, individuals like Amelda Shay's daughter are understandably apprehensive about visiting biomedical providers.

Language also plays a central role in the following poignant account wherein Mrs. Hale clearly blames the progression of her paternal grandmother's cancer on Indian Health Service surgeons not being allowed to remove enough cancerous tissue during surgery. The situation was in part exacerbated due to mistranslation. The doctor obviously meant for Beverlianna's grandmother to be told that they would need to take the breast, some muscle and tissue over the ribs, and some lymph nodes from the underarm but as she explains:

BH: My grandmother, on my dad's side, this is my Nali, she died of breast
    cancer.... When she went to have her cancer removed from her breast,
    a lot of people scared her, people that were supposed to translate for her
    didn't translate right, and they told her that to remove the breast they
    were going to take the breast, the muscle, the ribs, and part of her arm—
    that is how they translated for her, which actually was not what was going
    to happen. And she got scared and said, "No, just take that little piece."
    Just have a lumpectomy?

MS: Un-huh.

BH: But it was so advanced, it had spread, I don't think they got all of it back
    out. And she had a hard time of it and it never healed. Her surgery spot,
    it never healed, it was open, and we used to have to clean it and patch it

for her. And she would sit there in the hooghan and cry and tell us, you know, "Just stay away from me, I smell. It smells. I smell ugly, you should just stay away." We'd say, "No grandma, you don't smell." And we'd go over there and clean it for her and repack it. We'd try to bring her spirits back up. But after that, I think she only went through two or three chemo treatments and she got really sick and her oldest son turned around and said, "Why are you even going? It is just making you sick, so forget it." So that is why she didn't go back. And then she started getting sick on the medication. So we took her back to the hospital and she got some more radiation. But hers got so advanced that they finally said there was nothing more that they could do. So she got transported back into Gallup and stayed in the hospital for a while and then she finally asked if she could just go home. So we transported her from the hospital back to the house. And then a couple of days later, she passed away. My grandmother died of breast cancer. So we buried her in February of 1985.[17]

Mrs. Hale's commentary indicates she is convinced her grandmother would have survived if the surgery had been performed as planned and if it had been followed by a full regiment of chemo and radiation therapy. Most important, this grants curative powers to the biomedical treatments her grandmother failed to complete and that—as will be shown, having tried virtually every other option at her own disposal (traditional ceremony, Native American Church, and Christian prayer)—she was relying on saving herself at the time that we spoke. As her vivid description of chemotherapy reveals, this is not an enviable position for any woman to be in. With her characteristic good humor, Beverlianna Hale told me:

I got my first treatment, man that is something I would never want anybody to go through. It is terrible, it made me so sick. You are just laid out. You are vomiting, the smell of food just doesn't smell right to you no more, you lose your taste buds; you can't taste anything. You try to drink a soda and it just burns your mouth. You can't drink sodas no more. And then some of the medicines get you so constipated. You are suffering from the other end! (Laughs). And then sometimes, some of them give you the runs. So you are just miserable for about a whole week and a half. And just right when you are getting back to being yourself it is time to go back again. So you go back for treatment again and you go through the same process again. The second time I went back, I was sitting there thinking, "God this stuff is horrible, now I know why they give up. Now I know why some people only come for one treatment and never go back [Referring to her paternal grandmother]. Now I know why. This stuff is not good. It is nasty. But," I said, "I can't do that. I have to do this for my kids. I don't care how sick it makes me, I just got to keep trying." You know? Thinking of my kids.[18]

Although essentially subjected to the same treatments, each cancer patient's experiences are highly personalized both in how they are lived and how they are shared. Consider for example the contrast between the account given by Beverlianna Hale and the following given by Sarah Harvey, of Many Farms, Arizona. Mrs. Harvey is a wife and mother, who is also a breast cancer survivor. Her father was the founder and pastor of the Friendship Church. Like Mrs. Hale, after her diagnosis Mrs. Harvey underwent a full schedule of chemo and radiation treatments, however, she chose to downplay these aspects of her experiences in our conversation.

Mrs. Harvey remembers casually stopping by the Indian Health service clinic because she had a pain in her foot. "I couldn't stand so I thought maybe I might have a spur in my foot so I went over there and instead of checking out my foot and focusing on the pain in my foot, they—you know how they do the examination? And the doctor said they noticed a lump on my breast."[19] She continues,

> SH: I didn't think anything else could be wrong. And then he says, "It doesn't seem normal. So why don't we schedule an appointment for you to come in." And so I did and everything just happened so fast...I did go in and they said to me, "Can you come back in the next couple of days for surgery?" I am going, "Well OK." So I just went, well I didn't really know, I didn't think anything like this would happen to me. Of course nobody thinks like that.

> MS: Right.

> SH: And I didn't think anything of it,...I took doctor's advice so I went in for surgery a couple of days after that. And I had the lump removed and he said it takes like two weeks or so, for tests that goes out somewhere—I think he said Tucson. So within like a week later or so he told me that I was diagnosed with cancer. So I had other surgeries and he recommended that I have, he did say mastectomy, but I didn't want to. I didn't, I didn't want to do that. And I started going to treatment to, I wanted to get better because I have my kids....I have four girls and one boy....And they had to implant a port for me here (shows me her left forearm) because my veins were really thin. They couldn't do the IV's on me. So when I came back from there I learned that I was pregnant again. When I had one treatment done. I don't know how they didn't even check me for that....They wanted to abort the pregnancy for me and all that—terminate my pregnancy. I didn't want to. I really didn't want to and when I told the doctor that I didn't want to he got kind of upset with me. But I said, "How did you not know? I come here and make sure I am OK to go for the treatment. I want to go through with the pregnancy...." And well he says, "Well it is your life or the baby."...Well he said that, "If you go through with the pregnancy, it will be your life, but it is a very early pregnancy and then the chemo treatment is very toxic." He said "There is probably damage to the fetus."...I guess especially during the pregnancy with cancer, estrogen is one thing that can make the cancer grow faster.

> MS: Oh no.

> SH: And so even more it was not good. Then I talked with Ray [her husband] and we didn't, well I didn't want to go through with it, but then I decided

that, you know, I have my other kids and I really didn't want to, but I did.... I don't even know what they did.... The report says that they scraped me out.[20]

While listening to Mrs. Harvey, I was simultaneously stunned to hear of the child lost to chemotherapy and surprised at her complete lack of attention to the actual pain and discomfort brought on by the biomedical treatments she personally underwent. She obviously endured vomiting, diarrhea, constipation, and loss of appetite like that described so vividly by Mrs. Hale yet she chose not to discuss it. Rather, after her loss, Sarah Harvey's concerns center on changes in her reproductive capacity, which for her are marked by disruptions in her menstrual cycle. Like Mrs. Harvey and most cancer patients, once she had completed her chemotherapy Beverlianna Hale began radiation treatments. Unlike Mrs. Harvey, she chose to share the sheer brutality of the process endured.

> BH: And after that, they started me on my radiation treatment. So that is an everyday treatment. You go Monday through Friday, everyday. And it depends, the area where the cancer is at, it determines how long you go. Since mine was in the breast and mine was so advanced, I had to go for eight weeks. Monday through Friday I drove to Farmington to get my radiation treatment. I would come here, work half the day, leave here by noon, drive all the way over the mountain, all the way to Farmington, get my treatment in the afternoon—which only took five minutes to do—and then drive home.... That one is a little easier to do than the chemo but toward the end, like the last week you get radiation burns. Yeah, you get radiation burns, and they really hurt. Toward the last week you get them really bad. But they were really nice over there. They showed you how to take care of it, and wash it and dress it, you have to really keep it clean. But for a while I had to have my arm up (lifts her arm to illustrate) because I was all burnt. It kind of looks like a second or third degree burn. It is really nasty. And once you get done with the radiation, you are like that for about a week and a half, but then it is OK. And after you are done with that, your skin gets so dry that if you don't put ointment or something on it it starts to crack and that was another problem, so I had to buy like aloe vera gel, the 100 percent kind. I just kind of put it on there to just make sure that it healed up. I didn't really want those ugly scars.
>
> MS: Un-huh.
>
> BH: Even though I got treated here (indicates her breast area), I got creases here, it burned me up here—around my neck. Yeah, kind of like a wide range. So, after I got done with that, I thought, "OK, I am finished! The cancer is gonna be gone. Yea!!!"[21]

In this account, Beverlianna clearly places great expectations in biomedical treatments to cure the cancer that has sickened her body. As will be demonstrated, however, this is not the only source of power to which she turns for a cure; rather, like many Navajo cancer patients, she seeks help from a diverse array of religious and medical options to complement biomedicine.

RELIGIOUS PLURALISM

> AS: She was in the hospital...and there was a church just a few yards from the hospital so I went over there and I told them, so we pray over there with the nuns and the priests.
>
> MS: So you sought help from the Catholics?
>
> AS: Ah huh and that was just me and the priests.
>
> MS: And they offered prayers on her behalf?
>
> AS: Yes, but it was too late.[22]

The narrative strands of language and power dynamics fully converge in pluralistic therapeutic practices. Even Navajo consultants who characterize biomedicine as potentially effective such as Mrs. Shay, understand it to be spiritually bereft, therefore they seek out various modes of spirituality and prayer to complement it. Narratives from Navajo consultants of various religious persuasions highlight how indigenous or Christian approaches to healing engage the spirit thereby producing more effective cures than bio-medicine alone. Navajo accounts that claim the efficacy of indigenous healing techniques—traditional ceremonies, herbal remedies, or Native American Church meetings—*with the codicil that the rite must be performed before the allopathic physician touches the patient*—serve to affirm indigenous identity and culture, thereby empowering the disempowered. Being a devout Catholic, Amelda Sandoval Shay sought comfort from this religious community in addition to the previously mentioned traditional ceremonial treatments during her daughter's crisis with cancer.

Like Mrs. Shay, Julia Mathis is also a Catholic, unlike Mrs. Shay however, she did not limit herself to that denomination alone when seeking spiritual assistance during her illness and recovery. Instead, as she details below, she sought help from a variety of Christian groups while battling cancer. Furthermore, as found with other consultants, she did not use the power of Christian prayer alone; rather, she melded it with her traditional beliefs for greater benefit.

> MS: And have you ever sought help from the Catholic Church when you were facing medical problems?
>
> JM: Yeah, I usually do....I feel that I am a strong Catholic because, not only do I pray in the church, but I pray here at home. Not just through the Lord God, but when I am here I use my corn pollen, I use both the corn pollen, and then I go to church as well. So, I pray, with different things in mind— the Lord, Jesus, and then all the Holy People. I have gone, I've asked for prayers from the church and they help me....I sought help not only from

the Catholic Church but the Baptist Church, the different churches that offers prayers.[23]

In marked contrast to the above examples in which patients seek spiritual comfort from Christianity as a supplement to biomedicine, Rose Mary Wade, a devout Catholic from Pine Springs, Arizona, recalls how in desperation her very traditional mother sought a cure from a fundamentalist Christian group when faced with cancer late in life. As Mrs. Wade describes the situation her mother turned to this option after pursuing all available biomedicine options:

> She had cancer of the colon. And they tried to remove part of it, but I guess they just, it just didn't help, she died soon after that. It got through her system real fast.... She kind of turned to a religion, not the Catholic. She kind of turned to a religion for the—I am not really too sure what type of a religion that is, but she kind of turned to them. I think hoping that she gets well. She wanted to live, is what I understand. But the cancer was too far advanced. They couldn't control it.[24]

As the daughter of a church pastor, Sarah Harvey's biomedical treatments were supplemented by prayers from many people recruited through her father's associates. As she recalls, "Mom would ask for a prayer request from these other pastors that dad affiliated with—other churches. He knew a lot of people. One is from Page [Arizona], one is at Rough Rock [Arizona], they all prayed for me."[25] Mrs. Harvey's experience of accepting prayers solicited by others on her behalf rather than soliciting them herself mirrors that of Beverlianna Hale who told me:

> BH: My mom's a Christian and she wanted to have a prayer meeting. So I said, "OK."
>
> MS: Do you know what denomination she is?
>
> BH: No, I really don't. They just came over and they had a prayer meeting for me and talked to me. And that helped me too, you know, spiritually.
>
> MS: When you say they, do you mean members of her congregation?
>
> BH: Yeah, yeah. Members of her congregation came up to my house. And then my husband belongs to the Mormon Church, so the elders come by and they would do blessings for me. And we would go to the church and they would do a blessing for me.[26]

Clearly for Beverlianna Hale, all forms of supernatural power—regardless of their specific denominational source—are welcomed allies in her battle against cancer. She is not alone, for the accounts by Sarah Harvey, Julia Mathis, Amelda Shay, Rose Mary Wade, and others are also distinguished by a general eagerness to engage in a variety of spiritual practices—including various forms of Christianity, Native American Church meetings as well as traditional Navajo rites or ceremonies, and herbal remedies.

While discussing their treatment strategies, numerous consultants present Navajo approaches to healing as especially effective at meeting physical as well as spiritual needs—either alone or in combination with biomedicine. As noted by the ceremonial practitioner advising the Shay family, patients are urged, however, to seek traditional care before biomedicine. This is interesting in terms of what it suggests for the relationship between healing, religion, and identity: by going with Navajo medicine *first* individuals are signifying that it is their dominant identity, that they have support within the family or community, and that biomedicine/Euro-American culture comes second for them.

When and how individual Navajo people actually choose indigenous care varies. Consider for example the case of Mrs. Harvey, a fundamentalist Christian claiming no understanding of traditional ways, who decided to follow her regimen of biomedical treatments, which was supplemented by Christian prayer, with traditional herbal treatments. This decision was in part inspired by having witnessed her paternal grandfather's battle with cancer when Mrs. Harvey was a young girl. As she explains: "My grandpa was a medicine man and he had skin cancer,...I seen him. He had cancer, skin cancer and he did have all that traditional, some things done like that for him, but at that time, you know,..I think, maybe it was too late to treat, but I really think that herbs does help, because I have tried that myself."[27] Although as she notes, her grandfather did not seek help until his case was too far advanced to respond well to available biomedical treatment, this childhood experience led her to consider herbal remedies for her own care.

No traditional Navajo ceremonies have ever been done on her behalf as she notes below, even though on one occasion during her allopathic care Mrs. Harvey reached out to a traditional practitioner for help. Two years after the completion of chemotherapy, when she was contemplating seeking a traditional herbal remedy because of all the physical changes in her body resultant from the biomedical treatments, her mother-in-law brought such a remedy to her.

> SH: I didn't take the herbs until, what is this, like maybe two years after that.... I thought about getting it, but I was just waiting thinking what would be the right time and then she, one day she brought some herbs for me and I thought, "Maybe, this is probably the right time it is like almost two years now." So I started taking that.... No ceremonies just the herbs.... One time I asked this one gentleman, medicine man but he just, I don't know how he forgot or something. He didn't show up.
>
> MS: Oh boy.
>
> SH: And I didn't, the next time I didn't want to ask him.

MS: Was this during the time that you were going through the cancer treatment?

SH: Yes, but for some reason he didn't show up. I don't know, I thought he said, "I will come to your house," but he didn't come, but I didn't want to ask him again. So I don't really know much about traditional things so I would usually ask mom here.

MS: Yes your mother-in-law.

SH: Mom, because she is traditional, but I never did. I never had any ceremonies done at all, ever. Just the herbs.[28]

In like fashion, Don Mose provides an account of how traditional herbs healed his aunt of a second bout of cancer.

I have an aunt; she got cancer, colon cancer. When she got back where they were planning whatever needs to be done, here they spotted that she has liver cancer and they told her, "Well we are going to have to go back, as soon as you get up, we are going to have to come back and we are going to have to clean that up too." She said, "No, I've had it. I don't want to go to the doctor no more. I can't. I just can't anymore. It's weakened me; it's not helping me. I know that it's helping me to live some, but I'm sick. Let me just go home." She went home. Well her daughter was like, "Mom I'm going to take you to the medicine man."...So she takes her mother. She went all over and over until she finally found one in Klagetoh, [Arizona], or somewhere. He said, "I will make you medicine that will help you." So they go out somewhere toward the Grand Canyon where plants hardly grow any more....He does it. The plant, they got it and she's there with him and he tells her exactly what to do, you know, it is a medicine man and a patient's thing. They come together and they go back to Mother Earth for guidance and for help. From above (Father Sky) and from Mother Earth you see two humans standing, they're asking this plant for guidance and so they offer. And then he gave her a whole bottle of herbal medicine and said "Drink this, it is going to be your food." Two months later she got used to drinking that stuff. *Two months later she went back to the doctor, the doctor can't figure out where the cancer went.* But if it were just plugged out and made into a pill I don't think it's going to work. It has to be this ceremony this balance thing. It has to be the Father Sky and Mother [Earth] coming together with the two human beings and then it works you see.[29]

At first glance, Mose's explanation appears to simply lend insight into the Navajo healing system's focus on harmony and balance. Further consideration, however, reveals that Mr. Mose is actually stating that the efficacy of the cure depends on harmony and balance. Furthermore, his statement that the medication would not be effective if it were just "made into a pill," can be seen as a subtle critique of biomedical methods of treatment, which lack the holistic approach evident in the Navajo ritual he describes. It demonstrates, therefore, a form of resistance to the power dynamics inherent to the ongoing colonial context in which Navajo people find themselves embroiled.

Patterns are readily discerned when listening to accounts such as this about use of herbal remedies by cancer patients. After being diagnosed with cancer at an Indian Health Service Hospital, for example, Julia Mathis sought out and received help from a traditional herbalist before beginning the recommended chemotherapy. As she explains, she continued to use the herbal remedy throughout the chemo and radiation therapy as well. As with Don Mose's aunt, Julia Mathis is directed to consume the remedy in place of regular drinking water.

> I was diagnosed with cancer back in 1996. And I have an aunt, she is also an herbalist. And I went to her, and I explained to her my condition and she and I, like you and I are doing now, sat down and she wanted me to explain everything to her, you know, what kind of cancer I was diagnosed with, where it was at, you know, what part of my body it was gonna affect, so I explained this whole thing to her, and the reason for that is, um, when you go to see an herbalist, and you want them to do an herb for you, you have to give them your traditional name, because, you know, they have to go out there and they have to find the right kind of herbs. They don't just go out there and, you know, just start pulling herbs. It has to be specific ones that they use. It is only made for that patient, the one patient.[30]

It is worth noting here that, as demonstrated in the account presented by Don Mose, herbal remedies are individualized rather than standardized like biomedicine pharmaceuticals. Mrs. Mathis further clarified this process as she continued:

> JM: So you have to give them [the herbalists] your traditional name and then you give them a certain amount of money, and they go out and they find the herbs. And they go out and they pray and they tell them [the Holy People] your name and they also call the Mother Earth, the Father Sky, you know, all the Holy People, and then they pray as they gather these herbs. And after they collect it, they bring it back.... She gathered it and all I had to do was put it in a glass container and that was my only source of drinking water. So anytime that I wanted to drink water, that is what I would drink. She told me to do that for 30 days. "If it is really effective," she said, "It will start doing strange things to your body. You will feel like your blood is rushing." You know, how when you go for a test and they give you a shot and it kind of gives you a—what do you call it? When it opens up your blood vessels. You get this rush. Your blood starts to rush in your body. And that is what it does. So she said, "When it starts to work like that, that's when you know it is effective. That's when you know that the medicine, the herbs are working." So that is what she did for me and I drank that for 30 days.
>
> MS: Un-huh.
>
> JM: And then after that she came back and she checked on me and she wanted to know how it was. And then I went ahead with the chemotherapy. And then she came back and she had all of that prepared for me, so that was

maybe 1995 I had treatment, so 1996 she gave me the herbs and from that day on I've been cancer free. So you know, I just count my blessings everyday.[31]

These various accounts clearly demonstrate what Navajo approaches to healing offer to patients that biomedical approaches do not: they offer a connection with family tradition, they offer a spiritual worldview of balance and harmony, and they offer a spiritually empowered source of healing. Furthermore, in specific ways, Navajo approaches also are more individualized than standardized biomedical treatments. They also speak volumes about how Navajo people understand and negotiate the unequal power dynamics of the day-to-day colonial context in which they live. Consider, for example, the following narrative in which Mae Ann Bekis explains how herbal remedies were administered to one of her sister's daughters under the direct supervision of the practitioner within the controlled context of a ceremony. As Mrs. Bekis points out:

Like my niece. Her mom took her to a medicine man who diagnosed that she had a sore in her uterus that was about to turn into cancer, he diagnosed that by shaking of the hand. He said that "There is medicine from the mountains that can be used to cure that, but that it is very expensive." Her mother said, "Go ahead." He did the ceremony and gave her lots of herbs to drink. About the middle of the night, a lot came out from the bottom and I guess she was vomiting too. *She went back to the doctor and it was gone.* I guess all that was inside came out, including what was the sore and all that. So, *if it is just becoming cancer the medicine men can cure it with herbs but if it has already started growing it is probably too late* and there is no chance.[32]

Two points raised by Mae Ann Bekis are worthy of further discussion. First, an intriguing feature common to both Mrs. Bekis and Mr. Mose's accounts is the fact that they each mention in passing that patients treated by traditional means returned to their allopathic providers for rechecks whereupon it was discovered that the cancer was no longer discernable by biomedical technology. This understated point is of major significance because it firmly places the efficacy of the cure in traditional Navajo medical doctrine and practices thereby demonstrating the power of Navajo tradition to powerbrokers in an Indian Health Service hospital.

Mae Ann Bekis also notes that if treated in an early stage cancer can be cured with traditional herbs, but once it has started growing it is too late.[33] This coincides with the testimony of Julia Mathis who reports her mother used to tell us, "In each one of us, there is a cancer cell, and it can be cured if you get it in an early stage. Before it starts to bloom, before it starts to grow."[34] Mrs. Mathis did not mention what if anything she was told instigates the cancer's growth. Readers will recall that Beverlianna Hale as well as the ceremonial practitioner advising the Shay family attributed cancer to inappropriate contact with lightning.[35]

After recalling for me the specific childhood incident in which she and her uncle had a close call with lightning while out herding sheep, Beverlianna Hale went on to tell of other experiences she had with lightning during her life. In the process of this conversation, she told me what traditional ceremonial procedures were prescribed and performed for her. As she explains:

> I know my uncle was real scared of lightning and I am too. We are scared of it. Every time we hear the thunder we Awwhh!. Go run to hide. But ever since then [when she and her uncle encountered lightning while shepherding as children] lightning kind of like follows me around. And when I was in high school, I would be watching my brothers. We used to live at Continental Divide and it rained a lot up there and it never failed, the lightning would always strike the pole beside our house all the time. And when I was pregnant with my son, I was working at Gallup Medical Center and the lightning struck the building I was in. So that lightning has always followed me. But ever since I had that Lightning Way done, I haven't had any problems! So I guess I should have had it done maybe earlier. But yeah, I had a Lightning Way done.

> MS: Did they do the Lightning Way for you before or after you had the mastectomy?
> BH: After. After I started my treatments and everything.[36]

As she states, Beverlianna Hale's Lightning Way took place *after* her mastectomy. This is a critical point, for as noted by Amelda Sandoval Shay in the account about her daughter Carmella Shay, according to traditional Navajo healers this is not ideal. Ceremonial practitioners maintain that their best chance of curing cancer is if they have the opportunity to perform the Lightning Way *before* biomedical doctors touch the cancer, otherwise *the physician's contact with the emergent cancer will cause it to spread quickly.*[37] Beverlianna Hale's cancer returned one year after her mastectomy, this time in her spine. By the time we met two years later it had spread to her ribcage, face, and skull. Based on comments made by her such as "I guess I should have had it done maybe sooner," one could assume that Beverlianna Hale is granting curative power to the Lighting Way. The previously shared story about her paternal grandmother's battle with breast cancer, may, however, lead one to conclude otherwise.

Collectively these testimonies emphasize that traditional Navajo approaches are efficacious—either alone or in combination with biomedicine. Ceremonial practitioners advise their patients that they should seek traditional care before biomedicine. This is interesting in terms of what it suggests for the relationship between healing, religion, and identity; it emphasizes indigenous forms and de-emphasizes syncretic and colonial forms.

In regard to indigenous approaches to healing—both traditional Navajo ceremonies or herbal remedies and Native American Church ceremonies are only guaranteed to *work*—if they take place before contact with an allopathic physician. This suggests that indigenous modes of cure are seen as effective, particularly in contrast with biomedical treatments. Rather than focusing purely on the physical body, as Euroamerican medicine does, traditional Navajo practices and Native American Church ceremonies work to restore the whole person while affirming indigenous identity and cultural values.

NATIVE AMERICAN CHURCH

Native American Church approaches to healing are also presented in consultants' testimonies, which brim over with enthusiasm for engagement in a variety of spiritual practices. These examples reveal what the Native American Church has to offer to its practitioners and patients—presumably, a spiritually infused form of medicine that is more powerful than biomedicine. Intriguingly however, in many cases after-the-fact *validation* of such cures is frequently sought through biomedicine.

When we met, Beverlianna Hale told me that out of concern for her condition her husband's uncle held a Native American Church meeting on her behalf. This particular narrative speaks again to the power of language and its importance in the Navajo world. As she explains:

> He told me, "I want to have a peyote meeting for you." And I told him, "I have no idea what to do in a peyote meeting." And he said, "Don't worry, we will show you." So, I did. I had a peyote meeting. He did one for me. And a lot of people talked and it was real interesting. It kind of made me feel better. Thinking to myself, "You know, I am not the only one that has a hard time in life, there are other people worse off than me. Why am I griping about this?" I think it helped me, it brought me back up, and, my husband's uncle turned around and said to me, "You will be here a long time. Don't worry about it. You will be just fine." I hope so.
>
> MS: When was it that they had the peyote meeting for you?
> BH: They had that for me in December of 2003. I had a peyote meeting then.
> MS: And did he give you peyote to ingest?
> BH: Yeah, he told me that it was up to me if I wanted to try it or not. And I told him that I had never taken the stuff before so I don't know. So, the first time when it went around, I was kind of hesitant, then the next time it came I took a little bit. But I think that was the only time, was that one time just to see. But other than that I think it did help me. It has gotten me this far.[38]

A critical aspect of Beverlianna Hale's experience in this Native American Church meeting results from the language used by the road man when speaking to her about her condition and her future. She emphasized that he said, "You will be here a long time. Don't worry about it. You will be just fine." In contrast to the negative language experienced by her in conversations she has had with biomedical providers, his outlook was 100 percent positive, which resulted in lifting her spirits and offering her a sense of hope.

In addition to patients, I had the opportunity to speak to Native American Church road men on multiple occasions about cases in which people with cancer have come to them for help. Over and over consultants regaled me with accounts about patients with what seemed like every imaginable form of cancerous growth—in the brain, uterus, breast, etc. In addition to offering perspectives on healing logistics, these accounts lend further insight into how practitioners negotiate the complex power dynamics inherent to the ongoing colonial context in which they are entangled.

Interestingly, whereas Jonah Nez, a road man from Lukachukai, Arizona, told me about the use of numerous traditional herbs in the healing of other conditions such as diabetes or broken bones, he only documents the use of peyote in combination with prayer to heal patients who come to him with carcinomas.

> MS: So can you tell me about people that have come to you for help who have cancer?
>
> JN: Yeah, just like one of my brothers named Andrew Henderson Jr., had a throat cancer. And that one there is very, very difficult to deal with. Still, we gave him a little of this medicine peyote. We brewed him the tea, he couldn't swallow because of that cancer, and he started losing weight, so we made this medicine into a tea. We give him a little bit of it at a time. And after maybe fifteen minutes apart. And pretty soon, he starts drinking, starts drinking and within two and a half hours he starts eating food. So that shows that the cancer is out. So we sent him into Gallup. Gallup Hospital didn't want to help him so they sent him down to Phoenix. And when he got down to Phoenix, they took some more x-rays and there was nothing there.
>
> MS: The cancer was gone?
>
> JN: The cancer was gone.
>
> MS: Wow.
>
> JN: And his wife said, "But they have folders, they have x-rays of that cancer that was in his throat." And, I said "And they took some more x-rays down there too. There's nothing there anymore!" So, any part of the person can be cleared of it.[39]

A notable feature of these accounts—*also evident in some of the above-referenced accounts about patients treated by traditional herbal remedies*—is that after the Native American Church treatment the patient returns to the Indian Health Service hospital or clinic for retesting whereupon it is discovered that the cancer is no longer discernable by biomedical technology. Slight variations on this theme occur. For example, in the account shared next by Thomas Deschene, a road man from Kayenta, Arizona, what was thought to be a cancerous tumor is found to be a benign tumor after the patient is treated in a Native American Church meeting.

> I remember this one lady, she lived down at Salt Lake. I did a ceremony for her, she was saying, she was going back on Sunday. They were going to operate on her for cancer. They found a cancer in her uterus and she was going in for an operation on Monday. We did a ceremony for her. And she went back and we heard nothing from her for about two or three months then I saw her sister and I said "What's going on with her?" The doctors, she had got a second opinion to get that operation, and they did find a tumor and they were really sure it was a cancer and they retested her. I think they had been testing her for I don't know how long and they were really sure that it was a cancer and it turned out to be a benign tumor, somehow. And she's alright. I make a lot of prayers for those kinds of things.[40]

In each case the patient is first told by biomedical doctors that he or she has terminal cancer, but is then treated by a Native American Church road man with peyote, which cures him or her. The most compelling aspect of these accounts is that the patient returns to the hospital and gets rechecked whereupon he or she learns that the cancer is indeed gone. The question of agency remains vague in terms of exactly whose decision it is for the patient to return to the hospital or clinic to be rechecked. Jonah Nez notes that the family sent Mr. Henderson back to the hospital for a recheck on his throat cancer. In contrast, Mr. Deschene appears to have had nothing to do with his patient's return to the hospital after he performed over her.

Even seasoned healers who have served countless patients find it difficult to relay information about cancer patients with whom they have had contact; the situation is only more complicated when the patient is also a relative. This was brought home to me by the tortured look on Jonah Nez's face as he told me of his sister-in-law's situation:

> You come across some very hard cases. Dorothy's sister ... They say all of a sudden she started losing weight. She got really thin, all of a sudden like. They sent her down to Phoenix and here they found that she had a cancer right between her anus and vagina. Right there in-between them was a cancer. . . . a real bad one too. And that one is one of the hardest to cure.[41]

The biomedical physicians declared her cancer inoperative. As Jonah noted, "And, ah, so we asked the doctor if we could bring her back to the house to see what maybe we could do. We had to sign some papers."[42]

> JN: We brought her back and put her in the tipi. There was just a few of us. I said, "Never mind about other things, just try to pay attention to that cancer that she's got. We prayed and gave her the medication all night.

We done that four times, the fifth time that we had a meeting, it came morning time about like 3:00, somewheres in the morning, she had to go out. I guess somehow, what was in there, just burst out. We took her back to the hospital. We went back down there two or three days later. And the cancer was gone. So she says to me, "This is a miracle."

MS: It sounds like a miracle.

JN: And it can happen. Miracles can happen. Or, that is how I understood it. You really have to have faith in the Great Spirit. That is how I believe. You don't just go to the person and give them medication. Some of these medicine men, they think they are qualified to give medicine. They just give them a whole bunch of medicine. And you can't do that, you got to know just how much medication to give to a person to deal with that cancer. And then sure enough that person might get well.[43]

After treating her with peyote during five separate Native American Church meetings, she reported that the mass drained. They subsequently took her back to the hospital for a recheck. The cases described by Deschene and Nez, as well as those of Don Mose's aunt and Mae Ann Bekis's niece who each returned to hospitals or clinics for rechecks after being healed with traditional herbs, are examples of a form of empowerment for the disempowered, through demonstrating the efficacy of their indigenous traditions.

CONCLUSIONS

This foray into contemporary Navajo perspectives on cancer provides a window into how this group of people comprehends its current moral and political landscape. Testimonies from a diverse range of Navajo consultants describing their personal experiences with cancer as patients or healers reveals the means by which they negotiate power dynamics in a colonial context of religious and medical pluralism.

Particular focus on the critical narrative strands of language, power relations, and religious pluralism reveals care and treatment as the realm in which tension is most evident between biomedical guidelines and procedures on the one hand and traditional or Native American Church beliefs and practices on the other. This is revealed in Amelda Sandoval Shay's account of her daughter's reluctance to be seen by an allopathic physician. Like many Navajo patients, she fears receiving a negative prognosis from the doctor because of the performative power language has in her world. Power dynamics are further complicated by the fact that the ceremonial practitioner advising her family attributes instigating powers over what appears to be latent cancer to the biomedical doctor's touch. He points out that the traditional Lightning Way must be done before surgery to ensure the success of the ceremony. If surgery is performed first, as in the case of Carmella Shay and Beverlianna Hale, the doctor's touch will cause the cancer to spread rapidly and the ceremonial practitioner will not be able to control it by traditional means.[44]

Navajo consultants welcome a variety of spiritual approaches to healing (including Christianity), but to varying degrees demonstrate resistance to biomedicine. Biomedicine, while presented as potentially effective but painful and aggressive, is contrasted with indigenous and syncretic approaches to healing that address issues of the spirit, of balance and harmony, of community, and of hope.

The fact that those cured by traditional herbal remedies or peyote through the Native American Church return to the hospital to be retested and have doctors verify that the cancer is gone is very telling. The Native American Church roadman, the traditional practitioner, the patient, and his or her family may each have different reasons to want to prove to biomedical providers at Indian Health Service hospitals and clinics the efficacy of the traditional herbal remedy or the peyote and the validity of the traditional healing complex or the Native American Church. In either case, they want to do this in as public of a setting as possible.

Significantly, no consultant ever mentions a power struggle between a Native American Church road man and a traditional practitioner or between a traditional herbalist and a road man. Rather in each case, the conflict is between a bilag1ana (Euro-American) health care provider and a traditional herbalist, a ceremonial practitioner, or a Native American Church road man. This makes the patients being sent back to the Indian Health Service hospitals for rechecks all the more meaningful, for it casts these return visits as efforts at demonstrating the efficacy of these respective Native forms of healing in an Indian Health Service hospital run by the United States Federal Government. Affirmations of successful indigenous cures act as a way of claiming power for and pride in indigenous identity and traditions. That is, it is a way to claim indigenous power and competence in a stronghold of the colonizers.

NOTES

1. Interview with Amelda Sandoval Shay conducted by the author, Lukachukai, Arizona, June 6, 2005.

2. Whereas many consultants label cancer as recent, other Navajo exegeses reveal the origin of cancer to be firmly rooted in Navajo oral history. These connections are made most specifically to the story complexes associated with sexual aberrations, game animals, and abnormal growth, but important connections also lie within accounts of incest and arthritis deformans.

3. Interview with Amelda Sandoval Shay conducted by the author, Lukachukai, Arizona, June 5, 2005.

4. Dan Huff, "Ancient Wisdom, Modern Medicine: Navajo Cancer Inquiry," *Arizona Alumnus* (Spring 2003): 34–39.

5. Interview with Beverlianna Hale conducted by the author, Tsaile, Arizona, June 13, 2005.

6. Interviews conducted by the author with Mae Ann Bekis, To'tsoh, Arizona, on July 22, 2004 and Eloise Watchman, St. Michaels, Arizona, June 21, 2005.

7. Interview with Amelda Sandoval Shay, June 5, 2005.

8. Three cases of cervical cancer and one case of sarcoma were documented at Sage Memorial Hospital in Ganado, Arizona, during the 1930s, see Clarence Salsbury, "Disease Incidence among the Navajos," *Southwestern Medicine* (July 1937): 230–33. An outbreak of lung cancer amongst Navajo uranium miners in the 1960s brought national attention and a heightened awareness of the disease among Navajo people, see Thomas Csordas, "The Sore That Does Not Heal: Cause and Concept in the Navajo Experience of Cancer," *Journal of Anthropological Research* 45, no. 4 (1989): 463 and Doug Brugge et al., *Memories Come to Us in the Rain and the Wind: Oral Histories and Photographs of Navajo Uranium Miners and Their Families* (Boston: Tufts University School of Medicine, 1997).

9. Gladys Reichard, *Navaho Religion: A Study of Symbolism* (New York: Pantheon, 1950).

10. I direct the reader to Csordas, "The Sore That Does Not Heal," 459 and Huff, "Ancient Wisdom, Modern Medicine" on these points, respectively.

11. Interview with Larry Todachinee conducted by the author, Chinle, Arizona, June 28, 2005.

12. Not wishing anyone ill, I began interviews with introductions and routinely asked Navajo people to tell me what they considered to be the Navajo view on *as'ah na'adl*, or *living a healthy life*, before pursuing any questions about illness or illness narratives; that is, consultant's own commentaries on disease progression, curative action, and related events, see Evelyn Early, "The Logic of Well Being: Therapeutic Narratives in Cairo, Egypt," *Social Science and Medicine* 16, no. 16 (1982): 1491–97. This strategy worked and people were generally willing to discuss their views on health and illness as well as cancer in the contemporary Navajo world.

13. On what people can literally *do* with words see John Austin, *How to Do Things with Words* (London: Oxford University Press, 1962); John Searle, *Speech Acts* (Cambridge, UK: Cambridge University Press, 1969); and Judith Butler, *Excitable Speech* (New York: Routledge, 1997). On language as a form of social action, a cultural resource, and a set of sociocultural practices see Bambi Schieffelin, *The Give and Take of Everyday Life* (Cambridge, UK: Cambridge University Press, 1990).

14. Laura Ahearn, "Language and Agency," *Annual Review of Anthropology* 30 (2001): 110.

15. Mikhail Bakhtin, *The Dialogic Imagination* (Austin: University of Texas Press, 1981), 293.

16. Joseph Carrese and Lorna Rhodes, "Western Bioethics on the Navajo Reservation: Benefit or Harm," *Journal of American Medical Association* 274 (1995): 826.

17. Interview with Beverlianna Hale conducted by the author, Tsaile, Arizona, June 13, 2005.

18. Ibid.

19. Interview with Sarah Harvey conducted by the author, Lukachukai, Arizona, July 17, 2005.

20. Ibid.

21. Interview with Beverlianna Hale, June 13, 2005.

22. Interview with Amelda Sandoval Shay, June 6, 2005.

23. Interview with Julia Mathis conducted by the author, Chinle, Arizona, June 11, 2005.

24. Interview with Rose Mary Wade conducted by the author, Pine Springs, Arizona, June 17, 2005.

25. Interview with Sarah Harvey, July 17, 2005.

26. Interview with Beverlianna Hale, June 13, 2005.

27. Interview with Sarah Harvey, July 17, 2005.

28. Ibid.

29. Interview with Don Mose conducted by the author, Kayenta, Arizona, June 13, 2005, emphasis added.

30. Interview with Julia Mathis, June 11, 2005.

31. Ibid.

32. Interview with Mae Ann Bekis conducted by the author April 4, 2006, emphasis added.

33. Interview with Mae Ann Bekis conducted by the author April 4, 2006.

34. Interview with Julia Mathis, June 11, 2005.

35. Interviews with Beverlianna Hale, June 13, 2005, and Amelda Sandoval Shay, June 6, 2005.

36. Interview with Beverlianna Hale, June 13, 2005.

37. Interview with Mae Ann Bekis, April 4, 2006, and Amelda Sandoval Shay, June 6, 2005.

38. Interview with Beverlianna Hale, June 13, 2005.

39. Interview with Jonah Nez conducted by the author, Lukachukai, Arizona, June 12, 2005.

40. Interview with Thomas Deschene conducted by the author, Kayenta, Arizona, June 15, 2005.

41. Interview with Jonah Nez, June 12, 2005.

42. Ibid.

43. Ibid.

44. Interview with Amelda Sandoval Shay, June 6, 2005, and Beverlianna Hale, June 13, 2005.

BIBLIOGRAPHY

Ahearn, Laura. Language and Agency. *Annual Review of Anthropology* 30 (2001): 109–37.

Austin, John. *How to Do Things with Words.* London: Oxford University Press, 1962.

Bakhtin, Mikhail. *The Dialogic Imagination*, ed. M. Holquist, trans. C. Emerson and M. Holquist. Austin: University of Texas Press, 1981.

Brugge, Doug, Timothy Benally, Phil Harrison, Martha Austin, and Lydia Fasthorse. *Memories Come to Us in the Rain and the Wind: Oral Histories and Photographs of Navajo Uranium Miners and Their Families.* Navajo Uranium Miners Oral History and Photography Project. Boston: Tufts University School of Medicine, 1997.

Butler, Judith. *Excitable Speech.* New York: Routledge, 1997.

Carrese, Joseph, and Lorna Rhodes. Western Bioethics on the Navajo Reservation: Benefit or Harm. *Journal of American Medical Association* 274 (1995): 826–29.

Csordas, Thomas. The Sore That Does Not Heal: Cause and Concept in the Navajo Experience of Cancer. *Journal of Anthropological Research* 45, no. 4 (1989): 457–85.

Early, Evelyn. The Logic of Well Being: Therapeutic Narratives in Cairo, Egypt. *Social Science and Medicine* 16, no. 16 (1982): 1491–97.

Huff, Dan. Ancient Wisdom, Modern Medicine: Navajo Cancer Inquiry. *Arizona Alumnus* (Spring 2003): 34–39.

Reichard, Gladys. *Navaho Religion: A Study of Symbolism*. New York: Pantheon, 1950.

Salsbury, Clarence G. Disease Incidence among the Navajos. *Southwestern Medicine* (July 1937): 230–33.

Schieffelin, Bambi B. *The Give and Take of Everyday Life*. Cambridge, UK: Cambridge University Press, 1990.

Searle, John. *Speech Acts*. Cambridge, UK: Cambridge University Press, 1969.

CHAPTER 3

—— ✵ ——

"This Path Will Heal Our People": Healing the Soul Wound of Diabetes

Michelle M. Jacob

Fitness Walk

It was a brisk autumn morning on the reservation. Perhaps 40 people gathered in the lobby at the site of the Tribe's Annual Diabetes Conference. We were comfortably chatting and sipping small cups of coffee under the warm lights, laughing at our "fitness walk" we would all do in a few minutes. The reason we were laughing was because it was *early* in the morning. The sun had not yet risen. The lights in the parking lot were not working. Inside the lobby it was warm and comfortable, but we gazed out the lobby's glass door into pure darkness. Some wondered aloud why they weren't home in bed or eating a big, comforting breakfast.

Our fitness walk consisted of walking around the adjacent field for a couple of laps in order to complete our communal exercise. We silently wondered why the diabetes program didn't bring flashlights for us...and why we hadn't thought to bring our own. But, we were happy we'd made a commitment to our health. We *would* walk that morning. We *would* support one another. We *would* encourage each other to keep up healthy living habits. We shared a hope that we would all control or prevent diabetes in our families. As I joined in the fitness walk, I smiled as I thought about the dedicated people who attended the conference that year. I smiled as I thought about the countless hours the diabetes program staff put in to make the conference happen. I smiled as I realized that this walk, in early morning darkness, around a bumpy field, was part of the path to good health for our Tribal people.

Diabetes is currently described as an epidemic sweeping through America. As childhood obesity numbers rise and overweight/obese adults become the norm, many are wondering—what are the implications of *supersizing* our bodies? The popularity of projects such as *Super Size Me* and *Fast Food Nation* indicate growing concern with health problems such as diabetes. Additionally, the American Diabetes Association estimates that diabetes costs the

American economy 39.8 billion dollars each year, due to factors including health treatment costs and missed work/loss of productivity in the economy.[1]

While diabetes is a concern for American society in general, not all groups within the United States bear an equal burden with regard to this health problem. American Indians are one group that has long been recognized as bearing disproportionally heavy diabetes burdens. Sadly, American Indians seem to be leading the way in demonstrating how damaging this disease can be to individuals, families, and communities. In my own family, I have seen the damages of diabetes in the two previous generations. I am hoping that my brothers and I can break that cycle and eliminate the disease from our family. As our Tribal people become more aware of diabetes' causes and consequences, we are hopeful that we can indeed stay on the path that will heal our people. The hope is that efforts to discuss the context and meaning of diabetes, such as this chapter, will help all peoples find more complex ways to understand and improve their own health.

Drawing from my work on an American Indian reservation in the Pacific Northwest, this chapter critically assesses the contemporary diabetes epidemic as part of a larger *soul wound*. Soul wound is a concept that is growing in popularity and use in order to understand and explain deep-seated problems within marginalized communities. In this chapter, *diabetes* as soul wound is viewed as an effect of colonization; that is, colonization has devastated traditional, spiritual relations with sacred foods and life ways. The result of this soul wound is that the community is out of balance and illnesses are a manifestation of that imbalance.

This chapter examines ways in which community members actively grapple with concepts of traditionalism, colonization, modernity, and consumerism. Community members themselves consistently point to colonization and assimilation as explanatory factors for diabetes and imbalance within the community. In considering how the soul wound can be healed, community members point to notions of collectivism, valuing experiential knowledge, and caring for future generations as hallmarks of a healthy reservation community. This chapter explores the ways in which community members construct diabetes as a social problem, engage in activisms to revive healthy life ways amongst the people, and imagine ways in which the community will heal their soul wound.

Diabetes is often thought of as a *physical* disease. But what *social* meanings does it carry? I try to answer this question by focusing here on diabetes within an American Indian reservation on the Columbia River Plateau in the Pacific Northwest. In doing so, I share community members' arguments that the changes brought by colonization, including government's influence on our life ways, serve as the cause for imbalance and poor health within the community. The loss of balance within the community is viewed in spiritual terms. Traditional culture does not subscribe to the Western notion of the mind/body split, and indeed the spirit is viewed as primarily important for wellness. Our bodies' illnesses (e.g., diabetes) can be viewed as an outward effect of the damages done to our spiritual well-being as a community and as individuals. I link this spirit-illness with the theory of *historical trauma*.[2] As one of the first scholars to build on the idea of *soul wound* and apply the concept of *historical trauma* to American Indian populations, Maria Yellow Horse Brave Heart clarifies that "historical trauma is the cumulative trauma over both the life span and across generations that results from massive cataclysmic events."[3] Here, I focus on a top community health concern, Type II diabetes (also known as adult onset diabetes or non-insulin dependent diabetes mellitus) as a case around which to theorize the impact of colonization on the community's health and well-being. I also analyze the community's contemporary activisms to heal the soul wound of diabetes.

BACKGROUND: POWER, HISTORY, AND RACE RELATIONS

If one is to understand diabetes among American Indians, one must critically analyze power relations and their impact on marginalized people's bodies. I find Paul Farmer's concept of *structural violence* useful for doing so.[4] To explain, in studying health among marginalized peoples, Farmer concludes that advanced capitalism is *designed* to inflict suffering, illness, and death on those who are most disenfranchised within a global economic system. To draw on Farmer's notion of structural violence is to point out that modern-day reservations, while embedded within the richest country in the world, still have widespread poverty, in which poor health abounds. Winona LaDuke has similarly discussed the exploitative relationship that our sovereign nations must endure with the U.S. and State governments, noting how Native peoples' land, food, and spiritual practices are consistently assaulted by policies that privilege corporate interests rather than Native peoples' rights.[5] If one analyzes the odds that American Indians have overcome in order to survive, one is quick to see that our survival is nothing less than a brilliant negotiation with a system wrought with violence and inequality. It is simply no accident that a diabetes epidemic rages in Indian communities. Rather, when one analyzes the structure of reservation life, it is by design that our people suffer with the diseases of poverty.

My analysis also draws on Nancy Scheper-Hughes and Margaret Lock's discussion of the *mindful body*.[6] In their argument they state that "mind and body are inseparable in the experiences of sickness, suffering, and healing."[7] In crafting their argument against a dualistic mind/body split, they offer a definition of the *social body*. Examining the various ways that non-Western societies have understood bodies as social (versus a Western idea of bodies as individual, physical entities), the authors state that "social relations are understood as a key contributor to individual health and illness. The body is seen as a unitary, integrated aspect of self and social relations. It is dependent on, and vulnerable to, the feelings, wishes, and actions of others."[8] This resonates deeply with traditional American Indian knowledge, as indigenous peoples recognize the *spirit* not only of the people in one's environment, but also, as our elders say: the four-leggeds, winged, water, tree, plant, and land people/spirits.[9] This aspect of traditional knowledge is important to understand when thinking about the spiritual significance and costs of the diabetes epidemic; if the peoples' relationship with the spiritual is disrupted, then we should expect a result of widespread illness.

Diabetes did not become a problem in Indian communities until the mid-twentieth century.[10] It is common in Indian communities, including on my reservation, to hear people talk about the "old days" when Indian peoples did not have to deal with the problems that resulted from colonization and Americanization. Indian leaders and elders also urge tribal peoples to "get back to our old ways of doing things," implying that our traditions will help protect us from the tragedies of colonization. When analyzed scientifically, the elders are speaking the truth: when our people were able to practice our old ways we were not sick with diabetes.

Coupled with the sedentary lifestyles that many Indians now have, the general increased fat content in readily available food on the reservation has most certainly contributed to the high obesity rates in Indian communities. When these sorts of issues are brought into the discussion, a more complete understanding of the diabetes epidemic is possible. Rather than focusing solely on individual issues, the broader context of colonization and dominance of American culture should be included in the discussion as well. As traditional indigenous cultures—the heart of Indian identity—are challenged by American consumerism, Indian peoples face a troubling decision—which cultural way will they follow? This dilemma can be understood through the application of W.E.B. Du Bois's concept of "double consciousness."[11] That is, with each introduction of an American commodity into Indian communities, the double consciousness of Indian peoples becomes more complex, as Indian peoples make decisions that attempt to resist or assimilate into the American world.

Unfortunately, double consciousness of body image can be devastating in Indian communities as rates of diabetes grow. There is an extremely important contradiction: How can one have both a healthy Indian body *and* a healthy American body, when the two cultural systems have such different attitudes and norms? In a related discussion about the challenges that this question poses with regard to diabetes management and prevention, Brooke Olsen writes, "it is not surprising that there may be adverse reactions to advocating that [Indian] people should lose weight and be thin. The unwritten text here is that they should aspire to look like skinny white people, an understandably dubious suggestion when viewed with a cultural perspective that includes a prominent history of neocolonial and imperialist agendas for American Indians by whites."[12]

Double consciousness is at the heart of this critique. In public health messages and programs, perceptions of cultural relevance are important. Participation is influenced by whether prevention and treatment efforts honor Indian traditions and culture versus (white) mainstream U.S. culture. Efforts to heal soul wound must be culturally relevant, otherwise efforts can be perceived as neocolonial attempts to control Native bodies. Issues of controlling one's body are very important given the long history of conquest and violence Native communities have faced.

If one is to understand the diabetes epidemic on the reservation, one must understand what "control over one's body" means. In considering the diabetes problem, I began to see how being a *good diabetic* or even a *healthy eater* might be at odds with being a *good Indian* or a *good host/ess*. Medical understandings of diabetes point to two main causes of the disease—sedentary lifestyle and obesity, followed by a less significant cause—genetic predisposition.[13] However, these medical explanations often ignore important factors such as the social meaning of food and being able to control one's body in a relative place of disempowerment. As one diabetic interviewee told me, he wants to "go to his grave knowing he ate what he wanted." Such utterances can seem backward to health professionals who struggle to understand their Indian patients' noncompliance to medical orders of diet and exercise. But, when one understands the on-going colonial relationships and setting of the reservation, one can begin to understand how, for a man who has lost his job, lost many of his traditional ways of claiming an important role within the community, and lives constantly with overt and covert racist relations—"eating whatever I want" can seem to be an empowering stance within a very disempowered context. For this individual, and the many who share his view toward consuming American commodities, the medical orders of improved diet must be reframed so that one can feel empowered by choosing to do "what the government doctor says."

RACE AND THE RESERVATION

It is important to understand the significance of race and race relations when considering the content of this chapter.[14] I am focusing on a modern-day rural, federally recognized Indian reservation in an economically poor and agricultural area. The reservation was created because of the colonial relationship between the U.S. government and the Indian peoples in the area, with the Treaty of 1855 establishing the reservation boundaries, resulting in the people being forced to live on just a small fraction of traditional hunting, gathering, and fishing areas. Many of the tragedies of reservation life are a direct result of colonization, as Indian peoples have many so-called vices that are responses to historical trauma, suppression of traditions, and all of the violence and pain associated with racist, colonial governance by the United States.[15] A particularly important example of modern-day racist governance includes the consistent underfunding of the Indian Health Service, the branch of the federal government's Public Health Service on whom American Indian peoples rely for health care. Community members and clinic workers alike consistently state that the reservation clinic is understaffed, does not have enough medical supplies, and does not always offer needed services for community members' medical needs. It is within this context that I sought to understand the contemporary effects of colonization on the community's health and the ways in which community members are attempting to heal the soul wound of diabetes.

In the research project, I drew on the community-based research approach proposed by Linda Tuhiwai Smith, meaning that the community's needs would be the center of inquiry and would frame the entire project.[16] During initial inquires about a topic of interest, community members repeatedly shared their concern about the prevalence of diabetes among our people. Additionally, I found that these concerns were shared across Indian country, as I traveled to Indian health conferences in places such as Albuquerque, San Diego, and Winnipeg. Diabetes was repeatedly raised as an urgent problem facing Indian communities today. Secure in the knowledge that this topic had a high general importance amongst our peoples, I did not have to look far to see the personal relevance of the topic, with several family members suffering from the disease at home on the reservation.

This chapter draws from previous work,[17] but my ongoing and critical engagement with health issues on the reservation continues to inform my thinking and analysis. For the original study, I used a mixed-methods approach, including 11 months of field work, 18 in-depth interviews with community members, and a multiple regression analysis of tribal health data. For this chapter, I draw most heavily on data and interviews conducted in 2003–2004.

I believe that communities themselves have the wisdom to solve their own problems (as opposed to honoring only outsider's knowledge). Accordingly, I share the ways in which community members construct a collective vision of what a healthy community would be. How can our soul wounds be healed? What are community members doing to actively seek the healing of their soul wounds? In analyzing community member's actions and responses, I find that resisting colonization's effects, including consumerism and American consumption patterns, serves as the essential effort in restoring wellness. Community members consistently view diabetes as an illness of the body and spirit; thus, managing and/or preventing diabetes is viewed in spiritual terms.

DIABETES AS SOUL WOUND

It is important to make connections between historical, economic, political, and relational effects of colonization and the resulting imbalance within the Tribal community. I argue that the imbalance has led to the people experiencing what Eduardo Duran terms *soul wound*. In his most recent work, Duran writes about the suffering in indigenous communities, that the "psyche of the community recognized the wounding of the environment, and that this awareness in turn was perceived as a wounding of the psyche...the problems that were manifested and verbalized were merely symptoms of a deeper wound—the soul wound."[18]

And indeed, the Tribal community on which I focus has historically faced drastic economic and political change—much of which has been imposed by outside (colonial) influences. Before contact, the people survived on traditional foods of salmon, roots, berries, and game. In today's traditional and religious ceremonies on the reservations these First Foods are still recognized and honored.[19]

The relationships between the First Foods and the people, however, have been dramatically changed over time. One of the most striking examples is with the salmon. Traditionally, the people harvested salmon on the big river and dried quantities to ensure food would always be plentiful. Today, the environment of the salmon has changed: The building of large dams along the river, a nuclear reservation that dispenses waters into the river, and other poor environmental effects have all led to the tremendous decrease of salmon runs in the river. The people's most sacred fishing ground, a natural falls on the big river, was permanently flooded in the 1950s with the backwaters of one of the large hydroelectric dams built by the Army Corps of Engineers. Instantly, life ways were lost or severely challenged, as many men within the Tribe suddenly lost their traditional occupation as fishermen and many people lost their traditional relationship with one of the sacred foods. Thus, a Western idea of "progress" to produce inexpensive electricity actually has a very high cost to Indian peoples and social order within Indian communities. Additionally, the same waters of the sacred fishing grounds are downstream of a nuclear reservation that has had problems of leaking storage tanks of radioactive material.[20] Today the people struggle with historically low salmon runs and the constant threat of losing their healthy and sacred relationship with a food that has sustained generations upon generations.

I discuss the importance of the salmon at length here to make a point about diabetes as soul wound. The traditional foods diet is healthy and, if followed, will prevent diabetes. Tribal peoples did not struggle with diabetes until after contact and the changing (declining) relationships with traditional foods. On the reservation, the Tribal Diabetes Program makes efforts to educate the people on the high nutritional value of traditional foods and distributes lean game meat as part of their programming. More importantly, I would like to point out the larger effects of the salmon decline. Traditionally, religion and life ways are interwoven within the culture.[21] When viewing the culture from an indigenous perspective one can see how the devastating effects of history harm the spirit of the people.[22] One can see, through the case of the salmon, that an upset in important traditions will lead to imbalance and greater susceptibility to illnesses such as diabetes.

COLONIZATION AND HEALTH

Throughout the study, community members articulated the importance of understanding history in order to understand contemporary health problems on the reservation. Lori Jervis and colleagues take a similar approach in their ethnographic health research among Northern Plains Indians, and ask readers to "consider the impact of hundreds of years of colonialism...including more than 130 years of reservation life. The legacy of colonialism brought with it a number of historical traumas, such as the disruption of tribal members' traditional way of life, the loss of much of their territory to white encroachment."[23]

Community members had their own ways of articulating the importance of history and power relations. For example, one respected elder stated in a speech at a community wellness conference that his family, after seeing the ill effects of boarding school on his older sibling, went to great lengths to keep him away from that method of education. Instead, he lived his boyhood with his aunt, who taught him the traditional ways. This was an example of resisting colonization. The elder praised his aunt (now deceased) for teaching him the traditions. Commenting on today's reservation youth, the elder publicly denounced the ways in which many contemporary youth are losing their culture largely due to a lack of interest in learning their traditional ways. Instead, the elder views many of today's youth as being, "up to no good."[24] This elder articulated that knowing the indigenous language is the single most important aspect to knowing one's culture. He urged the audience to return to the longhouse religion and to learn the language. Simultaneously, he spoke of the ill effects of colonization, including the spread of Catholicism and Christianity in general on the reservation. He viewed these religions as distractions for our people from learning our language and the traditional ways, including alienation from our sacred foods.

It is important to note that the imbalance and poor health resulting from diabetes have disrupted the social relations amongst human beings as well as the social relations between humans and the plant, fish, and animal people. Because of the upset that colonization has brought, community members, out of economic necessity, spend less time hunting, fishing, and gathering traditional foods and materials. The elder who spoke at a recent wellness conference lamented that many people do not know the traditional names of our relatives (plants, fish, animals) and that we could not communicate with them if we wanted to (they should be communicated with using the traditional language). Also, the elder stated the importance of having an

Indian name (as opposed to a Christian name) and knowing the language so we could speak with the Creator when we pass into the afterlife. Well-being, for this elder, is highly centered on language. We cannot have healthy relationships with our environment, the Creator, or our culture without the language. It leaves little doubt that our spirits and bodies cannot be healthy without embracing our traditions. Although the elder was not talking specifically about diabetes, one can easily draw the conclusion that if we do not have a healthy relationship with the Creator and our food, then our bodies and spirits stand little chance of being in good health. In the elder's view, many tribal people are keeping themselves from good health because of a lack of desire to live the traditional ways. He advises learning the language and traditions in order to heal our soul wounds.

This elder is not alone in his view of what is needed to heal our people's soul wound. There are examples of community members carrying on traditional ways, keeping social relations within families strong. During my initial fieldwork, one chilly spring evening, I spent a restless night trying to get some sleep in the passenger seat of a pickup truck. It was that night that I began to see the importance of traditions and healing soul wounds. What follows is a lengthy field note excerpt that I have titled

An Ethnographic Salmon Story

"You'd better sing a good nusux song," my brother told me that windy day down by the big river. I'm not sure if he was teasing, since I don't know any salmon songs well enough to sing but I just smiled and walked down to the water. I would have liked to ask him if he'd teach me a song, but it didn't really seem like the best time and place to do so, with the cold spring wind howling and his friend ready to launch the boat we'd be using to fish that night. So I walked down to the water, half wondering if the strong spring wind, probably at least 50 miles per hour, would pick me up off the ground. Despite the extremely windy conditions, I was nevertheless happy that the grogginess that I had been feeling from the 2-hour drive to the fishing spot was momentarily gone. Just then, when I was standing down by the water, thanking the water and the salmon for all they do for us, asking the spirits to keep us safe, to keep all the people fishing safe, to protect us and protect our food, I felt calm and awake and happy. I wondered how many salmon would give their lives for us that night. After our prayers, we worked a little on my brother's friend's small old boat that would bring salmon in (if we caught any); the nets were already loaded on the boat.

"No, like this," my brother instructed me, as his friend silently watched, "you want it to cover up the jagged plastic on the top of the boat's railing," he further explained.

Oh, I had been wasting some of the duct tape, not realizing that the bottom edge of the jagged plastic railing was unimportant. Of course, now it seems logical, the nets scrape more on the top of the rail when the men hoist the nets, heavily loaded with salmon, onto the tippy little boat. Eventually we finished duct-taping the tops of the rails on both sides. After that it was just a matter of waiting until 9 P.M., because that is when the first net-fishing of the year was being allowed.

My mom had warned me to take an ample bag of snacks, because the men would likely "just smoke and drink diet Pepsi all night." She was right, and before long I was digging in the back seat of the pickup for some food, while the men smoked and talked about the different places they'd put in their nets in previous fishing trips....

Salmon is a precious, precious resource. One way that the Tribe is working to protect the salmon is to limit fishing. That night we were fishing for the first run of the spring Chinook salmon. We were near the mouth of the big river, so those are the freshest salmon. They would be just coming in from the ocean, swimming upstream to spawn, and lucky for us, some of them would offer their lives to sustain us. For this first run of salmon, a lottery was held, and only 20 Tribal members were drawn. Those 20 people could fish in this first run of salmon, or have a Tribal member fish on their behalf. My name was one of 20 drawn out of nearly 10,000 Tribal members. Pretty good. So my brother and his friend were fishing on my behalf and for one of their friends who was also drawn. The people who were drawn need to either fish for themselves or sit on the banks of the water while a tribal member fishes for them. Since I am a woman, and slightly built, I got to sit in my brother's pickup, a definite luxury considering the strong winds and rain that lasted through the night. My brother and his friend are both former football and basketball players, very strong and much better suited to pull the nets up into the boat in order to take the salmon out of the nets. The salmon, some nearly 30 pounds, necessitate a strong upper body in order to pull the beautiful silver fish out of the water. My job became backing the pickup onto the boat ramp after every time they ran the nets, so they could take the salmon out of the boat and place them into the ice coolers in the back of the truck. Also, I did a coffee run in the middle of the night, to try and help them warm up after being in the wind and rain out on the water, although the nearest small (redneck) town with a mini-mart was so far away that I'm not sure how warming the lukewarm coffee actually was after the 25 minute drive back to the fishing spot. Nevertheless, I was happy to be able to get them to drink something that was non-carbonated....

From this fishing story, a major lesson that I learned is that, to our people, food is social for a reason. Food and eating is not (or should not) be a quick, solitary experience that one does out of convenience. There should be stories around food, and these stories are meant to be shared with loved ones, stories to be told while eating together as a way of honoring the food and each other. Everyone should have an important role to play around food, to be a part of the food process. Such actions bring healing to the people involved and to the relationship between the people and the sacred foods. Living traditions such as these help to restore balance and heal the soul wounds of the people. This traditional knowledge resonates with the present-day understandings of diabetes that circulate in our community.

When people talk about diabetes, it is inevitable that discourses about colonization, traditional ways, and social meanings of food will enter into the discussion. People on the reservation are very savvy social theorists. They know what the problems are with health and society. "Colonization has made us sick" they say. To me, that statement is enough. But such a seemingly simple statement left unanalyzed perhaps hides the richness of their understanding.

A fancy word that I have learned in my readings of medical and social science literature is "etiology" which means "the beginnings of" or "how something started." Diabetes is a social problem on my reservation. So, how did this social problem start? How did it come about? The answers to these questions are complex, and community members shared their views of the etiology of diabetes in our community.

> "The white men came and brought the white flour and the sugar, and that is what made us sick."
>
> "We didn't have pop and all this junk food before. Now we do and that is all the kids want to eat, so that is why we have diabetes."
>
> "We used to be so active, now we just sit at a desk to do a job, or for a lot of people there are no jobs and we just sit at home and watch TV. So people aren't as active as we used to be and we have these diseases now that you never heard of before."
>
> "We used to go hunt and fish and dig and gather all of our foods. But now who has the time? Who has the money to drive up to the mountains to do all that? We're all so busy and have no time for any of that, so we just eat what is *convenient*, what is quick and easy."

Such statements are demonstrative that diabetes is a soul wound that is a result of the imbalance brought by colonization. Diabetes is, too often, framed as an individual health problem, in which the *person* who has diabetes needs to change their *own individual* eating habits and their *own individual* exercise habits. In the language of public health, diabetics need to "manage" their diabetes. But by considering stories, such as the salmon story, and listening to the rich narratives of diabetes etiology in the community, diabetes can be reframed as a problem of the soul wound caused by colonization, due to the destructive social and structural changes brought by modernity.[25] And, by critiquing diabetes as such, we can begin to imagine possibilities for decolonization.

The salmon story discusses the issue of diet and social relations built around food. Truly, our bodies are social. In reclaiming traditions surrounding our foods we will be able to heal the soul wound of diabetes. The other important piece of the diabetes story is exercise.[26] Our people are actively seeking to not only look to our relationship with food as a way to heal, but also how we actively use our bodies to exercise our way to health. Next I will share a field note excerpt in which a decolonized approach to exercise is constructed. I call this excerpt:

An Ethnographic Story of the Woman in Red Stretch Pants

An American Indian woman is sitting center stage in the tribe's casino events center. She is probably in her 40s or early 50s, has a round, cheerful face, and she's dressed in tight, bright red stretch pants and a t-shirt. The pants leave little for imagining what is underneath, as they fit snuggly over the ample rolls of fat in her mid-section. I think my mom has told me that is considered a woman's "apron," an interesting gendered reference to the kitchen and food preparation work that women do on the reservation. I think to myself—that woman is so brave to sit up there all exposed, I wouldn't want to be in her shoes, even in less revealing clothes, I'd be too self-conscious to sit on the stage in workout clothes—in front of perhaps 300 people! But she seems to be unafraid, unembarrassed, and eager to do her part for the tribe's annual diabetes conference. It is her time to shine on the stage, and I am about to find out just how much of a star she is. We, the audience at the diabetes conference, are told that she, the woman in red stretch pants, is there to lead us in some exercises. The conference speakers have repeatedly told us that exercise is probably the best way to prevent or control diabetes, a disease that is running rampant in many communities, including ours on the reservation.

The exercise leader herself resists the stigma of diabetes by performing (rather impressively) the role of "exercise expert" on the stage today. Diabetes usually spoils one's identity as a healthy person, eliminating any possibility for one to be a health expert of any sort. She doesn't claim any particular training or expertise, just that she loves exercising and she hopes to get us moving a little bit today. She has staff members go around and pass out paper plates that we'll use in our workout session. How funny that we are using this symbol of eating to workout with! After introducing herself, the woman in the red pants thrusts herself (literally!) center stage to perform. There is simply no other way to put it besides this—she is an aerobic goddess. She jokes and teases her way through what must be close to an hour of low impact aerobics and stretching, with several hundred of us sweating there in the awkwardly narrow rows of banquet tables and chairs. But everyone seems to be really enjoying ourselves, as wide, toothy grins fill the faces in the events center. Some of the men look like they might be embarrassed to be doing aerobics for exercise, but they are also looking like they enjoy it too much to sit down and be passive. So there we are, hundreds of us waving our arms up and down, up and down, those paper plates clutched in our hands. At the end of her routine, the red pants woman has many, many newfound fans and admirers, several of whom use the open mic time to make comments—mostly women pleading with her to make exercise videos of her captivating "rez robics" routine. I sit there smiling ear to ear, agreeing with my neighbors "that was fun!" and fanning my sweaty face with that paper plate.

I use the rez robics woman as an important figure to shape discussions of creative resistance against the diabetes epidemic. By doing her exercise routine with community members, this Indian woman uniquely got several hundred people to "comply" with medical orders to exercise; her efforts helped us learn how we can heal the soul wound of diabetes by drawing on our strength of collective identity. She made exercising an activity that was thoroughly "Indian" as it was *our* rez robics we were doing that day, complete with Indian-humor jokes peppered throughout the routine. She is an example of how we can win control over our bodies. She has successfully resolved the "double consciousness dilemma" in an effective way by mastering the gaze and drawing upon indigenous consciousness. She is a brilliant example of reclaiming one's body from the sicknesses of colonization and serves as a model for how soul wounds can start to be healed. Because collective identity is central to accepting a cultural practice, the rez robics woman is providing an important possibility for spiritual and physical wellness. Diabetes is an illness that has arisen, according to many community members, because we have forgotten who we are and we no longer hold fast to enough of our traditions. The rez robics woman, although not "traditional" in many ways, is helping community members to think of themselves as people who can be healthy, exercising, and defeating diabetes. This is an important, and I would argue, essential, first step to healing the soul wound of diabetes.

CONTESTED MEANINGS OF LIFESTYLE CHANGES: THE WEATHER AND THE DOGS

I met the woman in the red stretch pants at the Tribal Diabetes Conference, an annual two-day event focused on diabetes prevention and treatment. In my analysis of the conference interactions, I found two important ways that community members resisted the stigma and spoiled identities of being a person with diabetes: (1) they pointed out ways in which structural aspects of reservation life, such as weather and poor animal control, were barriers that perpetuated aspects of their spoiled identities as "unhealthy people"; (2) they resisted the view that diet was an *individual* health problem, instead recasting it as a problem that is *socially* meaningful, thus raising important questions about the gendered nature of the diet problem on the reservation. In analyzing these resistant interactions, one can gain a better understanding of the processes involved in the meanings and constructions of diabetic selves.

At the conference there were times when the audience members resisted the ways in which presenters addressed issues pertaining to their diabetic selves. These moments of resistance happened during the open microphone times, when audience members responded to what speakers had said in the previous session. It was during these times of contestation that audience members sometimes had questions, comments, and analyses that demonstrated that their lived experience of having a diabetic self differed from the (medical expert) speaker's "official" diabetic self. At times, I felt audience responses during open microphone sessions created a sense of conflict and uneasiness in the room, probably because the normally accepted (hierarchical) meaning of "medical professional as expert" was in question.

Instances in which this happened occurred when audience members went into detail about the meanings of everyday barriers that prevent them from being *appropriate* or *responsible* diabetic selves. One example of such resistance happened after one medical doctor's presentation about making lifestyle changes. In her presentation, the doctor, a seemingly kind and humble woman (she was a soft-spoken Native from another tribe, and seemed genuinely concerned with trying to share ideas for lifestyle changes) had gone through her Power Point presentation telling us to do things like make lists of our goals for change, keep track everyday of how we're making progress toward our goals, and write down the things that may be keeping us from achieving our goals for lifestyle change, especially for eating healthier and exercising.

After her presentation the audience applauded kindly, and we then waited to see if anyone would have something to say during the open mic period. One late-middle aged man in the audience stood up and waived his arm, letting the staff know he had something to say. Once he had the microphone, the man spoke about the meanings of two important barriers to physical activity that the doctor had ignored in her presentation—the packs of large dogs that roam the reservation and the harsh weather. The man sounded a bit frustrated as he wondered aloud how he was supposed to start a walking regimen, as the doctor had advised, when the big dogs and cold weather made it difficult to want to go outside. While he was saying this the audience members seemed to listen even more attentively, I presume out of respect for the man who was sharing his thoughts, and out of interest in how the doctor would respond to the man's comments. The doctor responded by giving a brief sympathetic comment, giving an affirming message something like "change is difficult" but also reinforced her presentation's message that "it's worth it to keep trying."

What is important to note is that, rather than passively accepting the doctor's presentation (and authority), the audience member publicly raised concerns about the meanings of barriers to such lifestyle changes. He was challenging the ways in which the meaning of a *diabetic self* was being constructed by the doctor. The physician's presentation painted a portrait of a diabetic as someone who needs to have more discipline in tracking one's habits, successes, and failures for behavior change, while the audience member did not recognize the problem in the pencil-and-paper tracking of habits. Instead he shared a different meaning of what diabetic selves are—social actors who are struggling to be healthy in a social environment that presents significant barriers for doing so. The medical doctor's presentation stood in sharp contrast to the rez robics approach, as rez robics emphasized collective identity and experiential knowledge, two aspects that resonated with conference participants. It is not coincidence that these are also two pillars of traditional culture—thus, it is evident that any attempts to heal the soul wound of diabetes must take into account the importance of collective identity and experiential knowledge.

In my qualitative interviews with community members, I specifically asked interviewees about barriers to exercise. I wanted to learn more about people's views of their opportunities to be healthy. Many people mentioned how few safe places there are to exercise on the reservation. However, during my time in the field, a walking path was constructed and opened in one of the isolated communities on the reservation. I wrote in my field notes:

Today I went out and walked four laps on the new walking path. The Tribal Diabetes Program had an opening ceremony for the walking path. From the diabetes community advisory board meeting, I remember the woman in charge of the ambulance center out there saying that it was really hard to get that path built. It took many years with her asking and saying "the community needs this." People are always saying how there's no place to walk out there and now they've got a place. It's a nice paved path, it's a third of a mile long. So the diabetes clinic women—all the workers in the clinic are women—they were all out there this morning and they had an opening ceremony. I heard them doing the longhouse prayer with the bell. Right when I walked up they were just finishing that. One of the men, a tribal leader, was saying a few words. He was saying "This path is what's going to save our people. Things like this are what will save our people, save our children." He was talking about diabetes and the need to be healthy and how we've got to start doing things to be healthier. So the diabetes program had flyers out and they gave me one yesterday. (I had also seen it in the tribal newspaper.) The announcement said that if you came this morning from 7 A.M.–10 A.M. they were going to be there for the grand opening of the path and if you walked three laps, which is a mile, you get a free t-shirt. So they had beautiful t-shirts. They had red, turquoise and blue; you could have your pick, and all kind of sizes. They had beautiful artwork on the front, with three feathers and on the side of the feathers they had an elder man and women either walking or jogging. A local artist made the artwork for the shirts. On the back the t-shirt says "Just Keep Moving." It also says "Pathway to a Healthier Life." The t-shirts were a really great idea. All kinds of people were out there for the grand opening: young people before school starts, parents, elders, workers, people out there walking and talking. I walked and talked with one woman who lives in the projects there right by the path. She was telling me that she used to walk on the track at the school; she used to do 5 miles in the morning and 5 miles at night. Which is amazing. She said she lost 51 pounds that way but she gained it all back. So she said she's got to start walking again, because she said she's not getting any younger. (She was middle aged perhaps in her 50s.) In total I saw about 40 people out there.

BRAIDED TOGETHER: STRUCTURAL CONSTRAINTS
AND COMPLACENCY

I learned from listening to community members that barriers to exercise are a combination of: (1) structural constraints (nowhere "safe" to exercise on the reservation) and (2) complacency (I used to walk a lot, but haven't been lately). While the present-day *structural constraints* are surely a combination of social, economic, and historical forces (e.g., lack of economic infrastructure in rural reservation communities due to isolation of communities, ongoing effects of racist policies, purposeful breaking of traditional economic systems, and settlement patterns); the roots of *complacency* are perhaps less obvious.

In analyzing the complacency phenomenon, three key areas of focus emerge. First, the ways in which the idea of a healthy body has been socially constructed on the reservation have sometimes been problematic. I discussed earlier the double consciousness concept, in that there are sometimes contradictory images of a *healthy Indian body* (versus a *healthy White body*). For example, overeating, being obese, and shunning White forms of exercise and fitness patterns are sometimes praised. The second area of focus is related, in that there simply need to be more ideas of *Indian* ways of being fit and healthy. The ethnographic examples provided in this chapter are shining examples of Indian people constructing themselves as healthy people. With more efforts and support from existing health and cultural programs, more models can be developed and the burden associated with wrestling with a double consciousness can be alleviated—but more importantly, diabetes rates and associated illnesses will decrease and the health of the people can be restored. The third area of focus, also related to both the double consciousness and soul wound concepts, is the need to understand how *structural constraints* and *complacency* are not separate problems, but are in fact braided together. This is to say that complacency and structure work together in contributing to poor health. Historically, our people were fit because of the tremendous caloric output involved in leading a "traditional" lifestyle. As these ways were eroded, due to extermination, reservation, and assimilation policies, our people both chose and were forced to partially assimilate into a Western lifestyle, dependent on the wage economy, with limited access to traditional foods and cultural practices. Today's reservation population has inherited that historical legacy, leaving many families to depend on the convenience stores and fast food outlets to feed themselves, while also, perhaps ironically, lamenting the loss of cultural ways. In fact, contemporary reservation life is such that it is easier to grab something quick to eat rather than blocking out chunks of time to gather traditional foods to use as staples. This is a phenomenon that will perhaps resonate with all contemporary Americans—that it is too time-consuming and difficult to be healthy. The main difference to Indian people is that *being healthy* is not just something that needs to be done to prevent diabetes or heart disease, but rather it is something that needs to be done to heal our soul wounds.

Understanding the intertwining of structural constraints and complacency is crucial if contemporary efforts to curb the diabetes epidemic are to be successful. Too often, the focus is placed on one or another aspect of the problem. For example, drawing from the earlier point from the diabetes conference, while suggestions for tracking one's eating and exercise habits may help to change complacent attitudes and behavior, such solutions do nothing to address structural constraints that act as barriers to healthy living. This is a theme I comment on below when I suggest solutions to the diabetes epidemic on the reservation.

In my analysis, I have highlighted two particular ways in which community members resisted the spoiled identities associated with having diabetes. Diabetes, too often, is perceived as an illness that results from the irresponsible, unhealthy behavior of an individual. I learned that community members reject this oversimplified conception of the diabetes epidemic on the reservation. As I think about meanings of the conference interactions and their implications for the future of diabetes on the reservation, I am struck by the meaningful differences I observed between the "expert presenters" and the resistant audience members. One possible reason why discrediting information is resisted by diabetics is perhaps because the people who share that information, the *experts*, oftentimes seem like they don't know what they are talking about because they might lack the experiential knowledge to be able to share a common perspective with those members of the stigmatized group. In a culture that highly values experiential knowledge, this seems to be one point that simply cannot be overlooked when considering future program and policy implications.

Additionally, as the woman in the red stretch pants illustrates, we need to master the gaze and operate from an indigenous consciousness. Anything that deals with the body must come from an indigenous framework. As community members know, to hear medical orders regarding the body from government doctors, often does not provide a true path for self-determination; quite simply, our soul wounds will never heal with this approach. We must work collectively and with our allies to push for the resources and freedom to run our institutions from an indigenous consciousness.

CONCLUSION

In considering evidence, such as the ethnographic stories about the salmon, the Tribal Diabetes Conference interactions, the rez robics, and the walking path, I argue that within this community we can see the resistance to colonization, the first steps of healing soul wounds, and the hope for true self-determination. Some practical ways of building on existing community strengths could include: work with the schools to create learning activities around the fishing runs, including how food is important socially; work to restructure school and work schedules so that family and community encampments can happen at the sacred fishing places; and work to provide resources for revitalizing traditional ways of harvesting and preserving salmon, including teaching and learning across generations and genders. In limited ways, these community activities are alive and well. But, due to contemporary stressors of modern work and school schedules and activities, not to mention an overall lack of resources on the reservation, these decolonizing activities are not widespread. By imaginatively resisting structural barriers that prevent these decolonizing activities from more readily happening, we can begin to heal soul wounds. We can decolonize our bodies, reclaim healthy relationships with food, and subvert the diabetes epidemic in our community.

By listening to the community, I have learned the simplest answer to the diabetes epidemic. Like many social problems, diabetes will be solved with love and respect. When society, social programs, and health care are less focused on the modernity-blessed terms *efficiency* and *cost-effectiveness* and more focused on *caring* and *connectedness*—this is when diabetes rates will finally level off and start to dwindle. This is also when our souls will heal: we will reclaim our bodies and our tribes will be truly self-determined, sovereign nations.

NOTES

1. "The Effects of Diabetes." *Diabetes Forecast* (November 2007): 42–43.

2. See Maria Yellow Horse Brave Heart "Oyate Ptayela: Rebuilding the Lakota Nation Through Addressing Historical Trauma Among Lakota Patients," *Journal of Human Behavior in the Social Environment* 2, no. 1/2 (1999): 109–26. See also Eduardo Duran and Bonnie Duran, *Native American Postcolonial Psychology* (Albany: State University of New York, 1995); and Eduardo Duran, *Healing the Soul Wound: Counseling with American Indians and Other Native Peoples* (New York: Teachers College, Columbia University, 2006).

3. Brave Heart, "Oyate Ptayela," 111.

4. See Paul Farmer, *Pathologies of Power: Health, Human Rights, and the New War on the Poor* (Berkeley: University of California Press, 2003).

5. See Winona LaDuke, *All Our Relations: Native Struggles for Land and Life* (Cambridge, MA: South End Press, 1999). See also Winona LaDuke, *Recovering the Sacred: The Power of Naming and Claiming* (Cambridge, MA: South End Press, 2005).

6. Nancy Scheper-Hughes and Margaret M. Lock, "The Mindful Body: A Prolegomenon to Future Work in Medical Anthropology," *Medical Anthropology Quarterly* 1, no. 1 (1987): 6–41.

7. Scheper-Hughes and Lock, "The Mindful Body," 30.

8. Ibid., 21.

9. See Duran, *Healing the Soul Wound*.

10. K. M. Venkat Narayan, "Diabetes Mellitus in Native Americans: The Problem and Its Implications," in *Changing Numbers, Changing Needs: American Indian Demog-*

raphy and Public Health, ed. Gary D. Sandefur, Ronald R. Rindfuss, and Barney Cohen (Washington, D.C.: National Academy Press, 1996), 262–88.

11. W.E.B. Du Bois, *The Souls of Black Folk* (New York: Signet, 1995[1903]).

12. Brooke Olsen, "Meeting the Challenges of American Indian Diabetes: Anthropological Perspectives on Prevention and Treatment," in *Medicine Ways: Disease, Health, and Survival Among Native Americans*, ed. Clifford E. Trazfer and Diane Weiner (Lanham, MD: AltaMira Press, 2001), 172.

13. See Narayan, "Diabetes Mellitus in Native Americans."

14. Some material in this section was drawn from earlier descriptive work of the reservation. See Michelle M. Jacob, *The Gendered Sports Experiences of Yakama Females*, unpublished Master's thesis, California State University, San Marcos, 2001.

15. See Brave Heart, "Oyate Ptayela." See also M. Brave Heart and L. M. DeBruyn, "The American Indian Holocaust: Healing Historical Unresolved Grief," *American Indian and Alaska Native Mental Health Research* 8 (1997): 56–78.

16. Linda Tuhiwai Smith, *Decolonizing Methodologies: Research and Indigenous Peoples* (New York: Zed Books, 2001).

17. Michelle Marie Jacob, *An Embodied Social Problem: Understanding Diabetes on an American Indian Reservation*. PhD dissertation, University of California, Santa Barbara, 2004.

18. Duran, *Healing the Soul Wound*, 195.

19. See Jovana J. Brown, "Fishing Rights and the First Salmon Ceremony," in *American Indian Religious Traditions, Vol. 1*, ed. Suzanne J. Crawford and Dennis F. Kelley (Santa Barbara, CA: ABC-CLIO, 2005). See also Joel Geffen and Suzanne J. Crawford, "First Salmon Rites," in *American Indian Religious Traditions, Vol. 1*, ed. Suzanne J. Crawford and Dennis F. Kelley (Santa Barbara, CA: ABC-CLIO, 2005).

20. Russell Jim, "The Nuclear Waste Issue in the State of Washington and a Tribal Response," *Wicazo Sa Review* 3, no. 1 (1987): 26–30.

21. This is in contrast to Western ideas of religion as a separate institution.

22. For more detail on the relationship between Native peoples well-being and the environment, see LaDuke, *All Our Relations* and LaDuke, *Recovering the Sacred*.

23. L. L. Jervis, P. Spicer, S. M. Manson, and AI-SUPERPFP Team, "Boredom, 'Trouble,' and the Realities of Postcolonial Reservation Life," *Ethos* 31, no. 1 (2003): 48.

24. For more detail on the troubles of reservation life, see Jervis, et al., "Boredom, 'Trouble.'"

25. For more on the link between colonization, modernity, and diabetes among Native peoples, see Jennie R. Joe and Robert S. Young, eds., *Diabetes as a Disease of Civilization: The Impact of Culture Change on Indigenous Peoples* (Berlin: Mouton de Gruyter, 1993). Also see Clifford E. Trazfer and Diane Weiner, eds., *Medicine Ways: Disease, Health, and Survival Among Native Americans* (Lanham, MD: AltaMira Press, 2001).

26. Diabetes treatment and prevention discourse focuses on two aspects of health lifestyles: diet and exercise.

BIBLIOGRAPHY

Brave Heart, M. and L. M. DeBruyn, "The American Indian Holocaust: Healing Historical Unresolved Grief," *American Indian and Alaska Native Mental Health Research* 8 (1997): 56–78.

Brave Heart, and Maria Yellow Horse. "Oyate Ptayela: Rebuilding the Lakota Nation Through Addressing Historical Trauma Among Lakota Patients," *Journal of Human Behavior in the Social Environment* 2, no. 1/2 (1999): 109–26.

Brown, Jovana J. "Fishing Rights and the First Salmon Ceremony," in *American Indian Religious Traditions, Vol. 1*, ed. Suzanne J. Crawford and Dennis F. Kelley (Santa Barbara, CA: ABC-CLIO, 2005).

Du Bois, W.E.B. *The Souls of Black Folk* (New York: Signet, 1995[1903]).

Duran, Eduardo. *Healing the Soul Wound: Counseling with American Indians and Other Native Peoples* (New York: Teachers College, Columbia University, 2006).

Duran, Eduardo and Bonnie Duran, *Native American Postcolonial Psychology* (Albany: State University of New York, 1995).

"The Effects of Diabetes." *Diabetes Forecast* (November 2007): 42–43.

Farmer, Paul. *Pathologies of Power: Health, Human Rights, and the New War on the Poor* (Berkeley: University of California Press, 2003).

Geffen, Joel and Suzanne J. Crawford, "First Salmon Rites," in *American Indian Religious Traditions, Vol. 1*, ed. Suzanne J. Crawford and Dennis F. Kelley (Santa Barbara, CA: ABC-CLIO, 2005).

Jacob, Michelle Marie. *An Embodied Social Problem: Understanding Diabetes on an American Indian Reservation.* PhD dissertation, University of California, Santa Barbara, 2004.

Jacob, Michelle M. *The Gendered Sports Experiences of Yakama Females*, unpublished Master's thesis, California State University, San Marcos, 2001.

Jervis, L. L., P. Spicer, S. M. Manson, and AI-SUPERPFP Team, "Boredom, 'Trouble,' and the Realities of Postcolonial Reservation Life," *Ethos* 31, no. 1 (2003): 48.

Jim, Russell. "The Nuclear Waste Issue in the State of Washington and a Tribal Response," *Wicazo Sa Review* 3, no. 1 (1987): 26–30.

Joe, Jennie R. and Robert S. Young, eds., *Diabetes as a Disease of Civilization: The Impact of Culture Change on Indigenous Peoples* (Berlin: Mouton de Gruyter, 1993).

LaDuke, Winona. *All Our Relations: Native Struggles for Land and Life* (Cambridge, MA: South End Press, 1999).

LaDuke, Winona. *Recovering the Sacred: The Power of Naming and Claiming* (Cambridge, MA: South End Press, 2005).

Narayan, K. M. Venkat. "Diabetes Mellitus in Native Americans: The Problem and Its Implications," in *Changing Numbers, Changing Needs: American Indian Demography and Public Health*, ed. Gary D. Sandefur, Ronald R. Rindfuss, and Barney Cohen (Washington, D.C.: National Academy Press, 1996), 262–88.

Olsen, Brooke. "Meeting the Challenges of American Indian Diabetes: Anthropological Perspectives on Prevention and Treatment," in *Medicine Ways: Disease, Health, and Survival Among Native Americans*, ed. Clifford E. Trazfer and Diane Weiner (Walnut Creek: AltaMira Press, 2001).

Scheper-Hughes, Nancy and Margaret M. Lock, "The Mindful Body: A Prolegomenon to Future Work in Medical Anthropology," *Medical Anthropology Quarterly* 1, no. 1 (1987): 6–41.

Smith, Linda Tuhiwai. *Decolonizing Methodologies: Research and Indigenous Peoples* (New York: Zed Books, 2001).

Trafzer, Clifford E. and Diane Weiner, eds., *Medicine Ways: Disease, Health, and Survival Among Native Americans* (Walnut Creek: AltaMira Press, 2001).

PART II

⸻ ✠ ⸻

Cultural Reprise, Identity, and Social Well-Being

CHAPTER 4

———— ✖ ————

Alcohol Abuse Recovery and Prevention as Spiritual Practice

Dennis F. Kelley

On the eve of Prohibition, between the period of ratification and implementation of the eighteenth amendment to the U.S. Constitution making alcohol an illegal substance, some American towns were so convinced of the connection between alcohol and crime that many of them sold their jails.[1] Clearly, the relationship between alcohol abuse and social ills was considered fairly universal, not merely the bane of some ethnic groups or social strata. Nonetheless, alcohol abuse has become most clearly associated with two subsections of American social history: Irish immigrants and American Indian tribes. What these two groups share might be fairly obvious (social and economic marginalization and stereotyping), but less obvious (from the point of view of the general history of America) would be the role that this association has had on the ethnic and cultural self-identity of the people that comprise those contemporary communities. The literature on the role that alcohol and its abuse has played in American cultural consciousness points to the assumption by the society at large of moral failing in the abuser, thus making alcohol abuse an effective tool for oppression. In addition, both of these subcultures (Irish immigrants and American Indians) have had to contend with a bias toward their natural tendencies toward alcohol abuse in that alcoholism is seen as an inherent trait of both American Indians and Irish people. This not-so-subtle connection between a perceived low moral character and the basic nature of these two groups continues to affect them, in that very real social and physical problems associated with alcohol abuse plague both Irish Americans and American Indians disproportionate to the society as a whole,[2] thereby perpetuating stereotypes and making real progress toward long-term solutions for alcohol abuse recovery and prevention difficult to realize. This process may in fact be more pronounced among Native people as a result of their persistent presence at the bottom of all demographic indicators of social and physical health.[3] What I suggest here is using the role of practice, especially religious practice, as a theoretical model for viewing American

Indian efforts to counter the effects of alcoholism in their communities in a culturally relevant way. In other words, it is through a return to, and maintenance of, traditional activities that the positive effects of contemporary approaches to alcohol abuse recovery and prevention can take hold in Indian Country.

The lens through which I will approach this set of issues is the history of American Indian approaches to alcohol abuse recovery and prevention—approaches which emphasize the role of traditional Native practices—highlighting how this process fits into the larger discussion of the role cultural practice plays in the resurgence of American Indian religious identity, a resurgence that I term "reprise." In effect, this term, borrowed from the vocabulary of musical composition, describes what I see as being the key to what some analysts have variously called *revival, renewal,* and *revitalization.* As these terms tend to draw upon imagery that plays into the "vanishing Indian" fantasy in that their use assumes a sort of death—or at very least, a cessation of traditional values and ideas in Native communities as a result of European contact and American colonization—I find *reprise* begins to highlight the far more accurate reality that many of the values, rituals, and identities now experiencing resurgence among American Indian communities have never really gone anywhere. Rather, they have continued, albeit in new clothing, within the very personalities of Native communities. My own grandmothers carried the ideas and lifeways relevant to their Native ancestry with them in their daily approaches to the universe. Like the Salinas River where their mothers drew water, the dry season of the dominant culture did not cause evaporation, but rather, drove the flow underground. Thus, the musical term *reprise* is a more fitting term in that it alludes to the rearticulation of an earlier theme whose basic elements remained present throughout. The process of alcohol recovery in Native communities draws upon the spiritual practices and values relevant to Native communities, making recovery an opportunity to reexperience a sense of "Indianess." Alcohol and other drug abuse prevention and recovery processes provide fertile ground for Indian communities—both those addicted and those who support them—to access these values and spiritual ideals in support of their larger reprise efforts.

Prior to discussing the context of recovery, a brief history of the relationship between Native America and alcohol abuse will be offered, along with an overview of the approaches by Indian communities directed at sustaining abuse prevention and recovery. Finally, the role that cultural relevance and traditional practices play in what has come to be called *wellbriety* will be described and added to the overall discussion of Native reprise through traditional healing.

INDIANS AND ALCOHOL

There exists a story that has become nearly iconic in the overall discourse on American Indians and alcohol abuse recovery, namely, the story of the

Alkali Lake Shuswap Indian Reserve in north-central British Columbia.[4] As the story goes, the reserve was free of alcohol until just prior to World War II, when a trading post/general store was opened by a non-Indian. Alcohol made its way into the community from this source, and by the 1960s, the reserve had a severe alcohol abuse problem, in that nearly every person on the reserve was drinking alcohol to some degree by the time they were in early adolescence. Dubbed "Alcohol Lake" by local communities, the notorious nature of the reserve was augmented by local media reports of arrests by the Royal Canadian Mounted Police (RCMP) for alcohol-related offenses as well as domestic violence and child abuse/neglect. However, there was virtually no response from the Canadian government, and the sole religious authority on the reserve, the local Catholic priest, was virtually mute on the subject. Then, in the summer of 1972, the seven-year-old daughter of tribal members Phyllis and Andy Chelsea refused to return home with her parents (from a stay with her grandmother) until her parents stopped drinking. Both parents did quit, Phyllis first with Andy following four days later, becoming the only two non-drinking adults on the entire reserve.

The Chelseas made contact with an Oblate Brother, Brother Ed Lynch, an Alcoholics Anonymous (A.A.) counselor from a nearby town, who visited the couple and provided the basic format for working the Twelve Step Program. While it took more than a year to attract any more Shuswaps to the kitchen table A.A. meetings at the Chelsea's home, Andy was elected tribal chair shortly after his sobriety became community news. That first year was a struggle for the Chelseas, owing in part to Andy Chelsea's implementation of radical changes on the reserve designed to curb alcohol consumption, provide safe childcare, and return the reserve to some semblance of health. Among his programs was the refusal of access to the reserve to anyone selling alcohol, especially the "Dog Creek Stage," little more than a flatbed truck full of beer and hard liquor that came to the reserve three times a week. In addition, the RCMP was brought in to arrest and prosecute illegal alcohol production and trafficking on the reserve (Andy Chelsea's own mother was arrested), and a voucher system was established with stores and businesses in nearby Williams Lake, wherein the government subsidy checks to some tribal members were sent to a central tribal bank, which issued vouchers redeemable at participating stores. These stores were strongly encouraged to refuse to honor vouchers for alcoholic beverages, with nearly complete compliance. Finally, the Catholic priest on the reserve was forcibly removed when he openly opposed the programs of Chelsea and his group. By 1973, the group had increased to 12, and by 1975, 40 percent of the reserve was sober. That number reached 98 percent by 1979. Though the A.A. process was clearly behind much of this success, the tribe also endeavored to revitalize the traditional spiritual life of the community. As the people of Alkali Lake had allowed this knowledge to fall out of the communal memory, the tribal council began to invite leaders from surrounding reserves to help them restore traditional spiritual traditions.

This is, of course, where the purposes of this chapter enter into the mix. One could rightly ask questions about the relationship between traditional revitalization and cultural construction when a tribe must learn traditional religious practices from neighboring tribes, tribes that may have historically practiced different spiritual traditions. Many commentaries regarding the Alkali Lake situation remark on the return of the community to "the Sacred Pipe" and "the Sweat Lodge," both important elements of "pan-Indianism," without critically analyzing the role that ritual construction plays in the reprise process. These two ritual complexes, that of the communal act of smoking a pipe and the generic sweat ceremony, provide a context within which pan-Indian elements can be seen to provide a set of religious practices which are specific to Native American and First Nations people and aid in the process of building discreet spiritual communities. Pan-Indianism is a somewhat controversial area in the larger American Indian religious discourse, given that it is ironic that the historical Euro-American colonial conflation of the hundreds of distinct tribal cultures extant prior to European arrival into the monolithic category "Indian" has provided an impetus for tribal-specific cultural survival. As English became a sort of *lingua franca* for Indian Country, the ability to make connections across tribal divides and all over the continent created the possibilities for political activism that has shaped contemporary Native America. Discussed by such luminaries as Vine DeLoria, Jr., this process is somewhat of a double-edged sword. On the one hand, important inroads to achieving sovereignty, including land and resource protection, as well as civil rights goals such as religious freedom and protection from police brutality, have come as a direct result of the ability of Indian people to see themselves as sharing a common set of issues attached to their indigenous status. On the other, the development of pan-Indian identity is viewed by some American Indians as an erosion of tribal-specific traditions. Language proficiency, sacred knowledge, community identity, traditional family structures, etc., are viewed as essential to the survival of tribal nations, and adherence to a set of ideologies and cultural practices that are dominated by Plains-oriented imagery are viewed as counterproductive to the cultural retention goals of particular non-Plains tribes. Key among the elements that tend to make up a pan-Indian spirituality are the Lakota *inipi*-style sweat ceremony, Plains-style *Calumet* Sacred Pipe and its ceremonial structures and meaning, and the "Medicine Wheel" theology, which will be discussed later. These are also connected to the development of the "pow wow" gathering, again a Plains-style set of dances associated with the Plains council-drum, a large horizontally played drum with several players who accompany themselves on it while singing dance songs from around the Plains region.

These elements inform the larger category "spiritual practices," providing an Indian-specific cultural vocabulary for the construction of religious identity. In the case of Alkali Lake and the notable turnaround experienced by that community, it is clear that the reduction of alcohol-related problems was truly a first step, to borrow from A.A. parlance, with the ultimate goal being to move toward a communal renaissance of Shuswap spiritual identity. What the above example suggests is that alcohol abuse recovery and prevention in Indian Country has a feature unique to itself, wherein the return to communal spiritual health is seen as essential to the process of individual sobriety and vice versa. Shared religious identity, learned, expressed, and validated through traditional practices, is the foundation for this collective wellness. However, one issue remains before a discussion of Native approaches to recovery, which draw from traditional practices can occur, namely, what is the role of alcoholic behavior in Native communities generally? A deeper understanding of the relationship between Indians and alcohol can provide a clearer sense of the *reasons* for a specifically Native American approach to recovery, and therefore the conscious effort to employ Native symbols and practices.

A relatively new approach to the relationship between Native American history and alcohol has been articulated through the *determinants of health* point of view. This approach views both the physical and social environment as having as much influence on health as purely biological factors.[5] The key feature of this approach for the purposes of this discussion is the refocus of the discourse away from not only the physical health problems that result from alcohol abuse, but also on medical approaches to abuse interdiction, and places it in discussion with the issues that facilitate, cause, and/or exacerbate the abuse to begin with—social and economic marginalization. This approach will highlight the culturally significant factors within recovery and prevention movements in Native communities.

In addition to health-oriented studies, there have been many alcohol-specific behavioral studies,[6] which view drinking styles as learned from the ambient drinking community. Thus, the discussion of American Indian alcohol abuse must consider both the socioeconomic factors detrimental to Native people generally, as well as the history of Indian interaction with alcohol as an aspect of colonization. Generally speaking, the study of alcohol and culture divides drinking populations into groups with restrictive attitudes toward alcohol consumption, those with views that actively promote moderation, and communities with no official position on the matter. An example of the first category might be America's Mormon communities, the moderation group can be seen in French and Italian approaches to wine as a food, and the latter category operates in the basically permissive atmosphere of American popular culture and the personal choice/individual responsibility ethic. What these studies have shown is that, while the presence of alcohol-related health issues—such as liver problems—correlate to the latter category as suspected, the restrictive-type community tends to produce more alcohol-related *social* problems, especially significantly higher per capita arrest statistics for driving while drunk, public drunkenness, and so on.[7] The implication here is that severely restrictive communities tend to provide alcohol consumption with antisocial cachet. Individuals who react against the norm for their social order can use extreme alcohol consumption as a means for going against the status quo, and/or to express a subconscious realization of one's fringe status. In an article by John Frank, Roland Moore, and Genevieve Ames titled "Historical and Cultural Roots of Drinking Problems among American Indians,"[8] the relationship between this contextual approach to alcohol consumption and the identification of alcohol abuse and American Indians is revealed in American Indian alcohol consumption patterns throughout history. The authors highlight the insidious dynamic between the cultural and socioeconomic marginalization of Indians and the assumption that alcohol abuse is somehow inherent in Native drinking patterns.

What they show, rather, is that Native drinking patterns emerge as a direct result of the relative newness of recreational alcohol consumption to Native communities and the behavior of non-Indians in early European contact zones. The newness factor refers to a distinct lack of prior information regarding alcohol consumption in early contact Indian contexts, and the non-Indian behavior reference is to the presence of non-Indian transient drinkers, who tended to come from the "non-scriptive"[9] (those without either an abiding prohibitive, nor moderation value approach to alcohol consumption) category. Thus, Native communities possessed no inherent categories for proper alcohol use, but due to the frontier nature of their interaction with Whites, often had problematic drinking as a model. In my view, this may point to a dualism with regard to the restrictive use producing a marker for fringe status, and the non-scriptive style rendering long-term overconsumption as a possible trend for Indian drinking.

Further, the article posits a pattern, or sequence, that emerges in Native alcohol consumption from first experience to a fully ensconced alcohol presence. In the first phase, the community is assumed to have a positive view of altered mental states prior to contact, owing to the transcendent nature of tribal rituals. While these are rarely achieved through pharmacological means, the authors opine that the mental states, which characterize much of indigenous ceremony achieved through sleep deprivation, pain, fasting, and so on, produce sensations that provided early contact communities with a set of cognitive categories for understanding the effects of alcohol. These effects, in their traditional context, were most often viewed positively, thus the initial presence of alcohol failed to draw communal sanctions, and neither, in many cases, did excessive drinking. These factors characterize the entrance into the second phase, initial contact, which Frank and colleagues refer to as a "naïve period of grace."[10] The authors claim that this period was both brief and variable according to tribal circumstances, and point to the social learning aspect of their argument.[11] The variability refers to the fact that within the processes of colonization in North America, national character is key in the approaches to the exploration and exploitation of this continent. There were Spanish settlers in the southeast, southwest, and Gulf regions, French trappers and traders around the Great Lakes and in the Ohio River Valley, and English all along the eastern seaboard and to the Appalachian Mountains by the middle of the eighteenth century. Each of these regions represented a different approach to the interaction with Natives, as well as to drinking in general. Regardless of these differences, it was a relatively short time before effectively all Indian communities were experiencing alcohol problems to some degree, the central feature of the third phase. This third phase is further associated with certain hallmarks[12] reported on by multiple observers of Indian behavior with regard to alcohol consumption: group drinking, lone drinking, and maximal dosing[13] (drinking until all the alcohol is gone). Absence of social controls on alcohol consumption, a rapid rise in uncontrolled behavior and violence while under the influence of alcohol, an absence of either blame or remorse for these actions, and attributing the behavior to alcohol itself are all hallmarks reported on. Related to this final aspect can be found a near-fanatical opposition to the actual substance, viewing it as a demonic presence. While not universal in nature, these trends nonetheless represent a fairly consistent sequence throughout Indian Country.

Given the precontact cultural tendency to experience altered states of consciousness primarily in highly ritualized contexts, for example, with the use of psychotropic substances such as peyote and datura (jimsonweed) or through physical stress from fasting or inducing pain, as well as the nearly complete lack of distilled (as opposed to fermented) beverage consumption prior to European contact,[14] it can be posited that neither fundamental aspects of precontact Native cultures, nor inherent biological factors provide adequate evidence of a predisposition toward problem drinking by Natives. This leads Frank, Moore, and Ames to their ultimate thesis: that excessive drinking and violence were learned from Whites.[15]

Given that moderate-to-heavy drinking was fairly prevalent in the early national period (annual per capita alcohol consumption between 1800 and 1830 was nearly 9 gallons, compared to 2.6 in 1978[16]), and the frontier nature of all of the European-dominated regions, I believe this thesis provides much insight. What I would add, apropos to the task at hand, is that there existed a connection between European and later American cultural approaches toward life in general that contributed heavily to the erosion of traditional lifeways. As Natives increasingly saw themselves as *Indians* rather than through distinct traditional categories, and as the moniker *Indian* connoted a marginal status vis-à-vis Euro-American culture in general, the aboriginal population of this continent seemed uniquely positioned to the hazards of both excessive drinking and the adoption of radical alcoholic behaviors as a feature of their collective identity. It may be, in fact, that alcoholic drinking levels in Indian country can be considered an opportunistic infection related to the overall disease of colonialism. Further, it could be argued that the erosion of discreet cultural and spiritual identities of the various Indian nations is both the result of alcoholic drinking and of the genocidal tendencies associated with the marginalization inherent in the negativity associated with Indianess in the national cultural consciousness. The act of alcohol consumption (not only abuse of alcohol), became a marker for bad behavior in Indian Country, outwardly verifying internalized aspects of their marginalized status. Thus, the contemporary approaches to recovery focus attention on communal health factors and diminish, to a certain degree, the emphasis on individual transgression. As such, they are indicative of the reprise process.

It is this relationship between Native American alcohol abuse problems and cultural factors that provide the basis for the various approaches to recovery via religious identity occurring throughout Indian Country. Before exploring Native American approaches to alcohol abuse recovery and prevention, an exploration into the issues surrounding the application of traditional cultural practices within American Indian cultural revitalization is in order.

CONTINUITY AND REVITALIZATION MOVEMENTS

Within the study of American Indian religious traditions, the key examples of revitalization movements in the scholarship continue to be the Handsome Lake Tradition; the Ghost Dance; and the Peyote Religion, which provides the foundations for the Native American Church. What these all have in common is the assertion of the practitioners that participation in these rituals would bring about a radical change in the situation in which the Indians found themselves. In the case of the Ghost Dance, these changes would affect the whole continent, while in the Handsome Lake movement, the entire world would be transformed in an apocalypse in the true sense of that term. The consistent reference to these examples that employ radical change has tended to influence the way scholars have approached the issue of revitalization among contemporary American Indian communities. While these revival movements speak often of total transformation, I hold that totality was, at times, rhetorical, and that the intention was a much more localized change in Indian circumstances extending to regions within the purview of the initial movements. While total transformation of the entire universe is the overt goal for Indian communities,[17] in the majority of American Indian communities since the turn of the last century, revival movements have been manifestations of a much more subtle reprise process. In these instances, cultural and spiritual themes have resurfaced, continuing in different forms under the auspices of the dominant cultural systems (religious, political, or economic) for the betterment of localized communities with specific sets of circumstances.

REPRISE AND THE DEMOGRAPHIC PUZZLE

As an exemplary approach to contemporary Indian identity that provides insight into revitalization movements in Native America, I offer Joane Nagel's treatment in her book *American Indian Ethnic Renewal: Red Power and the Resurgence of Identity and Culture*.[18] In this important piece, the transformation process inherent in reprise is spoken of in terms of statistical data, rendering a clear notion of contemporary American Indian struggles with authenticity. Nagel addresses the interesting conundrum arising out of the 1990 national census in which people claiming American Indian ancestry jumped from half a million (in 1960) to two million people. As this jump is unexplainable via birth and death rates, Nagel deconstructs the census questions, and the possible responses[19] over time to ascertain some clue as to the shift during the decades between 1960 and 1990 that is clearly a result of a change in self-identification. Finding ambiguities in the way that the census packages concepts such as race, nationality, and ethnicity, the data clearly show that American Indian respondents shifted between categories in their individual responses, as well as identifying differently in 1990 than they did in 1960.

Noting these ambiguities, Nagel then casts about among sociological and political science categories for a theoretical explanation for the increase in the number of Americans choosing American Indian as at least part of their self-identity. Combining the aforementioned analysis of census figures with archival research into newsworthy mention of American Indians between 1960 and 1980, along with correspondence and telephone interviews (including with an incarcerated Leonard Peltier), she makes a fairly persuasive case for what she terms *ethnic mobilization*—ethnic groups organizing to litigate, lobby, and protest—as a suitable explanation for this phenomenon. Nagel also points to political and economic transformations that grew out of the Civil Rights movement such as Lyndon Johnson's War on Poverty, Nixon's push for Indian self-determination, and the Reagan-era explosion of reservation casinos as examples of Red Power joining similar Black and Chicano-American movements of the post-Civil Rights era. She asserts that it was "the federal government (who) promoted an Indian ethnic revival... by funding Indian organizations and by providing increased incentives for Indian ethnic identification and activism," to the tune of 1.98 billion dollars by 1980.[20] She also claims that the termination policies of the 1950s, which forced many American Indians into an urban working class away from reservation communities, served as an impetus for the pan-Indian "powwow" culture, as well as political movements produced by dispossessed young people of American Indian descent, which were linked to the general U.S. cultural renaissance of the 1960s. The Alcatraz occupation, in which a group of American Indians enacting an "Indians of All Tribes" protest movement took over the Alcatraz Island Prison site in San Francisco Bay for 19 months in 1969–71 was emblematic of such movements. Its leadership were essentially all enrolled in the first Native American Studies course at San Francisco State University, and as such represented educated, enculturated activists in the mold of Ghandi, or Martin Luther King, Jr., and the Nigerian leader N. Azikewe.[21] These leaders, then, were the ironic product of governmental assimilationist policies, rendering an Indian Country diaspora that was marginalized vis-à-vis the dominant culture due to the unique nature of American Indian history.

The significance of this situation described by Nagel for my purposes here is that the role general Indian self-identification played in the reification of Native political identity formation also led to a renewed interest in Native religious cultural practices, both pan-Indian and tribal specific. The political awareness associated with opposition to the social and economic ills experienced in Indian Country included increased awareness of alcohol abuse issues, and the totality of Indian spiritual, cultural, and economic health, which were in turn all linked to traditional religious practices. I believe that Nagel's neoliberal take on the process of Indian identity-building among indigenous Americans, while cogent and convincing, falls into the same trap as the scientific rationale for denying that very identity, namely, assuming there was a complete break in the transfer of American Indian culture at the turn of the twentieth century. Nagel draws upon the same biases in that her sense is that American Indians attempting to rearticulate their identity as Indian do so through cultural construction, rather than reconstruction. While she valorizes the efforts of Indian people to assert a relatively newfound Native identity in the modern world, she also assumes that these cultures were dead, and are now reanimated. By contrast, the reprise concept points to a continuity that actually strengthens Nagel's argument, and allows for a view of Native people that highlights an ongoing adaptive process. Nagel's take—important and informative as it is—depends upon the assumption that repression of specific practices associated with American Indian religiosity and the eclipse of traditional beliefs by those of the dominant culture (Christianity, market capitalism, primogeniture, etc.) was total.

This understanding is evident in the anthropological and historiographic use of the specific theological term "conversion" when referring to both religious and social adaptations by Indian communities over time. I have addressed this issue in the past with regard to the contemporary Chumash Indians of Central California and the dominance of the conversion concept in the academic discourse on them.[22] The dissolution of this bias has been championed by thinkers such as Michael McNally, who has asserted the role that Christianity and Christian practices such as hymn singing have promoted Ojibwa traditional cultural reprise.[23] McNally's emphasis on the role of active practice in the process of religion also provides a way to subvert the ethnocentric tendencies within the academy.

In a recent article,[24] McNally calls for a shift toward a practice-centered approach to American Indian religious traditions rather than focusing all attention on the beliefs to which these practices allegedly point. More than merely "theory-speak for its own sake,"[25] he suggests that this perspectival refocus will clarify the role that practice plays in the navigation of Native traditions through the consequences of colonization. He also implies that the academic treatment of Native spirituality has thus far been, in the main, a search for ethnographic authenticity, sifting through the constructed contemporary practices of Indian communities in search of "purer" aspects associated with precontact cultures.[26] Therefore, an attempt to "recalibrate our analysis in terms of practice rather than belief"[27] would open up the dialogue to include the growth and dynamism inherent in these communities and bring us closer to an understanding of the role that incorporating new ideas and practices has played in the continuity of Indian culture, and diminish to some degree the control over the discourse by academia that fails to appreciate the Indian perspective. To this cogent argument I would add that the refocus on issues of practice can also serve to shed light upon Native religiosity generally, and can clear the way for an appreciation of contemporary traditions and of ritual construction within the context of modern Native America.

NATIVE APPROACHES TO ABUSE RECOVERY/PREVENTION

While the focus here is on *contemporary* recovery processes inherent in Native American A.A. and the Wellbriety Movement, I have previously associated the academic obsession with "apocalypticism" in the analysis of American Indian cultural revivals with Handsome Lake and peyote use. No discussion of the role alcohol abuse recovery and prevention in Indian Country would be complete without discussing the historically significant contributions to this area by the Handsome Lake/Longhouse tradition, the "Delaware Prophets," and the Native American Church. These and other attempts,[28] took the loss of spiritual traditions as the source of the problems associated with alcohol, and the need for tradition retention and revival as the key to physical and cultural recovery and did so very early in the history of European presence on the continent. In fact, as early as 1737, reports of a Native "seer"[29] who preached against alcohol use to the Shawnee and Onondaga appeared in diaries and official documents, and by 1740, opposition to both alcohol use and the loss of Native traditions became the key feature of multiple itinerant Native preachers throughout the Northeast and Great Lakes regions.[30] However, six key individuals arose among the Lenni Lenape (Delaware) between 1744 and 1766, who came to be known as "the Delaware prophets," and are associated with not only sparking a revitalization of traditions in their respective places and times, but also with informing subsequent revitalization movements.[31] In addition, these prophets are often referred to as an initial articulation of a positive pan-Indian identity in the region.[32] The best known of these individuals, called Neolin, began to preach in 1755, building on previous prophets. Neolin articulates what is the most fully developed set of concepts in the Lenni Lenape prophet movement. These ideas are representative of both the themes of the Delaware Prophets, and are also indicative of later ideas including those of Handsome Lake regarding alcohol consumption. In an address to a Native audience in 1759, he stated:

> Hear what the Great Spirit has ordered me to tell you! You are to make sacrifices, in the manner that I shall direct; to put off entirely from yourselves the customs to which you have adopted since the white people came among us...and above all, you must abstain from drinking their deadly beson [liquor], which they forced upon us for the sake of increasing their gains and diminishing our numbers.[33]

Neolin regularly called for "unity, cultural purification, and personal purification,"[34] with the latter to be achieved through abstinence from alcohol and promiscuous sex, as well as the ritual use of the Black Drink,[35] a traditional (nonintoxicating) tea made from the leaves of the Yaupon Holly. This beverage is found among Native cultures of the North and Southeast, and its consumption is ritually regulated.[36] This conscious replacement of alcohol with the traditional Black Drink is particularly notable in that the ritual context of its consumption reinforces the precontact social structure, a central ingredient to both the Delaware Prophets' and subsequent approaches to alcohol abuse recovery and traditional spiritual revitalization.

Perhaps more well-known in the discourse on American Indian revitalization is the Handsome Lake tradition, begun by a Seneca named Ganiodaio (Handsome Lake) in the early nineteenth century.[37] Born in 1735, Handsome Lake had fought for the British during the Revolutionary War, and as a result, had a particularly difficult existence in the new America. The story of his life is one of a nomadic social outcast, partly due to his marginalization by Whites, and partly due to his Native community's reverence for his brother, Cornplanter, a Seneca war chief. By the time he reached his sixties, he was essentially hopelessly alcoholic and near death due to the physical ravages of his drinking. By all accounts of the time, Handsome Lake died on June 15, 1799. He lay "cold and breathless"[38] for seven hours, whereupon he awoke having had a vision in which the Great Spirit commanded him to pass on messages to his people. For the next 16 years, until his death, Handsome Lake abstained from alcohol and preached a process of cultural and spiritual revitalization that has come to be known as the Code of Handsome Lake, or Longhouse Religion, still a strong presence among the Haudenosaunee (Iroquois).

The key features of the Code are, of course, abstention from alcohol, but perhaps more central to Handsome Lake's purpose are elements that attempted to reestablish traditional practices, relationships, and beliefs. However, Handsome Lake preached a certain level of adaptation to European culture, especially in education, everyday dress, and farming style. This effectively shielded the Longhouse from overt criticism from Whites, while placing the Haudenosaunee traditions in a central position in the daily lives of the community. The Code, having derived from Handsome Lake's vision, also has the adaptive quality of syncretistic movements, in that much of the innovative elements have a clearly Christian patina. Handsome Lake was very well acquainted with Christianity, indeed, the region was one of the more heavily contested missionary territories in the country at the time of Handsome Lake's vision. Catholic priests and Protestant ministers of many denominational stripes competed for converts, putting pressure on the authority of traditionalists in the region. What Handsome Lake was able to do was place Haudenosaunee traditions in a position to compete with Christian theology, with the added element of tools to secure freedom from the concomitant problems associated with alcoholism. The narrative features of Handsome Lake's vision contain elements familiar to a heavily evangelized community: the death/resurrection scenario of Handsome Lake's story, images of both heaven and hell, along with the clearly apocalyptic aspect to the vision which describes a fiery end of the world if the people failed to maintain their traditions. In addition, Longhouse religious gatherings contained a confessional element, where public admissions of sinful behavior were encouraged. Indeed the concept of *sin* was new to Haudenosaunee culture, resulting from the preaching of Handsome Lake. Thus, the physical Longhouse provided a de facto church, which may have legitimated the practices therein to some of the Christian members of the surrounding non-Indian community (and perhaps to some of the converted Indians as well), and the theological Longhouse established a strong set of practices and behaviors that allowed for the continuing appeal to tradition in the Haudenosaunee cultural survival. The Longhouse Religion was eventually formally organized into a church, and by 1845 had begun implementing a standardized approach to alcohol abuse recovery, prevention, and the maintenance of cultural traditions.[39]

Another infamous and continuing viable means for recovery from alcohol abuse in Indian Country is the advocacy of peyote use, most often within the context of the Native American Church. Peyote, a mescaline-producing cactus indigenous to the southwestern United States and northern

Mexico, has been incorporated into religious ceremonies in those areas since pre-Columbian times.[40] The entrance of peyote into the Native American reservation system came as a result of the teachings of a Comanche named Zuanah, known most widely as Quanah Parker, who, like Handsome Lake, successfully recovered from alcohol addiction through the adoption of a Christian-influenced practice of Native traditions, these in a decidedly pan-Indian vein.[41] Parker had been given peyote by a Ute medicine man while suffering an infected wound received during a battle with the Texas Rangers. While under its influence, Parker had a vision of Jesus Christ, who told him he must reform his ways and spread the use of peyote to his people. Returning to the Staked Plains region and becoming the last war chief to bring his people to the reservation, Parker began to assimilate what he knew of the peyote theology of the north Mexican tribes into Comanche-style practices and beliefs, adding the appropriate Christian elements that he had been exposed to by missionaries. Thus, the peyote became a gift from Jesus to Indians in order that they might have a direct experience of Jesus, shared like communion among the assembled people at the appropriate ritual gathering, for the purposes of promoting love, peace, and understanding. Eventually, Parker, along with a companion and student known as John Wilson (Kiowa), spread the peyote-way ideology beyond his reservation borders, training what have come to be known as "roadmen," itinerant peyote-way practitioners, and defending the ritual use of peyote by Indians.

The Native American Church, incorporated as such in 1918,[42] varies somewhat from group to group and roadman to roadman. However, the basic approach remains consistent, wherein the use of peyote allows for a deep communal prayer experience in which one receives visions regarding one's own specific path. In the alcohol abuse recovery community, peyote use remains a controversial method within the Western interdiction model, given the counterintuitive nature of using an element characterized as a controlled substance by the federal government to promote sobriety. However, the Native American Church has as a basic tenet the total abstinence from alcoholic beverages. Further, peyote is only used during peyote meetings, which themselves are infrequent aspects of the overall *Peyote Way* (the set of principles associated with the Native American Church theology). Peyote, then, represents the sacrifice of Jesus, the need for close, personal contact with Him, and a medicinal herb that provides divine aid in the reformation of one's life and the strength to stay on the right path. Peyote use provides what Gilbert Quintero calls an "epistemological shift,"[43] a new way to conceive of alcohol, its use and abuse, one's personal identity, and one's purpose for living. The Church itself is a structured community of like believers, a key aspect of virtually all spiritually oriented recovery systems.

What the Native American Church also provides is a culturally unique set of beliefs and practices. In spite of the obvious Christian elements, the Church is uniquely Indian in symbolic representation, physical setting (meetings are often held in tipis, and even when not, contain Native expressions in music and decor) and the required Native heritage of its membership. The success of the Peyote Way in recovery from alcoholism has been documented in both Albaugh, and Anderson and Quintero. What is important here in regards to this chapter's thesis is that the focus is again on a traditional identity that depends to a large degree on traditional practice. The Native American Church provides the alcoholic with a new, specifically Native identity, complete with a set of practices and goals such as learning songs, and the adoption of regular sweat lodge and sacred pipe use. Such practices not only replace the averse behaviors that derive from alcohol abuse but replaces them with culturally satisfying ones that build on ethnic identification to provide a systematic spiritual complex that connects to, and validates that identification. This process, as I have stated, mirrors other types of recovery systems in that it has a spiritual component, it connects the alcoholic to a community of likeminded individuals, and it provides a regular setting for the expression of that unique community. Both standardized systems, such as Native American Alcoholics Anonymous and the Wellbriety movement, as well as individualized faith-based recovery processes draw to some degree or another from these elements in their approach to alcohol abuse recovery and prevention in Indian Country with varying degrees of success. What remains is an analysis of these approaches with regard to their tendencies to both draw upon *and* promote traditional American Indian spiritual values.

While no clear consensus exists as to the most effective means for preventing alcohol abuse, nor for the recovery from alcoholism,[44] one can identify two key paths taken by recovery programs in general: one that views alcohol and other substance abuses through the *disease model* and therefore somewhat beyond the abuser's responsibility, and those that view the behavior as *voluntary*, though irrational. In the latter group, programs such as Rational Recovery, founded by California social worker Jack Trimpy, and Moderation Management, a nonprofit organization based in New York City, oppose the disease model and defer to techniques developed in cognitive behavior therapy systems that attempt to give the abuser the tools to individualize their approach to moderation or abstinence. Alcoholics Anonymous and its 12-step spin-off groups such as Narcotics Anonymous best represent the disease model. These systems view the abuser as having some propensity (genetic, sociocultural, and/or psychological) toward abuse for which total abstinence from alcohol is the only appropriate watershed choice.[45] Alcohol abuse, then, becomes a symptom of a larger network of issues from which the abuser must recover. This remains a controversial position[46] in that the American Psychological Association fails to regard the abuse of alcohol as falling into the "disease or mental defect" category.[47] The Supreme Court, in *Traynor v. Turnage*, found no reason to compel the Veteran's Administration to provide payments to clients for whom alcohol abuse was their foundational issue.[48] Therefore, the view of alcohol abuse as a defect of character, linked to individual fortitude and moral standing, remains the prevailing official position, whereas the 12-step approach, which has at its core a strong spiritual component, has long been the more popular prescription for successful recovery. There are some common key features to the various "disease model" programs, care centers, and encounter groups that comprise the contemporary alcohol abuse recovery community. The most common of these is the utilization of the 12-steps employed by Alcoholics Anonymous. As this "recovery community" approach has both spawned a specifically Native American program and greatly informed the Wellbriety Movement, a brief discussion of the Alcoholics Anonymous approach is in order.

Alcoholics Anonymous officially began with the publishing of *Alcoholics Anonymous* in 1939, but within A.A. circles, the genesis was in the meeting of two men, known as "Bill W." (William Griffith Wilson) and "Dr. Bob" (Robert Holbrook Smith, MD), in May 1935. Both men were experiencing difficulties remaining sober, and both had embarked on separate quests for answers to their problems. Wilson was convinced by his doctor, William Silkworth, that alcoholism was a kind of *allergy* in which the alcoholic experiences symptoms from drinking not found in normal drinkers. In addition, Silkworth convinced Wilson that only the "Great Physician" could successfully heal alcoholism, leading Wilson to search out evidence of spiritual aspects of alcohol recovery. This came in the form of one of Bill W.'s former drinking buddies, Ebby Thatcher, who had apparently recovered from alcoholism through participation in a spiritual program pioneered by what the literature refers to as "The Oxford Group," an offshoot of the First Century Christian movement founded in 1919 by Dr. Frank N. D. Buchman.[49] Wilson sought out more information on this approach, eventually studying with the Rev. Samuel Shoemaker, a member of the Oxford Group. Wilson himself attributes most of the 12-steps (3 through 12) to Shoemaker's teaching.[50] Even with this information, however, Wilson relapsed, again winding up in the hospital for detoxification. It was during this stay that Wilson had what he believed to be a religious experience, in which he was overwhelmed by a spiritual presence that declared him a "free man."[51] Following this realization, Wilson became "born again" at the Calvary Rescue Mission.

The actual founding of the A.A. process, however, relied upon Wilson's meeting Dr. Bob. While on a business trip to Akron, Ohio, Wilson found himself on the verge of relapse. Phoning a local minister, he inquired as to the possibility of speaking with other alcoholics. This minister sent Wilson to the home of Dr. Bob Smith, who was in the midst of relapse and being prayed for by his Oxford Group congregation. Over the next three months, the two studied the Bible and Oxford Group ideas, eventually forming the pioneer Akron Group, the model for A.A. fellowships from that time forward. Together, the Akron Group formalized the 12-step approach and its central feature, the 12-step recovery meeting, which became known as Alcoholics

Anonymous meetings after the publication of the book by the same name.[52] Thus, the A.A. process encompasses the combination of an individual "spiritual awakening" as well as the fellowship and community one experiences through regular contact with other alcoholics. This feeling of community, formalized into the 12-step meeting protocol, is the feature which I believe most influences specific American Indian innovations of Native-specific recovery systems (Wellbriety meetings in particular) and provides the context within which to view the reprise process from a contemporary, pan-Indian perspective.

Regular non-Indian A.A. meeting protocol varies somewhat from group to group, and Alcoholics Anonymous claims no organizing superstructure. However, meetings tend to follow a standardized procedure in which a volunteer convener (secretary) announces the start of the meeting, opens with a prayer (usually the Serenity Prayer), reads aloud a standard (but optional) opening, reads, or ask for volunteers to read, sections of *Alcoholics Anonymous* (The Big Book) containing the 12-steps as well as other portions. What follows this process generally involves a brief sharing by someone usually chosen by the secretary in which they discuss their own story, usually identifying a theme from which to encourage additional sharing by the other participants. The one key caveat here is that the comments are in the form of a sort of monologue, in that no cross-talk is allowed. This separates the A.A. meeting from other encounter-type groups or group therapy. Speaking directly to another person violates protocol. This individual focus, juxtaposed with the communal nature of the A.A. meeting, renders an interesting mix of collectivity and individualism, community and isolate. It is this feature of A.A. that has proved dissatisfying to many American Indians, in that it brings a Protestant influence and focus on individual salvation in the form of a personal spiritual awakening that seems to violate the reverence for community found within tribal spirituality.

One attempt to reconcile this issue has been a movement within A.A. to formulate a Native American-oriented meeting style, along with a reevaluation of both the steps and the ideology behind them, which has met with some success. While the adaptation of the 12-steps of Alcoholics Anonymous to American Indian spirituality is not without some controversy,[53] the process has also been a notable success in Indian Country, especially among highly acculturated communities such as those found in urban centers. The Alkali Lake situation and other contexts show that reservations have also been able to at least begin the path to recovery.[54] What is significant for this study is the addition of symbols and practices that evoke a more specifically Indian approach to the A.A. process. The key differences in style are pan-Indian in nature, with the use of candles, burning sage bundles, circular seating arrangements, and other Native-themed motifs to create a more familiar atmosphere within the meeting space, as well as changes in the wording of the steps to reflect a pan-Indian lexicon of signification. An example of the wording changes in the 12-steps makes this point clear:[55]

Traditional A.A. Steps

We came to believe that a Power greater than ourselves can re-store us to sanity. (Step 2)

We admitted to God, to ourselves, and to another human being the exact nature of our wrongs. (Step 5)

Indian A.A. Steps

We come to believe the power of The Pipe is greater than our-selves, and can restore us to our Culture and Heritage. (Step 2)

We acknowledge to the Great Spirit, to ourselves, and to the Native American Brother-hood, our struggles against the tide and its manifest destiny. (Step 5)

Several differences are worth noting here, namely, the present tense use in the "Indian-step" language, as opposed to the past tense of the traditional steps, as well as overtly communal nature of the Indian A.A. ideology. While it is part of the A.A. process to see oneself in a community of fellow sufferers,[56] the Alcoholics Anonymous program is essentially a lone journey, with the exception of the encouraged employment of a "sponsor," a trusted, long-term 12-stepper that serves as a mentor and guide. Alcoholics Anonymous, deriv-ing as it does from Protestant Christianity, follows an individual-salvation model, in which the alcoholic is expected to have their own sobriety as their main goal, as well as an evangelistic element, bidding the now sober alco-holic to "carry this message to alcoholics,"[57] while acknowledging that their program and sobriety are their own individual responsibility. Also, the refer-ences to the role the dominant culture has played in the struggles of Indian people (manifest destiny) draw the individual alcoholic into the collective pan-Indian community, further emphasizing the uniquely indigenous nature of their issues, and therefore their relief.

Somewhat ironically, the introduction of the A.A. concepts into the general Native American consciousness came as a direct result of Bureau of In-dian Affairs programs designed to entice Indians off of their respective reser-vations and into urban centers for the purposes of enculturation through job training.[58] The jobs failed to materialize, and many Indians, especially men, found themselves worse off in the city, rather than better. The resulting de-pressive conditions, both emotional and economic, gave rise to alcohol abuse, and prompted the entry into treatment centers that drew upon or promoted the Alcoholics Anonymous paradigm, which was then communicated to res-ervation communities when many of these individuals returned home.[59]

Coyhis and White place the next fifty-plus years of Native American inter-action with A.A. into three overlapping stages: the participation in standard

A.A. meetings by Native people, the adaptation of A.A. for Indians, and the development of "broader cultural frameworks of recovery" by Native communities themselves. In the adaptation stage, both local and national offices of A.A. International attempted to address the structural needs (such as the language changes in the literature), while Native meetings were developing their own character without guidance from the official A.A. structure. These changes included meetings that started and ended much later than most traditional meetings, with long breaks for socializing in the middle; inclusion of children and other family members, the addition of singing, meals, sage-smoke smudging, eagle-feather or other markers for those who are speaking, and singing into the meeting format. It also included pan-Indian references such as "medicine wheel," and "the Red Road."[60]

This latter term, drawn from Plains Indian theology, especially that of Oglala Holy Man Hehaka Sapa (Black Elk), was further articulated by Gene Thin Elk (Lakota)[61] and developed into a bona fide approach to alcohol recovery by the nonprofit organization White Bison, founded by Don L. Coyhis (Mohican). The overt reference is to the southern direction in Black Elk's vision, which the Lakota people are said to be traveling when they live in balance, peace, and harmony with the creation.[62] With the emphasis of Plains imagery and ideologies in the development of pan-Indian concepts, the Red Road has come to mean a balanced and harmonious journey by all Indian people who adhere to it. The Red Road ideology is best described by Gene Thin Elk himself:

> The Red Road is a holistic approach to mental, physical, spiritual, and emotional wellness based on Native American healing concepts and traditions, having prayer as the basis of all healing.... The traditions and values of the Native American People ensure balance by living these cultural traditions through the Red Road. Healing is a way of life for the Native American who understands and lives the cultural traditions and values.[63]

The language of contemporary psychology and social work are obvious, owing to Gene Thin Elk's Master's of Arts training in these areas, as well as his work in developing portable concepts that can be communicated to mental and physical health practitioners who work primarily or exclusively with an Indian clientele. The Red Road concept informs and guides much of the Wellbriety Movement, combining with both pan-Indian and regionally specific spiritual practices to effect processes of healing appropriate to the needs of those communities employing Wellbriety and White Bison techniques and concepts. For the purposes of this section, I will draw from the published materials of White Bison in order to fully articulate what the Wellbriety Movement entails, its parameters and approaches, and role in the furthering of the Red Road philosophy.

The Wellbriety Movement drew upon Gene Thin Elk's notion that the Red Road approach to recovery from alcohol abuse provides "detoxification of the spirit as well as the body."[64] In particular, Don L. Coyhis, the founder of White Bison, drew strength from his grandfather, Joe Coyhis, and a visit with a Native Elder in New Mexico to envision an approach to alcohol abuse recovery that would take Native community concerns into consideration while drawing upon traditional Native values in the healing process. During his visit with the elder, Coyhis was given what the elder referred to as the "Four Laws of Change," which Coyhis incorporated into his thinking on the Medicine Wheel, and articulated as a path appropriate to Native Americans in general.

The Medicine Wheel derives its name from the Bighorn Medicine Wheel in Wyoming,[65] with similar stone examples found throughout the Great Plains. They are physically structured as a series of radii extending out from a central point at regular intervals. While little is known about the specific uses of these stone constructions,[66] they appear to have had a religious, ceremonial, and astrological significance, with many dating back over two thousand years before present.[67] Much of Plains spiritual teaching draws upon a circular, "sun-wise" motif (often deriving from the creation stories of the various tribal groups of the region), and has come to symbolize the unity and structure of the universe.[68] Medicine Wheel approaches to wellness vary, but the basic indigenous meanings associated with them, much like the Sacred Pipe, have found their way to pan-Indian discourse from Plains-specific religious traditions (with much appropriation from New Age practitioners along the way). The Medicine Wheel draws upon connotations of interconnectedness, balance, and directional symbolism found in many, if not most, tribal regions.[69] This latter aspect, directionality, has come to be a key feature of pan-Indian spirituality, with specific meanings associated with seven points: North, South, East, West, Zenith, Nadir, and inward. Colors are also generally associated with the directions, along with seasonal type and personality traits. What Coyhis and others have done is to apply what Gene Thin Elk has called an "innate" in Native Americans[70] to the process of communal approaches to recovery, further tying the freedom from the problems associated with alcohol abuse to traditional communal values. The Medicine Wheel is symbolized within the Wellbriety Movement by the Sacred Hoop, a physical hoop of 100 eagle feathers constructed by elders from around Indian Country and dedicated to the movement at the first Gathering of the Elders in 1994.[71] This hoop travels to various national gatherings associated with the Wellbriety Movement and provides a focal point for ceremonial observations during the gatherings.

The Four Laws of Change given to Coyhis provide the Movement with a set of ideological underpinnings that support the superstructure and facilitate localized entrance into the Wellbriety process. As gathered by Don Coyhis during his stay with the Elder from New Mexico,[72] the first law is that change must come from within, from the "within-side," giving the Wellbriety process a spiritual beginning that leads to physical healing. Second is the notion that development must be preceded by a vision. Not necessarily a spiritual vision, the reference here is to the conscious effort to create the reality of change, to plan on success. The third law refers to the fact that a "great learning" must occur in the change—that the entire community is in the process of learning and that no individual can get well unless all of the community is participating in the learning experience. Finally, the fourth law states that one must create a "healing forest." This is a reference to a story in which several ill trees in an ill forest leave the forest to get well, then having done so, return to the forest only to become re-infected. The emphasis here is obviously on the need to heal the entire community—that not only the individual who suffers from substance abuse, but the community as well and that the context that produces the illness must also be addressed. This is, of course, the key factor for the purposes of this study. From the Wellbriety perspective, the well community is envisioned as having a healthy communal and tribal spiritual identity, expressed through traditional practices. The "well" aspect of Wellbriety refers specifically to going beyond sobriety, committing as a community to work toward cultural as well as physical health as a means of prevention. Regular participation in tribal-specific traditional practices, augmented by *Circles of Recovery* (an outreach and gathering system that brings the Wellbriety structure to local sites),[73] is the suggested path. White Bison as an organization primarily serves as a unifying force, tying the various approaches to alcohol and other drug abuse recovery processes into a network that takes Native cultures to be the key factor in communal wellness.

CONCLUSION

What all of these approaches point to is both an early and ongoing connection between traditional reprise and the prevention of and recovery from social ills. This tension between the individual realm of abusive behavior and the communal sense of both the ultimate harm and possibility for recovery is a central concern of this project. What I feel the American Indian approaches to alcohol recovery show is the subversion of the "western" interdictive medical model for recovery which emphasizes the broken individual needing to be repaired in order to halt the ill effects of their behavior on the community, and instead highlighting what is a basic tenet of Native American traditional healing: the maintenance of individual wellness as inseparable from community. Traditional Indian religions tend to subsume the individual to the collective, and much of religious practice in these tribal contexts is geared toward ascertaining, analyzing, and communicating the spiritual nature of the people's responsibilities to the universe. In longer-lived systems such as those espoused by the Longhouse Religion, the "middle-passage" of the Peyote Way by the Native American Church, or the more recent developments of the Native American A.A., Red Road, or Wellbriety Movements, what is clear is the connection between a strong sense of wellness, proper position in the universal order, and traditional religious practices. Thus, a traditional identity, maintained through its associated practices, is seen by many contemporary Native communities as key to both physical and cultural survival.

NOTES

1. Anti-Saloon League of America, *Anti-Saloon League of America Yearbook* (Westerville, Ohio: American Issue Press, 1920), 28. Cited by Harold A. Mulford, *Alcohol and Alcoholism in Iowa, 1965* (Iowa City: University of Iowa, 1965), 9.

2. For examples of these data, see the Native Health Databases section of the University of New Mexico's Health Sciences Center Library at: http://hsc.unm.edu/library/nhd/index.cfm.

3. Ibid.

4. This story is often repeated in the literature, including a film titled *The Honor of All: The Story of Alkali Lake*, Phil Lucas Productions, 1985, video, 56:48 min. Here in this brief overview I have utilized The Four Worlds International Web page, which is devoted to the story, at: http://www.4worlds.org/4w/ssr/Partiv.htm.

5. For a collection of essays that view health from this perspective, see *Why Are Some People Healthy and Others Not?: The Determinants of Health of Populations*, ed. E. G. Evans, M. L. Barer, and T. R. Marmot (New York: Aldine de Gruyter, 1994).

6. See, for example, Howard D. Chilcoat and Naomi Breslau, "Alcohol Disorders in Young Adulthood: Effects of Transitions into Adult Roles," *Journal of Health and Social Behavior* 37, no. 4 (December 1996): 339–49; James F. Mosher and David H. Jernigan, "Public Action and Awareness to Reduce Alcohol-Related Problems: A Plan of Action," *Journal of Public Health Policy* 9, no. 1 (Spring 1988): 17–41; and Eric Single, "International Perspectives on Alcohol as a Public Health Issue," *Journal of Public Health Policy* 5, no. 2 (June 1984): 238–56.

7. Nii-K. Plange, "Social and Behavorial Issues Related to Drinking Patterns," in *Drinking Patterns and Their Consequences* (London: Taylor and Francis, 1998), 93–95.

8. John W. Frank, Roland S. Moore, and Genevieve M. Ames, "Historical and Cultural Roots of Drinking Problems Among American Indians," *American Journal of Public Health* 90, no. 3 (2000): 344–51.

9. R. F. Bales, "Cultural Differences in Rates of Alcoholism," *Quarterly Journal of Studies on Alcohol* 6 (1946): 482.

10. Frank, Moore, and Ames, "Historical and Cultural Roots," 345.

11. Ibid., 346.

12. Ibid.

13. Ibid.

14. There is one notable regional exception to this, namely the Southwestern tribal groups who began to drink a fermented cactus beverage derived from native Mexican groups. See P. J. Abbot, "American Indian and Alaska Native Aboriginal

Use of Alcohol in the United States," *American Indian Alaska Native Mental Health Resources* 7 (1996): 1–13.

15. Frank, Moore, and Ames, "Historical and Cultural Roots," 348.

16. M. E. Lender and J. K. Martin, *Drinking in America: A History* (New York: Free Press, 1982), 46–48.

17. See, for example, the Alkali Lake (Canada) Reserve transformation.

18. Joane Nagel, *American Indian Ethnic Renewal: Red Power and the Resurgence of Identity* (New York: Oxford University Press, 1996).

19. Ibid., 84–101.

20. Ibid., 123–24.

21. Ibid., 142.

22. Dennis F. Kelley, *Religion in Contemporary Native America: Traditional Practices, Modern Identities.* Unpublished Ph.D. dissertation, University of California, Santa Barbara, 2006.

23. Michael McNally, *Ojibwe Singers: Hymns, Grief, and a Native Culture in Motion* (Oxford: Oxford University Press, 2000).

24. Michael D. McNally, "The Practice of Native American Christianity," *Church History* (December 2000): 834–59.

25. McNally, 2000: 853.

26. McNally: 837.

27. Ibid.

28. For two other significant movements, see Thomas Lewis's treatment of the Sun Dance in *The Medicine Men: Oglala Sioux Ceremony and Healing* (Lincoln: University of Nebraska Press, 1990); and J. H. Howard's "The Plains Gourd Dance as a Revitalization Movement," *American Ethnologist* 3 (1976): 243–59.

29. Alfred A. Cave, *Native American Revitalization Movements in Eastern North America* (Lincoln: University of Nebraska Press, 1999), 14.

30. Don L. Coyhis and William L. White, *Alcohol Problems in Native America: The Untold Story of Resistance and Recovery* (Colorado Springs, CO: White Bison, Inc., 2006), 77.

31. Ibid.

32. Alfred Cave, *Prophets of the Great Spirit: Native American Revitalization Movements in Eastern North America* (Lincoln: University of Nebraska Press, 2006), 13.

33. Alfred Wallace, *The Death and Rebirth of the Seneca* (New York: Vintage Books, 1969), 120.

34. Coyhis and White, *Alcohol Problems in Native America*, 80.

35. Ibid.

36. Charles M. Hudson, *Black Drink: A Native American Tea* (Atlanta: University of Georgia Press, 1979).

37. Because this sequence of events is widely known and reported, I will be following the historical evidence as presented by Coyhis and White, *Alcohol Problems in Native America*, 93–99.

38. Coyhis and White, *Alcohol Problems in Native America*, 94.

39. Wallace, *Death and Rebirth of the Seneca*, 154.

40. Ake Hultkrantz, *The Religions of the American Indians* (Berkeley: University of California Press, 1979), 153.

41. Coyhis and White, *Alcohol Problems in Native America*, 116.

42. Omer Stewart, *The Peyote Religion: A History* (Norman: University of Oklahoma Press, 1987), 112.

43. Gilbert A. Quintero, "Gender, Discord, and Illness: Navajo Philosophy and Healing in the Native American Church," *Journal of Anthropological Research* 51, no. 1 (Spring, 1995): 69–89.

44. For much of this aspect of the overview, I draw from the excellent and informative report by Marja Korhonen, "Alcohol Problems and Approaches: Theories, Evidence and Northern Practice" (Ottawa: National Aboriginal Health Organizations, 2004).

45. For excellent overviews of the various approaches, see Larry Nackerud, "The Disease Model of Alcoholism: a Khunian Paradigm," *Journal of Sociology and Social Welfare* 29 (2002), and Herbert Fingarette, *Heavy Drinking: The Myth of Alcoholism As a Disease* (Berkeley: University of California Press, 1988).

46. For a discussion of the development and controversies surrounding the "disease model" of alcohol abuse recovery, see Roger E. Meyer, "The Disease Called Addiction: Emerging Evidence in a 200-Year Debate," *Lancet* 347 (1997): 162–66.

47. Fingarette, *Heavy Drinking*, 61.

48. U.S. Supreme Court, *Traynor v Turnage*, 485 U.S. 353 (1988): 535–50.

49. Bill W. [William Griffith Wilson], *Alcoholics Anonymous Comes of Age: A Brief History of A.A.* (New York: Alcoholics Anonymous World Services, 1990[1957]), 38.

50. Ibid., 39.

51. Ibid., 43.

52. Ibid., 57.

53. Coyhis and White, *Alcohol Problems in Native America*, 140.

54. For a more in-depth assessment of this point, see L. W. Anderson's *Wellness Circles: The Alkali Lake Model in Community Recovery Processes.* Doctoral dissertation, Northern Arizona University, Flagstaff, 1991; Don Coyhis, *Recovery From the Heart: A Journey Through the Twelve Steps: A Workbook for Native Americans* (Center City, MN: Hazelden. 1990); and L. Lilek-Aall, "Acculturation, Alcoholism, and Indian-Style Alcoholics Anonymous," *Journal of Studies on Alcohol* 9 (Suppl., 1981): 143–58.

55. Lawrence A. French, *Addictions and Native Americans* (Westport, CT: Praeger Publishers, 2000), 90.

56. Bill, *Alcoholics Anonymous Comes of Age*, 61.

57. Ibid., 65.

58. Coyhis and White, *Alcohol Problems in Native America*, 140.

59. Lisette M. Womack, "The Indianization of Alcoholics Anonymous: An Examination of Native American Recovery Movements," Master's thesis, Department of American Indian Studies, University of Arizona, 1996, 27.

60. Coyhis and White, *Alcohol Problems in Native America*, 142.

61. Ibid., 147.

62. John G. Neihardt, *Black Elk Speaks: Being the Life of a Holy Man of the Oglala Sioux* (Omaha: University of Nebraska Press. 1979[1932]): 39–54.

63. Doyle Arbogast, *Wounded Warriors: A Time for Healing* (Omaha, NE: Little Turtle Publishing, 1995), 319.

64. Coyhis and White, *Alcohol Problems in Native America*, 144.

65. For an overview of this structure see http://wyoshpo.state.wy.us/medwheel.htm (last accessed in March 2006).

66. For a general overview of the research on these structures see http://www.royalalbertamuseum.ca/human/archaeo/faq/medwhls.htm (last accessed in March of 2006).

67. Ibid.

68. Raymond Bucko, *The Lakota Ritual of the Sweat Lodge: History and Contemporary Practice* (Lincoln: University of Nebraska Press, 1998), 67.

69. Coyhis and White, *Alcohol Problems in Native America*, 158.

70. Arbogast, *Wounded Warriors*, 319.

71. See http://www.whitebison.org/wellbriety_movement/index.html (accessed on June 5, 2006).

72. Coyhis and White, *Alcohol Problems in Native America*, 156–58.

73. Ibid., 182.

BIBLIOGRAPHY

Abbot, P. J. "American Indian and Alaska Native Aboriginal Use of Alcohol in the United States." *American Indian Alaska Native Mental Health Research* 7 (1996): 1–13.

Anderson, L. W. *Wellness Circles: The Alkali Lake Model in Community Recovery Processes*. Doctoral dissertation, Northern Arizona University, Flagstaff, 1991.

Anonymous World Services. *Alcoholics Anonymous Comes of Age. A Brief History of A.A.* New York: Alcoholics Anonymous, 1990 (1957).

Anti-Saloon League of America. *Anti-Saloon League of America Yearbook*. Westerville, OH: American Issue Press, 1920.

Arbogast, Doyle. *Wounded Warriors: A Time for Healing*. Omaha, NE: Little Turtle Pub., 1995.

Bales, R. F. "Cultural Differences in Rates of Alcoholism." *Quarterly Journal of Studies on Alcohol* 6 (1946): 482.

Cave, Alfred A. *Native American Revitalization Movements in Eastern North America*. Lincoln: University of Nebraska Press, 1999.

Coyhis, Don. *Recovery from the Heart: A Journey Through the Twelve Steps: A Workbook for Native Americans*. Center City, MN: Hazelden, 1990.

Coyhis, Don L., and William L. White. *Alcohol Problems in Native America: The Untold Story of Resistance and Recovery*. Colorado Springs, CO: White Bison, Inc., 2006.

Evans, E. G., M. L. Barer, and T. R. Marmot, eds. *Why Are Some People Healthy and Others Not?: The Determinants of Health of Populations*. New York: Aldine de Gruyter, 1996.

Fingarette, Herbert. *Heavy Drinking: The Myth of Alcoholism As a Disease*. Berkeley: University of California Press, 1988.

Frank, John W., Roland S. Moore, and Genevieve M. Ames. "Historical and Cultural Roots of Drinking Problems Among American Indians." *American Journal of Public Health* 90, no. 3 (2000): 344–51.

French, Lawrence A. *Addictions and Native Americans*. Westport, CT: Praeger, 2000.

Howard, J. H. "The Plains Gourd Dance as a Revitalization Movement." *American Ethnologist* 3 (1976): 243–59.

Hudson, Charles M. *Black Drink: A Native American Tea.* Atlanta: University of Georgia Press, 1979.

Kelley, Dennis. *Religion in Contemporary Native America: Traditional Practices, Modern Identities.* Unpublished Ph.D. dissertation, University of California, Santa Barbara, 2006.

Korhonen, Marja. "Alcohol Problems and Approaches: Theories, Evidence and Northern Practice." Ottawa: National Aboriginal Health Organizations, 2004.

Lender, M. E., and J. K. Martin. *Drinking in America: A History.* New York: Free Press, 1982.

Lewis, Thomas. *The Medicine Men: Oglala Sioux Ceremony and Healing.* Lincoln: University of Nebraska Press, 1990.

Lilek-Aall, L. "Acculturation, Alcoholism, and Indian-Style Alcoholics Anonymous." *Journal of Studies on Alcohol* 9 (Suppl., 1981): 143–58.

McNally, Michael. *Ojibwe Singers: Hymns, Grief, and a Native Culture in Motion.* Oxford: Oxford University Press, 2000.

McNally, Michael D. "The Practice of Native American Christianity." *Church History* (December 2000): 834–59.

Meyer, Roger E. "The Disease Called Addiction: Emerging Evidence in a 200-Year Debate." *Lancet* 347 (1996): 162–66.

Mulford, Harold A. *Alcohol and Alcoholism in Iowa, 1965.* Iowa City: University of Iowa Press, 1965.

Nackerud, Larry. "The Disease Model of Alcoholism: A Khunian Paradigm." *Journal of Sociology and Social Welfare* 29 (2002).

Nagel, Joane. *American Indian Ethnic Renewal: Red Power and the Resurgence of Identity.* New York: Oxford University Press, 1996.

Neihardt, John G. *Black Elk Speaks: Being the Life of a Holy Man of the Oglala Sioux.* Omaha: University of Nebraska Press, 1979 (1932).

Quintero, Gilbert A. "Gender, Discord, and Illness: Navajo Philosophy and Healing in the Native American Church." *Journal of Anthropological Research* 51, no. 1 (Spring, 1995): 69–89.

U.S. Supreme Court. *Traynor v Turnage,* 485 U.S. 353 (1988): 535–50.

Wallace, Alfred. *The Death and Rebirth of the Seneca.* New York: Vintage Books, 1969.

Womack, Lisette M. "The Indianization of Alcoholics Anonymous: An Examination of Native American Recovery Movements." Unpublished Master's thesis, Department of American Indian Studies, University of Arizona, 1996.

CHAPTER 5

—— ❈ ——

Figuring It Out: Sundancing and Storytelling in the Lakota Tradition

Larissa Petrillo with Melda Trejo

The Sundance and other traditional ceremonies were effectively curtailed by the Bureau of Indian Affairs (BIA) in the late nineteenth century but have since been reintroduced and are now noticeably prevalent.[1] Specifically, the Sundance has a long history among the Lakota (Teton), also called the Oglala Sioux. The Lakota have been referred to as "the archetypal Indian in the American imagination" and have been popularized in many of the Native stereotypes associated with the Wild West.[2] At present, one now finds the Sundance in many Lakota communities, including Pine Ridge Reservation and the neighboring Rosebud Reservation.[3] Home to the Oglala Lakota nation, Pine Ridge Reservation, located in the plains of the southwestern part of South Dakota, is the second largest reservation in the United States.[4] With the proliferation of the Sundance at Pine Ridge, spiritual practitioners have had to balance conventional customs with emerging needs and new questions in their efforts to determine current practices. Accordingly, individuals often find themselves figuring out what constitutes tradition through interaction, debate, and storytelling. These discussions can best be understood within a system of interrelations that characterizes the Lakota traditional community more generally. In fact, the dialogue that takes place on the reservation about what counts as *traditional* can be regarded within a framework of prayer and storytelling that is indicative of tradition itself. Finding a shared sense of tradition and an identity associated with that tradition, is central to the healing process that has emerged since these ideals were first split apart with the advent of colonization.

Retraditionalization has been evident on Pine Ridge Reservation since the late 1960s and has been integral to the healing of the Lakota community. Any community that has been subject to systemic racist policies suffers from some fracturing of self and community identity. Specifically, the dichotomized stereotype associated with Indians—the noble Indian or the drunken Indian—functions in the erasure of the complexity of lived experience. Joyzelle Gingway Godfrey, Dakota educator, describes the dehumanizing effects of such colonial discourses and the persistence of these issues with the younger generation:

> So lots of "stuff" we're going to have to rethink…and think about what we want to be; who do we want to be? Who are we, truly? That's something we need, as Indian people; we need to look at our true history, the reality of who we really were, as human beings, so that we can be human beings, so that we're not trying to live up to those thoughts, pictures, something that we never were. My God, no wonder we have so much alcohol and drug abuse, no wonder we have suicide. Our teenagers are killing themselves in droves—what do they have to live up to? On the one hand, they see their parents, the alcohol and drug abuse that's horrible; on the other hand, they see themselves as supposed to be this noble Indian, you know. So for them there is no middle ground. There is no safety net. Yet there truly is.[5]

The internal pressures of racism and colonialism can be manifested in many negative ways but they can also lead to resistance and healing. Dakota scholar Elizabeth Cook-Lynn mentions the framework out of which resistance, and the hope associated with this resistance, might emerge:

> Like all people confronted with an oppressive government and racist colonialism, the Sioux are familiar with hatred. It begins with the hatred felt from others and the hatred felt for others, from outsiders, and, then, it sometimes turns into self-hatred, that is, internalized oppression, which eventually, and mercifully, can become the landscape of resistance.[6]

The Sundance is specifically part of this landscape of resistance because it allows for the restoring of an individual and community identity. This claiming of self is also a reclaiming of a sacred connection and one which the ceremony upholds. The loss of identity that followed from experiences of oppression is repaired as the community comes together in their effort to heal, in their renewal of identity.

This chapter explores the way in which oral storytelling, and the sharing of life experiences, functions in sustaining Lakota tradition and how this reconnection with tradition serves to heal the fractures of colonization. The work itself is informed by the life story narratives of Melda and Lupe Trejo. Melda Red Bear (Lakota) was born on Pine Ridge (Oglala Lakota/Sioux) Reservation in South Dakota (1939–). Her husband, Lupe Trejo (1938–1999) is Mexican and has been a long-term resident of the reservation. In their 40 years together, Melda and Lupe have raised 11 children and supported themselves as migrant workers. Since 1988, they have held a Sundance ceremony on the Red Bear land on Pine Ridge Reservation. In their life stories, Melda and

Lupe emphasize the importance of the Sundance ceremony and convey their understanding of Lakota tradition to their relations. They define themselves through their spiritual practice in the Sundance and situate themselves, and their Sundance, amid the controversies that surround authentic practices and the participation of outsiders in the ceremony.

For those who are unaware of the ceremony, the Sundance (*Wi wanyang wacipi*) should be distinguished from the popularly conceived image of the men's traditional dance of the contemporary powwow. Traditional, in reference to the powwow, entails a particular style of dance, most recognizable because of its use of the men's headdress. The intertribal powwow (*wacipi*), started in the 1930s, and became increasingly popular during the 1950s and 1960s (Melda and Lupe met at a powwow in 1957). By contrast, at the Sundance, dancers continually gaze at the sun while dancing and fasting having committed to do so for a one- to four-day period. The ceremony provides strength for the relations, namely all of creation. Each year the dancers individually make a pledge to dance "for the people" or for specific individuals in need. In the Lakota community, the pipe continues to be used "to remember White Buffalo Cow [Calf] Woman and serves as a medium of purification and prayer."[7] Prayers are made to the four directions and each direction is associated with a specific color and set of symbols. There are also many different sacred rites in Lakota tradition, including the sweat lodge (*inipi*) or purification rite, the funeral practices or keeping of the soul, the vision quest or crying for a vision (*hambleceya*), the adoption ceremony or making of relatives (*hunka*) and the puberty rites.[8] Additionally, the *yuwipi* ceremony involves a bound spiritual practitioner who "obtains release through the mysterious intercession of helping spirits" for reasons of "spiritual devotion and to find lost objects."[9] The *hambleceya*, or vision quest, is often called going up the hill and continues to be a key factor in ritual legitimation.

I was introduced to Melda and Lupe through a mutual friend in 1995 and developed an enduring friendship with them prior to our decision to collaborate in the recording of their storytelling sessions (1997–1998). In all, 10 tapes were recorded for 90 minutes each and further conversations, both social and for the purposes of this work, have continued since that time. I have been going to the reservation for 10 years now, both for weeks or months at a time. In our sessions, the process of recording was largely undirected. I avoided leading questions and allowed for an open-ended session. Over the course of our developing friendship, I had already heard Melda tell the stories that she values repeatedly to numerous people on the reservation. I only needed to prompt her recall of those stories. Melda served a similar function in eliciting stories from Lupe that she had already heard. The resulting work itself is based, in part, on feedback from the academic and reservation communities connected to the project.[10] Melda and members of the Trejo family have been involved in each step of the writing process and our relationship continues outside the context of research. Melda positions herself as a Lakota woman by claiming a set of experiences that are lineal, cultural, and political, while Lupe necessarily negotiates a different set of experiences in his life story as a Mexican-American. Melda's great-great-grandfather was an Indian Scout for the United States Army and the third cousin of the well-known Lakota warrior, Crazy Horse.[11] Howard Red Bear, her paternal great-uncle, was also an Indian Scout for the United States Army. He served under Company I, 2nd Regiment and was stationed at Fort Crook. Philip [Runs Along the Edge] Red Bear, Melda's great-grandfather, was born in the mid-1800s. As will be discussed, Philip Red Bear was influential in bringing peyote to South Dakota in 1914 and in establishing the Native American Church. The Native American Church is a pan-Indian Christian movement that involves the use of peyote and, in Red Bear's case, the traditional pipe. Melda attended Native American Church meetings that were run by her father until she was 16 years old. She grew up speaking the Lakota language, and she continues to speak Lakota with those who know the language.

Traditionalism "symbolizes for the Sioux what it is to be Indian" and has been described, in the contemporary era, as an "attempt to return to the 'old ways,' the 'traditional ways,' 'Lakota ways'...that provide historical links to the past."[12] The loss of the connection to these old ways, implicit with strategies of assimilation, has been tenuous but threatening. Bringing forth very deliberate connections between identity and tradition has been part of an important mending in the Lakota nation. However, while contemporary Lakota identity is often associated with traditional practices, these practices are frequently debated because an unchanging past is incommensurate with a present that necessitates change. Accordingly, tradition can often best be understood by attending to the pride or, alternatively, reticence that might be associated with specific practices. Anthropologist Raymond DeMallie notes, "[f]or the Lakotas of Pine Ridge...to be Lakota, 'Sioux,' or more generally to be *ikcewicasa*, 'common men,' that is, Indians (not whites), is an unwavering source of pride and strength."[13] In *The Lakota Ritual of the Sweat Lodge: History and Contemporary Practice* (1998), Raymond A. Bucko describes the use of *tradition* and *traditional* in contemporary political and cultural discourses:

> Tradition itself is a vital term in contemporary Lakota discourse and constitutes a key symbol in Lakota culture. Tradition is used on the reservation today both as a term to authenticate a legitimate link to the past and as a mark of legitimacy itself. People, behaviors, and ceremonies are often called traditional...The word *wichoh'a* "tradition" is used in several ways by the Lakotas on the reservation. The first meaning matches the English definition of the word; it implies the handing on of a body of material from the past. The second, more analogous to custom or habit, refers to actions in the present that represent generalized repetitive behavior. Finally, the English word traditional is used to mean "proper, correct, or accurate" and can imply one or both of the two Lakota meanings.[14]

In speaking about tradition as something essential, as well as something that has been eroded by colonial forces, individual sentiments about changes in tradition are both divisive and unifying. Despite the divisiveness that can ensue in these sorts of discussions, the ultimate process is one of healing in that the community works together in its renewal.

RETRADITIONALIZATION AND THE SUNDANCE

Melda and Lupe Trejo tell the story of how they came to hold a Sundance, but the timeline of Melda and Lupe's move towards the Sundance is some-times difficult to determine. This is because they are not speaking about time as a linear marker. Rather, they are describing life passages and ceremonial cycles—unexpected and exceptional events that take place over a 40 year period. It is a healing journey and one that has meant connecting in new ways to a community that was itself also continually moving towards the healing associated with retraditionalization. Melda and Lupe also discuss the changes in tradition that have occurred both historically and in the contem-porary era. They talk about the Ghost Dance, Christianity, and the Native American Church and they describe how they have constantly negotiated and learned about what they associate as Lakota tradition. Melda, who was socialized in a Lakota setting, has been to varying degrees dislocated from the Lakota community, especially in her capacity as a migrant worker, and she has increasingly moved towards Lakota tradition later in her life. However, these facts do not in any way imply an indistinct connection to what she un-derstands as Lakota tradition. It is by no means a given that those who move toward Lakota tradition later in life are less traditional and, likewise, it is by no means a given that those who have been raised within Lakota tradition necessarily claim an un-problematized identity. All too often there is a failure to seriously explore Indian identity as an emerging process over the course of an individual's life, or dislocation and its effects on Indian identity. Accord-ingly, Dakota scholar Elizabeth Cook-Lynn cautions against the tendency "to discuss the divisions on Indian reservations between half-breeds and 'tradi-tionals'" in the scholarship about the Lakota people.[15]

The Sundance itself is emblematic of ongoing retraditionalization efforts in many Native communities. While John Collier legislated against any in-terference with Indian religious life or ceremonial expression in 1934, there were continuing deterrents.[16] American Indian Movement (AIM) activist Russell Means describes the history of the Sundance in his autobiography: "As with many of our spiritual observances, Christian missionaries forced the BIA [Bureau of Indian Affairs] to ban it [the Sun Dance] in 1881. Our right to the sun dance was restored in the 1950s, but with so many restrictions that the ceremony was reduced to a mere shadow of what it had once been...but a few Lakota secretly conducted the holy rituals in remote parts of their reser-vations."[17] Carole Anne Heart Looking Horse (Lakota) says that "[i]t wasn't until 1978, when the American Indian Religious Freedom Act was passed, that our people felt finally they could practice their ceremonies openly in this country."[18] The Sundance was reintroduced in the 1970s and 1980s and is now prevalent on Pine Ridge Reservation. The Crow Dog Sundance, in 1973, was the first widely accessible autonomous ceremony. It was held on Rosebud Reservation by Henry Crow Dog (Lakota) and his son, Leonard Crow Dog, a medicine man who is often associated with AIM.[19] The Red Power movement of the 1970s was characterized by spiritual revitalization, political protests, and demands for treaty rights.[20] The activist movement grew out of the civil rights era of the 1960s and came to be associated with the reintroduction of spiritual practices.[21] Consequently, as Marjorie Schweitzer explains, "[s]ome [individuals] return[ed] to their native communities and enter[ed] again into Indian social and ceremonial life, learning as retirees what they had missed when they were young."[22]

The political, religious, economic, and cultural suppression of Native cultures has necessarily had an effect on the way individuals are connected to traditional ways. In *Standing in the Light: A Lakota Way of Seeing* (1994), Severt Young Bear (Lakota) describes four circles of people who are present at Sundances: those who are in the center (the dancers), those in the arbor (supporters/singers), those who are helping around the edge of the arbor, and those who remain further out in the parking lot.[23] In her life story, Melda similarly describes moving through these circles in her involvement with the Sundance. It is a movement that is part of a healing journey for many as they reconnect with the traditions of the Sundance. And, as the circles each support and reinforce the other, this movement becomes cyclical for each generation as the community heals itself. Specifically, Melda recalls going to the sanctioned Sundance in 1957, which was revived in a public display, associated with an annual fair and organized by the tribal council:

> [The Pine Ridge] Sundance was in the morning and powwow starts in, like, the afternoon. We always stay there. But, I never did go in the mornings. The old people were there. My mom used to tell us, "You should go there and sit there." And I really regret not having done that. Because, I was like probably sixteen. Probably seventeen. And we sleep late! We always sleep late in the tents. She takes off. Sometimes we get up and we catch the end of it. They do that. I remember Sundance, they dance every morning, I don't know why. They didn't dance all day...In those days, nobody really got into these Sundances.

In *Bead on an Anthill: A Lakota Childhood* (1998), Delphine Red Shirt (Lakota) describes her experience of the Sundance at that time in similar terms:

> Mom-mah and Kah-kah prayed while the carnival rides stopped and started as people purchased tickets for a quarter; the dust at the rodeo flew as the riders with numbers pinned on their backs, dressed in their cowboy boots and brand

new jeans, mounted and dismounted with each passing event. The vendors counted change and sold hamburgers, and the dancers danced. The dancers danced in the full sunlight, raising their arms to the sky, sage crowns upon their heads, sage bracelets upon their wrists and ankles. Some carried a hoop made of sage, others a fan made of sage. They danced, ignoring us, as we children ran from one event to the next, spending quarters as fast as we could get them. I was like everyone else there: I ate snow cones and cotton candy. I drank soda pop and ran around the sacred circle. I chased boys and ran to and from the carnival looking for quarters on the ground. I played and played, never once stopping, until the last day, to see the faces of the Sun Dancers...[including] the man in the long dark wig. I was no different from the tourists. I wanted to see what everyone else had paid to see.[24]

Both accounts attest to the restricted nature of the Sundance as well as the ways in which the younger generation was disconnected from Lakota tradition. The older generation supported the ceremony and encouraged others to learn from the Sundance and move towards the ceremony.

Melda's reconnection with Lakota tradition in the 1970s and 1980s demonstrates the degree to which healing identity and restoring tradition are dynamic processes. Melda asserts that she "grew up in a traditional way," but she also acknowledges that she "got into this Lakota religion" more earnestly later in life. She was raised in the Native American Church and grew up praying with the pipe. She has spoken the Lakota language since childhood. Her family ties to Pine Ridge are extensive. While I doubt that she would characterize herself as ever being disaffected from Lakota tradition, she has experienced dislocation both as a migrant worker and living in urban areas such as Denver, Colorado, and Scottsbluff, Nebraska. She began, in the 1950s, sleeping in her tent in the parking lot at the BIA Sundance. This type of support is essential to the ceremony. There is a network of people who work together in supporting the Sundance. All of the individuals, together, enact and propel tradition. James Fenelon says that "[s]ocietal integrity and group polity... grow out of and are essential to the sundance."[25] Melda's description of her initial estrangement from aspects of traditional practice, as was the case for many of her generation, accords honor to a tradition that both survives and impresses upon a new generation that they are able to move through the circles that encompass ceremony. As Joyzelle Gingway Godfrey says: "We are here, we are surviving, we are living our traditions, we do go to sweats, we do have *Wopila* [thanksgiving] ceremonies, people still sun dance, people still go on vision quests, all of these things we still have...we're still there. And we're still strong."[26]

In tracing her own healing as continually moving towards tradition, Melda encourages her children and grandchildren to do the same. Melda talks about her initial experiences with medicine man Ruben Fire Thunder in setting up the Sundance. She also describes the difficult task of preparing for a *yuwipi* ceremony in Scottsbluff, Nebraska. A young dog is ritualistically cooked for the ceremony as a way of according respect and honor in the Lakota tradition. As Leonard Crow Dog says, "The dog is sacred."[27] Referring to her experiences in the ceremony, Melda says: "[w]hen I was young I used to go there [*yuwipi*] but I've never actually cooked a dog and all these things." Melda emphasizes her role in cooking for the ceremony and, in fact, "[m]uch of the preparation that goes into a feast and give-away is in the hands of females."[28] Melda acknowledges that she had to learn how to be involved beyond being a participant; she had to learn about the preparations for the ceremony. Elsewhere she describes how she made *wasna* (pemmican) and *wojapi* (chokecherry pudding), foods that are used ritualistically in ceremonies. In describing her ability to cook *wasna* and her inability to cook a dog, Melda describes herself as both knowing and not knowing about traditional practices. She unsettles the totalizing discourses associated with Lakota tradition and demonstrates her own process of learning about traditional practices. Learning is necessarily involved as a community restores self and tradition in a process of healing the effects of colonization. Melda also highlights the effects of dislocation on Lakota tradition which is also implicit in the fracturing of the community. She says that "there was no way you were going to start a fire in Scottsbluff." This highlights the incongruity between a rural traditional past and the contemporary urban situation. Trying to live a traditional life in an urban locale is what makes her story seem ironic; or, more specifically, her story shows that living in a city makes traditional life seem somehow inconsistent. Being aware of these inconsistencies, and one's position in trying to mend these rifts, means that the community moves towards renewal.

The inconsistencies in the contemporary situation are also evident with the resurrection of the ceremonies themselves. Current Sundances maintain continuity with the past and also necessarily incorporate more recent changes. In 1979, there were several hundred people attending the tribal Sun Dance at Porcupine, South Dakota.[29] Mikael Kurkiala identifies the growing number of Sundances on Pine Ridge Reservation:

> From the mid-1970s, the number of Sun Dances has grown significantly...In the summer of 1993, approximately thirty Sun Dances were held on different locations on the Pine Ridge and Rosebud Reservations. In the summer of 1997, the number had increased to 43 on Pine Ridge alone.[30]

In 2000, including the memorial Sundance honoring Lupe Trejo, there were at least three simultaneous Sundances just in the immediate area of Allen, South Dakota. These ceremonies are held for a four-day period scheduled anytime throughout the entire summer period; the simultaneous ceremonies are therefore quite significant. Given this increase, the competition over viable ceremonies accelerates due to greater opportunities for comparison and also because there are simply fewer available medicine men to run the ceremonies. The dialectic surrounding authentic ceremonies is, in part, a corollary to the proliferation of traditional practices and the ongoing discourse surrounding correct practices. In *American Indian Ethnic Renewal: Red Power and the Resurgence of Identity and Culture* (1996) Joane Nagel says, "individual Indian ethnic renewal appears to be tightly connected to an interest and a participation in tribal traditions and ceremonial practices."[31] She also acknowledges the contested nature of traditional practices in the contemporary context. She says, "despite the well-known fact that identities and cultures change,... [t]o document the reconstruction, much less the new construction of an individual's ethnic identity or a community's cultural practices or institutions, is often an unwelcome, sometimes vilified enterprise."[32]

The Native American Church and Religious Diversity

Religious diversity on Pine Ridge Reservation further complicates traditional Lakota beliefs, both historically, and, in the contemporary context. Raymond DeMallie and Douglas Parks note that "among some Sioux groups traditional and Christian practices have become amalgamated; among others they are kept strictly separate."[33] At present, the reservation is dominated by religious pluralism, whether Christian or *Bah'ai* or some combination of Lakota beliefs.[34] For example, Bucko records a Lakota man's description of what he sees as a natural conflation of spiritual beliefs:

> These guys who come looking for a pure Indian way of life. They'll see this here picture of Christ and they can't understand it. My grandfather had an altar with his pipe and the statue of Mary. There's one God...*Tunkashila* and God are the same. They're just different words, different symbols. So I need both.[35]

I have often been unsettled in much the same way as those guys looking for a pure Indian way of life, when I have entered houses on Pine Ridge Reservation and found both Christian iconography and Lakota symbols of tradition. In this respect, Melda and Lupe's house is no exception. They adhere to Christian teachings *and* Lakota beliefs and practices. For example, Melda describes her associations to the Christian church, most specifically the Church of God in Scottsbluff, Nebraska. Melda does not comment on the apparent incompatibility of her adherence to both Christian and traditional beliefs. She focuses instead on prayer and the values that she associates with her life in church. The religious plurality on the reservation provides many different avenues for healing but can also be seen to threaten the healing that some might see as only aligned with one tradition, or another. In Melda's account, however, social life in the reservation community is also characterized by an attempt to accommodate competing religious beliefs and practices under the more overarching banner of prayer.

Melda additionally talks about peyote as traditional, despite its relatively current introduction, through a demarcation between peyote use and religious traditions associated with non-Native culture. The Native American Church, established in the early 1900s, integrates Christian beliefs, the use of peyote and, in some churches, the use of the pipe.[36] Again, this diversity in what might be regarded as a traditional practice for the community provides new avenues for healing, while also potentially challenging such a process for those who see only restricted avenues for retraditionalization. Melda acknowledges that the use of peyote is not a traditional Lakota practice because it was adopted from another tribe in the 1900s. She says, "I know that peyote is not traditional." In that sense, she defines "tradition" as having roots in precolonial practices. However, peyote use, especially in conjunction with the pipe, contests efforts to suppress Native spiritual practices. It also indicates continued adaptation and innovation of a persistent tradition, namely the use of the pipe. In that sense, Melda speaks with considerable pride about her paternal great-grandfather's role in establishing peyote use among the Lakota people. Melda describes how her great-grandfather brought peyote from Oklahoma to South Dakota. In *Peyote Religion: A History* (1987), Omer Stewart cites the involvement of Melda's great-grandfather in establishing the pan-Indian syncretic church at several points in his text.[37] He describes Philip Red Bear's use of the traditional Lakota pipe; he says, "the Lakota put their own traditional stamp on the [ceremony]...in Red Bear's use of the Pipe."[38] Philip Red Bear's role in sustaining Lakota spirituality is especially significant given that traditional practices were not supported by government policies at that time. Peyotists began to practice in South Dakota in 1914, the Native American Church was incorporated in South Dakota in 1922, and there are now many people on the reservation who belong to the Native American Church.

The diversity of religious expression is problematic for Melda only inasmuch as it threatens continuing traditional practices. For example, she makes derisive comments about Catholicism when she aligns the church with colonial practices. She associates these colonial practices with efforts to suppress traditional spiritual practices. These associations are evident in a story where Melda describes a Catholic preacher, riding on his horse "down east" trying to convert her family to Catholicism. She equates this man with what she regards as colonial imposition: "The *wasicus* came and told them they're going to go to hell if they're not baptized." The Lakota term for white people is *wasicu* and has come to mean "'clothes wearers,' 'fat takers,' or 'loud talkers,'" emphasizing white men's negative characteristics."[39] Although *wasicu* may have originally meant "'white' or 'snow' of the north, *Waziya*"[40] or, alternatively, the term *many*,[41] today, the term *wasicu* has come to stand as an abstract designation of "a mind-set, a worldview that is a product of the development of European culture."[42] Significantly, Melda also uses the term *wasicu* when talking about the suppression of the Ghost Dance. The Ghost Dance is a ceremony that promises to restore the precontact world and it was initiated in 1889 by Wovoka (Jack Wilson, Paiute).[43] The Ghost Dance came to the Dakotas in May 1890. It has been described by outsiders as a *ritual of militant resistance* and the massacre at Wounded Knee is connected, at least in part, to the threat associated with the ceremony.[44] The Ghost Dance was effectively discontinued after the massacre in December 1890 and was only reclaimed in the retraditionalization era of the 1970s and 1980s.[45] It is fitting then that Melda uses distinct terminology when she describes what has been lost with the erosion of the ceremony.[46] In Melda's narrative, she uses *wasicu* when referring to the historical incursion of Lakota spiritual practices; this is the *only* time she uses the term. When she uses *wasicu* in describing the Catholic preacher "down east," she is critiquing Catholicism inasmuch as it is associated with the historical suppression of Native American spirituality and practices. The suppression of these practices is a threat to the Lakota community and its ability to renew and heal itself and Melda highlights this tension with her framing of the issues.

Spiritual practitioners seeking to heal their communities must balance traditional and contemporary needs; interpretations as to how that balance is best achieved vary among individuals and communities. For example, there are debates on the Pine Ridge Reservation about whether or not non-Native people should be allowed to take part in the Sundance. According to some, Sundances are more traditional if only Lakota participants are involved in the ceremony. In this sense, that which is so-called traditional is defined through its resistance to a colonial presence. At the same time, individuals on the reservation, Melda and Lupe included, advocate that allies, or relations, are meant to pray together. Melda and Lupe welcome dancers and supporters of any racial or tribal designation at their Sundance. They have done so since the beginning of their Sundance, but their actions have taken on new meaning since the debate surrounding cultural legitimacy has emerged on the reservation.[47] When she talks about the Sundance, Melda advocates that no one should be excluded from the ceremony. Her view is based on traditional Lakota teachings on forming alliances and honoring relations. She refers to different races, such as white people and black people as well as different kinds of Indians and cites her father and medicine man Ruben Fire Thunder in addressing the issue. She says that praying "with everybody is the only way you're going to heaven." She disengages from the racial aspects of the debate by instead urging a spiritual understanding of human nature; the claiming of relations through prayer. The restoring of self is that much more powerful when understood as the unifying of all people and creatures, joined together in prayer.

STORYTELLING

Many of Melda and Lupe's stories depict their own individual processes of healing, of renewing identity through knowledge about tradition, of family and their own sense of themselves. In particular, Melda's stories often revolve around her experiences in not knowing about something. Accordingly, there is one particular story—one that she tells very, very frequently—that I have interpreted and reinterpreted on several occasions in the course of my own learning. It is about her grandson, Patrick, taking part in his first Sundance. I have heard the story many times in different contexts and continue to find in it new meanings. When Patrick was very young, he wanted to dance in the Sundance ceremony and he knew that he had to have a Sundance skirt in order to dance. Melda relates the discussion that she has with both her mother and daughter, Barbara, about this event. She speaks in a lighthearted tone and tends to laugh quietly at many points in the story. Here is that story:

Melda

You know, I want to talk on how Patrick, my grandson, started Sundancing. This is back when we started Sundance. My mom was there. And, I had all my kids there. We were all there. And I had my son, the one that died, was there too. He came and he was always helping out. He was always around there, helping out. And the first year was really good. And that's when my grandson, Patrick, started. First year. Yeah, and he was only like three and a half years old. And he was into the sweats. He was only going in with grandma and Lupe and all those old people. So he was really interested in this. He was just a little boy, but he was interested. Just like he was peeking in there saying, "What are you people doing in there? Can I come in?"

So the first year Sundance started and, well, Barbara's son, Patrick wanted to dance, you know. He kept asking my daughter, Barbara, "I want to dance. I want to dance beside grandpa." And, Barbara asked and I said, "He's too young." I said, "Wait 'til you get older." He says, "No, I want to dance beside grandpa."

So they already started to dance. It was early in the morning they started. So that morning when they first started dancing, I guess... We always sit in that cookshack. So we were all sitting in there. And, here, Patrick came. He came over and he said, "Did you get my skirt ready? Because I'm going to dance. I'm going to start today." And, here we were all sitting around there just looking at each other. And my mom was sitting there and Ruben's wife, Pansy, and all those old people. So, I said, "No, Patrick, you wait." And, then my mom said, "No, he's a boy. He's a Lakota boy. Make up his own mind. He want to dance, then let him dance." So he was really happy when my mom say that. She said, "I got this skirt for him." We still have that skirt. I don't know where she got it. I don't how she got it. But, she got this little skirt. Just small. A blue one. Yeah, and it had ribbons. She got that from her bag and she said, "I've got a skirt for him."

And, you know, the dancers have eagle feathers. And, Sole and my other granddaughters said, "Oh, boy, Patrick didn't have no eagle fan, so we're going to make one for him." And I was like...I thought they were just teasing. At that time, Rae-Ann and Sole was just small girls. So they were really happy that Patrick was going to dance. So they all said, "We're going to help you." So they went in the cookshack and one of Emma Waters's kids brought that turkey, wild turkey. They brought that wild turkey and they were plucking the feathers out. But, they got some feathers and they make a fan in a hurry. And here comes Sole and Rae-Ann and they say, "We make that feather for Patrick. The fan." It was just cute. Patrick was passing by with those turkey feathers and they have a red rag around them and he was really fanning himself!

And, I talked to Earl Swift Hawk, the medicine man. I said, "My grandson wants to come in." I said, "Is it all right?" I told him that he wanted to dance. He told him the same thing. He said, "Good. He's a boy. If he wants to do something then let him." So, I said, "Okay." So I put him out there. And, then my brother's son, Everett, came out right away and in Indian he said, "My cousin, *hanka si*." He said, "My cousin going in?" So, I said, "Yeah." So he came out and they went in the sweatlodge. And I think that was real cute. Two little boys. He was only three and a half.

And when they were resting, I think it was second round, they took Patrick in. He went all around there. And all those people stand up. They were saying, "Everyone stand up, the Sundancers are coming in." Everybody was looking and here Patrick was just small, walking in. And everybody say, "What?!?" So he danced. He finished his four days. He finished his four days and he was really strong.

Initially, when I first tried to find meaning in Melda's story about her grandson's first Sundance, I had focused on the gender issues that are prevalent in the story. In fact, I had initially regarded the entire project along gender lines that differed from Melda and Lupe's conception of the project. Consequently, I interpreted this specific story relating to *women,* in the *cookshack, having* to ask a medicine *man* about the commanding decision of a Lakota *boy.* I thought it indicated the authority that men have in all spheres of life, specifically the religious and spiritual. In that sense, I missed the point that both Melda's mother and the medicine man *corroborated* one another; that traditional authorities were supported in a network of relations. I now understand this story in terms of the changes in Lakota tradition and, more importantly, how to talk about and incorporate those changes. In that sense, it is a story about healing because the community came together to talk about renewal.

Melda tells her audience about the constant process of learning from stories and the importance of this practice. For example, in a story about her eldest brother, Albert, she says that she regrets not asking more of her eldest brother. She also indicates that her own brother felt this way about not asking more of his great-grandparents. He says, "I always wonder why." Melda includes these queries in her own account and we learn about the process of sharing stories, and their importance in the process of restoring self and collective identity. She has fittingly become an expert storyteller herself. She laughs, both quietly and out loud, at many points in her stories and her tone is overwhelmingly lighthearted. Even when she speaks of hardships, Melda tends to find them heartening and educational and this comes across in her strength and spirit. In this story about her grandson Sundancing, Melda recounts the discussion that took place among three generations of women, as well as with the medicine man, in order to determine how to maintain tradition. Melda's enjoyment in telling this story, and her enjoyment in storytelling in general, is integral to the meaning of the story. The dialogue that takes place is as significant as are her repeated efforts to perpetuate that dialogue. Melda repeatedly uses *she said* and other quotative verbs to convey the dialogic engagement that is critical to her story. She emphasizes her own learning, achieved through discussion, in coming to understand a traditional practice. In the story, Melda traces how an understanding of "tradition" was determined. Melda's telling of the story serves to promote a dialogue about traditional practices and, therefore, functions to perpetuate and sustain tradition. Dialogue is part of this negotiation and necessary for healing as the community works together on a shared sense of renewal.

In her storytelling, Melda recounts the people who were involved in their long path to the Sundance. She authorizes her own role in the Lakota community through her associations to specific individuals and practices. She does so, however, in an encompassing manner in that her "stories serve to both establish and legitimate the poles of the dialectic that creates tradition."[48] In *The Lakota Ritual of the Sweat Lodge: History and Contemporary Practice* (1998), Raymond A. Bucko elaborates that stories "not only guide the dialectical process but also become part of the process itself."[49] Accordingly, Melda's stories demonstrate the ways in which Lakota tradition is experienced as a dynamic and regenerative process. She shows how that process is spoken of and talked about. In this sense, one's relations as well as one's connection to those relations are essential to discussions that sustain tradition. In fact, knowing who you are, or claiming an individual identity, necessarily also involves claiming sacred knowledge. Accordingly, Dakota scholar Elizabeth Cook-Lynn says that the "question '*taku iniciapi he?*' or 'what is your name' is a sacred question which most often means 'who are you in relation to all the rest of us?'"[50] Melda traces her kinship ties and shows how her knowledge extends both into the past and future. She says, "I'm the seventh generation from my great-grandfathers." *Tiyospaye*, or smaller kin groups, are significant to the organization of the Lakota community. Cook-Lynn says that the *tiyospaye (tiospaye)* "is so much a part of the storytelling process for the Sioux... [because it is] a nationalistic forum for the people."[51] In using kinship ties, Melda is establishing herself within a national discourse; one which upholds the Lakota as a sovereign nation.

Melda and Lupe talk of praying in the traditional way and show us that tradition is something that is worked on and maintained. In Melda and Lupe's characterization of tradition, that which is "traditional" is necessarily constantly changing. These changes result from the responses to colonial impositions, but also because all cultural traditions must constantly change. Dakota scholar Vine Deloria, Jr. summarizes some of these ideas; specifically, he contests the idea that Lakota tradition, and I would suggest Indian identity, has ever only been associated with the past:

> We must be confident that in showing respect for our traditions we are acting responsibly. In a real sense we cannot "revive" a religion for that is going backward. What we can do is respect religious traditions and allow them to take us forward into the future. That is all the old ways ever promised they would do.[52]

As something that operates in the present, Lakota tradition necessarily functions within a system of dynamic interrelations. Given these relationships, individuals determine what constitutes tradition through interaction and debate. People make up tradition in both senses of the word; they comprise tradition and they construct tradition and they do this, in part, through the sharing of stories. These stories are ultimately encompassing to essential audiences—this one included—and, like the prayer *Mitakuye Oyasin* or "all my relations," function in invoking and sustaining the sacredness associated with what are, from a traditional Lakota perspective, the divine relations among all things.[53]

NOTES

Adapted from material in *Being Lakota: Identity and Tradition on Pine Ridge Reservation* by Larissa Petrillo in collaboration with Melda and Lupe Trejo published by the University of Nebraska Press, 2007.

1. John Collier repealed antireligion laws in the 1930s, but there is a continuing history of constraints and legislation. For a history of the Sundance, see Clyde Holler's *Black Elk's Religion: The Sun Dance and Lakota Catholicism* (Syracuse, NY: Syracuse University Press, 1995).

2. Raymond A. Bucko, *The Lakota Ritual of the Sweat Lodge: History and Contemporary Practice* (Lincoln: University of Nebraska Press, 1998), 34.

3. For more information on Rosebud Reservation, see Elizabeth S. Grobsmith, *Lakota of the Rosebud: A Contemporary Ethnography* (New York: Holt, Rinehart, and Winston, 1981).

4. The American Indian population of Pine Ridge Reservation is estimated to be between 14,295 (2000 census) and 39,734 (FEMA, 2004). See Federal Emergency Management Agency, Region VIII (2004), available at: http://www.fema.gov/about/contact/regions.shtm (accessed June 9, 2005). The territory of the Great Sioux Reservation was established with the revision of the Fort Laramie treaty in 1868. The

Lakota people began living inside the boundaries of the reservation primarily in the 1880s, although the order for Indians to return to tribal lands was issued in 1876. In 1887, the General Allotment Act (also known as the Dawes Act) legislated that land be divided into private allotments to be held in trust for 25 years.

5. Susan Gardner, "Speaking of Ella Deloria: Conversations with Joyzelle Gingway Godfrey, 1998–2000, Lower Brule Community College, South Dakota," *American Indian Quarterly* 24, no. 3 (2000): 464.

6. Mario Gonzalez and Elizabeth Cook-Lynn, *The Politics of Hallowed Ground: Wounded Knee and the Struggle for Indian Sovereignty* (Urbana: University of Illinois Press, 1999), 87.

7. Bucko, *The Lakota Ritual*, 55.

8. Many ethnographies have been written on some or all of these rites. For Black Elk's description, see Joseph Epes Brown's *The Sacred Pipe: Black Elk's Account of the Seven Rites of the Oglala Sioux* (Norman: University of Oklahoma Press, 1953). Julian Rice provides one of the most recent comprehensive analyses of Lakota belief and ritual in *Before the Great Spirit: The Many Faces of Sioux Spirituality* (Albuquerque: University of New Mexico Press, 1998). Many other prominent Dakota and Lakota ethnographies were written in the late 1800s and early 1900s. See, for example, James W. Lynd, "The Religion of the Dakotas," *Minnesota Historical Collections* 2 (1864): 150–74; Gideon H. Pond, "Dakota Superstitions," *Collections of the Minnesota Historical Society* 2 (1867): 32–62; Samuel W. Pond, *The Dakota or Sioux in Minnesota As They Were in 1834* (St. Paul: Minnesota Historical Press, 1986[1908]); Alice Fletcher, "Indian Ceremonies," *Report of the Peabody Museum of American Archaeology and Ethnology* 16 (1884): 260–333; Stephan R. Riggs, *Dakota Grammar, Texts, and Ethnography*, edited by James Owen Dorsey (Washington, D.C.: Government Printing Office, 1893); James O. Dorsey, *A Study of Siouan Cults* (Seattle: Shorey, 1972[1894]); James Mooney, *The Ghost-Dance Religion and The Sioux Outbreak of 1890* (Chicago: Smithsonian Institution, Bureau of American Ethnology Annual Report, no. 14, 1896); George Sword, "Dakota Texts from the Sword Manuscript," trans. Ella Deloria, [1896–1909] (Philadelphia: American Philosophical Society, 1938); James R. Walker, *Lakota Belief and Ritual*, ed. Raymond J. DeMallie and Elaine A. Jahner (Lincoln: University of Nebraska Press, 1980[1896–1909]); James R. Walker, *Lakota Myth*, ed. Elaine A. Jahner (Lincoln: University of Nebraska Press, 1983[1896–1909]); James R. Walker, *Lakota Society*, ed. Raymond J. DeMallie (Lincoln: University of Nebraska Press, 1982[1896–1909]); Clark Wissler, "Societies and Ceremonial Associations in the Oglala Division of the Teton-Dakota," *Anthropological Papers of the American Museum of Natural History* 11 (1912): 1–99; Charles A. Eastman, *Indian Boyhood* (New York: McClure, 1902); Frances Densmore, *Teton Sioux Music*, Smithsonian Institution Bureau of Ethnology Bulletin 61 (Washington, DC: Government Printing Office, 1918); Ella Deloria, *Dakota Texts* (New York: AMS, 1974[1932]); George Bushotter, *Teton Myths*, ed. and trans. Ella Deloria Boas Collection 30 (Philadelphia: American Philosophical Society, 1937); Eugene Buechel, *A Grammar of Lakota* (St. Francis, SD: Rosebud Educational Society, 1939); Ella Deloria, *Speaking of Indians* (Vermillion, SD: Dakota Press, 1979); Ella Deloria, *Waterlily* (Lincoln: University of Nebraska Press, 1988).

9. Holler, *Black Elk's Religion*, 230.

10. For the full life story accounts see Larissa Petrillo (in collaboration with Melda and Lupe Trejo), *Being Lakota: Identity and Tradition on Pine Ridge Reservation* (Lincoln: University of Nebraska Press, 2007).

11. Edward Kadlecek and Mabell Kadlecek, *To Kill an Eagle: Indian Views on the Last Days of Crazy Horse* (Boulder, CO: Johnson, 1981), 139, 161.

12. Raymond J. DeMallie, "Lakota Traditionalism: History and Symbol," in *Native North American Interaction Patterns*, ed. Regna Darnell and Michael K. Foster (Hull, Quebec: Canadian Museum of Civilization, 1988), 2.

13. Ibid., 4.

14. Bucko, *The Lakota Ritual*, 14, 98.

15. Elizabeth Cook-Lynn, "How Scholarship Defames the Native Voice...and Why," *Wicazo Sa Review* 15, no. 2 (2000): 88.

16. For further information on legislation around religious freedom in the United States see Lee Irwin, "Freedom, Law, and Prophecy: A Brief History of Native American Religious Resistance," in *Native American Spirituality: A Critical Reader*, ed. L. Irwin (Lincoln: University of Nebraska Press, 2000), 295–316.

17. Russell Means, *Where White Men Fear to Tread: The Autobiography of Russell Means* (New York: St. Martin's, 1995), 186.

18. Jane Katz, ed., *Messengers of the Wind* (New York: Ballantine, 1995), 292.

19. The American Indian Movement (AIM) is a pan-Indian national activist organization. For more information, see Joane Nagel, Troy Johnson, and Duane Champagne, eds., *American Indian Activism: Alcatraz to the Longest Walk* (Urbana: University of Illinois Press, 1997).

20. The interest in Native spirituality in the late 1960s and 1970s, in both Native and non-Native communities, fueled the writing and reissue of several popular books about Lakota culture. *Black Elk Speaks*, the collaborative life story of Nicholas Black Elk, was first published in 1932 and it grew in popularity with its reissue in 1961. Dee Brown's historical account of the Lakota people, *Bury My Heart at Wounded Knee* (New York: Holt, Rinehart, and Winston, 1970), also achieved popular success at that time. Shortly thereafter, Richard Erdoes told the story of John (Fire) Lame Deer in *Lame Deer: Seeker of Visions* (New York: Simon and Schuster, 1972) and, in the 1970s, Frank Fools Crow, in collaboration with Thomas Mails, also provided what were well-received narratives about his practices as a medicine man. See John G. Neihardt, *Black Elk Speaks* (Lincoln: University of Nebraska Press, 1961[1932]); Dee Brown, *Bury My Heart at Wounded Knee*; John Fire Lame Deer and Richard Erdoes, *Lame Deer: Seeker of Visions* (New York: Washington Square Press, 1972); Thomas Mails and Frank Fools Crow, *Fools Crow* (Garden City, NY: Doubleday, 1979).

21. See Joane Nagel's *American Indian Ethnic Renewal: Red Power and the Resurgence of Identity and Culture* (New York: Oxford University Press, 1996). Dakota scholar Elizabeth Cook-Lynn clearly differentiates between civil rights and the Native efforts towards self-determination and sovereignty that are associated with being constitutionally recognized nation(s) in the United States. For a further discussion, see Elizabeth Cook-Lynn's *Why I Can't Read Wallace Stegner and Other Essays: A Tribal Voice* (Madison: University of Wisconsin Press, 1996), 141.

22. Marjorie M. Schweitzer, ed., *American Indian Grandmothers: Traditions and Transitions* (Albuquerque: University of New Mexico Press, 1999), 16.

23. Severt Young Bear and R. D. Theisz, *Standing in the Light: A Lakota Way of Seeing* (Lincoln: University of Nebraska Press, 1994), 177.

24. Delphine Red Shirt, *Bead on an Anthill: A Lakota Childhood* (Lincoln: University of Nebraska Press, 1998), 69.

25. James V. Fenelon, *Culturcide, Resistance, and Survival of the Lakota ("Sioux Nation")* (New York: Garland, 1998), 290.

26. Gardner, "Speaking of Ella Deloria," 473.

27. Leonard Crow Dog and Richard Erdoes, *Crow Dog: Four Generations of Sioux Medicine Men* (New York: HarperCollins, 1995), 124.

28. Patricia Albers, "Sioux Women in Transition: A Study of Their Changing Status in Domestic and Capitalist Sectors of Production," in *The Hidden Half: Studies of Plains Indian Women,* ed. Patricia Albers and Beatrice Medicine (Lanham, MD: University Press of America, 1983), 214.

29. Paul B. Steinmetz, *Pipe, Bible, and Peyote Among the Oglala Lakota: A Study in Religious Identity* (Knoxville: University of Tennessee Press, 1990), 79.

30. Mikael Kurkiala, *"Building the Nation Back Up": The Politics of Identity on the Pine Ridge Indian Reservation* (Uppsala, Sweden: Acta Universitatis Upsaliensis, 1997), 227.

31. Nagel, *American Indian Ethnic Renewal,* 190.

32. Ibid., 63.

33. Raymond J. DeMallie and Douglas R. Parks, "Introduction," *Sioux Indian Religion: Tradition and Innovation,* ed. Raymond J. DeMallie and Douglas R. Parks (Norman: University of Oklahoma Press, 1987), 7.

34. Bucko, *The Lakota Ritual,* 15.

35. Bucko, *The Lakota Ritual,* 175.

36. Quanah Parker (Comanche), an Oklahoma peyotist, helped to bring the Half Moon style of peyote meetings to other tribes. The Half Moon ceremony deals less explicitly with Christianity than does the Big Moon (or Cross Fire) branch.

37. Omer C. Stewart, *Peyote Religion: A History* (Norman: University of Oklahoma Press, 1987), 87–89, 94–95.

38. Ibid., 167.

39. DeMallie, "Lakota Traditionalism," 9.

40. Kenneth Lincoln and Al Logan Slagle, *The Good Red Road: Passages into Native America* (San Francisco: Harper and Row, 1987), 104.

41. Esther Black Elk DeSersa, Olivia Black Elk Pourier, Aaron DeSersa Jr., and Clifton DeSersa, *Black Elk Lives: Conversations with the Black Elk Family,* ed. Hilda Neihardt and Lori Utecht (Lincoln: University of Nebraska Press, 2000), 5.

42. Means, *Where White Men Fear to Tread,* 28.

43. For a further description see Mooney, *The Ghost-Dance Religion.* For a timeline and history see William S. E. Coleman, *Voices of Wounded Knee* (Lincoln: University of Nebraska Press, 2000).

44. Rice, *Before the Great Spirit,* 2.

45. On December 29, 1890, 300 unarmed men, women, and children were killed by U.S. soldiers at Wounded Knee Creek. The site of the massacre was later occupied in 1973 by AIM members and Lakota traditionalists in an effort to grieve unjust conditions on the reservation.

46. For a more complete account of the story Melda relates about the healing effects of the Ghost Dance, see Crow Dog and Erdoes, *Crow Dog*, 43. The account is attributed to Howard Red Bear, Melda's great-uncle.

47. In 1993, Lakota spiritual and political leaders passed the "Declaration of War Against Exploiters of Lakota Spirituality," which was brought to the attention of the United Nations. See Fenelon, *Culturcide, Resistance, and Survival*, 295. The Sundance controversy proliferated in 1997 with several articles in *Indian Country Today*, the national Indian newspaper, which listed medicine men accused of selling the Sundance to non-Native participants. For example, see K. Marie Porterfield, "The Selling of the Sun Dance," *Indian Country Today*, July 28, 1997: A1

48. Bucko, *The Lakota Ritual*, 145.

49. Ibid.

50. Gonzalez and Cook-Lynn, *Politics of Hallowed Ground*, 189.

51. Cook-Lynn, *Why I Can't Read Wallace Stegner*, 93.

52. Vine Deloria, Jr., *For This Land: Writings on Religion in America*, ed. James Treat (New York: Routledge, 1999), 268.

53. Portions of this chapter are adapted from material in *Being Lakota: Identity and Tradition on Pine Ridge Reservation* by Larissa Petrillo in collaboration with Melda and Lupe Trejo published by the University of Nebraska Press, 2007.

BIBLIOGRAPHY

Albers, Patricia. "Sioux Women in Transition: A Study of Their Changing Status in Domestic and Capitalist Sectors of Production." In *The Hidden Half: Studies of Plains Indian Women*, edited by Patricia Albers and Beatrice Medicine, 175–234. Lanham, MD: University Press of America, 1983.

Black Elk DeSersa, Esther, Olivia Black Elk Pourier, Aaron DeSersa Jr., and Clifton DeSersa. In *Black Elk Lives: Conversations with the Black Elk Family*, edited by Hilda Neihardt and Lori Utecht. Lincoln: University of Nebraska Press, 2000: 42–72.

Brown, Dee. *Bury My Heart at Wounded Knee*. New York: Holt, Rinehart, and Winston, 1970.

Brown, Joseph Epes. *The Sacred Pipe: Black Elk's Account of the Seven Rites of the Oglala Sioux*. Norman: University of Oklahoma Press, 1953.

Bucko, Raymond A. *The Lakota Ritual of the Sweat Lodge: History and Contemporary Practice*. Lincoln: University of Nebraska Press, 1998.

Buechel, Eugene. *A Grammar of Lakota*. St. Francis, S.D.: Rosebud Educational Society, 1939.

Bushotter, George. *Teton Myths*, edited and translated by Ella Deloria. Boas Collection 30. Philadelphia: American Philosophical Society, 1937.

Coleman, William S. E. *Voices of Wounded Knee*. Lincoln: University of Nebraska Press, 2000.

Cook-Lynn, Elizabeth. "How Scholarship Defames the Native Voice...and Why." *Wicazo Sa Review* 15, no. 2 (2000): 79–92.

Cook-Lynn, Elizabeth. *Why I Can't Read: Wallace Stegner and Other Essays: A Tribal Voice*. Madison: University of Wisconsin Press, 1996.

Crow Dog, Leonard, and Richard Erdoes. *Crow Dog: Four Generations of Sioux Medicine Men.* New York: HarperCollins, 1995.

Deloria, Ella. *Dakota Texts.* New York: AMS, 1974 (1932).

Deloria, Ella. *Speaking of Indians.* Vermillion, SD: Dakota Press, 1979.

Deloria, Ella. *Waterlily.* Lincoln: University of Nebraska Press, 1988.

Deloria, Vine, Jr. *For This Land: Writings on Religion in America,* edited by James Treat. New York: Routledge, 1999.

DeMallie, Raymond J. "Lakota Traditionalism: History and Symbol." In *Native North American Interaction Patterns,* edited by Regna Darnell and Michael K. Foster, 2–21. Hull, Quebec: Canadian Museum of Civilization, 1988.

DeMallie, Raymond J., and Douglas R. Parks. "Introduction." In *Sioux Indian Religion: Tradition and Innovation,* edited by Raymond J. DeMallie and Douglas R. Parks, 3–22. Norman: University of Oklahoma Press, 1987.

Densmore, Frances. *Teton Sioux Music.* Smithsonian Institution Bureau of Ethnology Bulletin 61. Washington, D.C.: Government Printing Office, 1918.

Dorsey, James. *A Study of Siouan Cults.* Seattle: Shorey, 1972 (1894).

Eastman, Charles A. *Indian Boyhood.* New York: McClure, 1902.

Federal Emergency Management Agency. 2004. Region VIII. June 9, 2005. Available at: http://www.fema.gov/regions/viii/tribal/oglalabg.shtm.

Fenelon, James V. *Culturcide, Resistance, and Survival of the Lakota ("Sioux Nation").* New York: Garland, 1998.

Fletcher, Alice. "Indian Ceremonies." *Report of the Peabody Museum of American Archaeology and Ethnology* 16 (1884): 260–333.

Gardner, Susan. "Speaking of Ella Deloria: Conversations with Joyzelle Gingway Godfrey, 1998–2000, Lower Brule Community College, South Dakota." *American Indian Quarterly* 24, no. 3 (2000): 456–81.

Gonzalez, Mario, and Elizabeth Cook-Lynn. *The Politics of Hallowed Ground: Wounded Knee and the Struggle for Indian Sovereignty.* Urbana: University of Illinois Press, 1999.

Grobsmith, Elizabeth S. *Lakota of the Rosebud: A Contemporary Ethnography.* New York: Holt, Rinehart, and Winston, 1981.

Holler, Clyde. *Black Elk's Religion: The Sun Dance and Lakota Catholicism.* Syracuse, NY: Syracuse University Press, 1995.

Irwin, Lee. "Freedom, Law, and Prophecy: A Brief History of Native American Religious Resistance." In *Native American Spirituality: A Critical Reader,* edited by L. Irwin, 295–316. Lincoln: University of Nebraska Press, 2000.

Kadlecek, Edward, and Mabell Kadlecek. *To Kill an Eagle: Indian Views on The Last Days of Crazy Horse.* Boulder, CO: Johnson, 1981.

Katz, Jane, ed. *Messengers of the Wind.* New York: Ballantine, 1995.

Kurkiala, Mikael. *"Building the Nation Back Up": The Politics of Identity on the Pine Ridge Indian Reservation.* Uppsala Studies in Cultural Anthropology 22. Uppsala, Sweden: Acta Universitatis Upsaliensis, 1997.

Lame Deer, John Fire, and Richard Erdoes. *Lame Deer: Seeker of Visions.* New York: Washington Square Press, 1972.

Lincoln, Kenneth, with Al Logan Slagle. *The Good Red Road: Passages into Native America.* San Francisco: Harper and Row, 1987.

Lynd, James W. "The Religion of the Dakotas." *Minnesota Historical Collections* 2 (1864): 150–74.

Mails, Thomas, and Frank Fools Crow. *Fools Crow*. Garden City, N.Y.: Doubleday, 1979.

Means, Russell. *Where White Men Fear to Tread: The Autobiography of Russell Means*. New York: St. Martin's, 1995.

Mooney, James. *The Ghost-Dance Religion and The Sioux Outbreak of 1890*. Washington, D.C.: Government Printing Office, 1896.

Nagel, Joane. *American Indian Ethnic Renewal: Red Power and the Resurgence of Identity and Culture*. New York: Oxford University Press, 1996.

Nagel, Joane, Troy Johnson, and Duane Champagne, eds. *American Indian Activism: Alcatraz to the Longest Walk*. Chicago: University of Illinois Press, 1997.

Neihardt, John G. *Black Elk Speaks*. Lincoln: University of Nebraska Press, 1961 (1932).

Petrillo, Larissa, Melda Trejo, and Lupe Trejo. *Being Lakota: Identity and Tradition on Pine Ridge Reservation*. Lincoln: University of Nebraska Press, 2007.

Pond, Gideon H. "Dakota Superstitions." *Minnesota Historical Society* 2 (1867): 32–62.

Pond, Samuel W. *The Dakota or Sioux in Minnesota As They Were in 1834*. St. Paul: Minnesota Historical Press, 1986 (1908).

Porterfield, K. Marie. "The Selling of the Sun Dance." *Indian Country Today*, July 28, 1997: A1.

Red Shirt, Delphine. *Bead on an Anthill: A Lakota Childhood*. Lincoln: University of Nebraska Press, 1998.

Rice, Julian. *Before the Great Spirit: The Many Faces of Sioux Spirituality*. Albuquerque: University of New Mexico Press, 1998.

Riggs, Stephan R. *Dakota Grammar, Texts, and Ethnography*, edited by James Owen Dorsey. Washington, D.C.: Government Printing Office, 1893.

Schweitzer, Marjorie M., ed. *American Indian Grandmothers: Traditions and Transitions*. Albuquerque: University of New Mexico Press, 1999.

Steinmetz, Paul B. *Pipe, Bible, and Peyote Among the Oglala Lakota: A Study in Religious Identity*. Knoxville: University of Tennessee Press, 1990.

Stewart, Omer C. *Peyote Religion: A History*. Norman: University of Oklahoma Press, 1987.

Walker, James R. *Lakota Belief and Ritual*, edited by Raymond J. DeMallie and Elaine A. Jahner. Lincoln: University of Nebraska Press, 1980 (1896–1909).

Walker, James R. *Lakota Myth*, edited by Elaine A. Jahner. Lincoln: University of Nebraska Press, 1983 (1896–1909).

Walker, James R. *Lakota Society*, edited by Raymond J. DeMallie. Lincoln: University of Nebraska Press, 1982 (1896–1909).

Young Bear, Severt, and R. D. Theisz. *Standing in the Light: A Lakota Way of Seeing*. Lincoln: University of Nebraska Press, 1994.

PART III

━━━━ ✠ ━━━━

Native American Notions
of the Embodied Self

CHAPTER 6

— ✵ —

Restoring Sacred Connection with Native Women in the Inner City

Denise Nadeau with Alannah Earl Young

We acknowledge our place in Creation and remember the Ancestors who have gone before and the teachings they left with us for the benefit of the future generations. We acknowledge the sacred gifts of the earth, the air, the fire, and water that give life and sustain us. We acknowledge the minerals, plants, animals, and the humans as our relatives. We acknowledge the traditional ancestral territories in which we visit, work, live, and we honor where our original Ancestor's lineages come from and the gifts they offer in our lives as they continue to direct our intention to reflect our spiritual teachings in practice.

—*Denise Nadeau and Alannah Earl Young*

In the darkness and rain of a windy Vancouver night 100 women with candles have gathered around the circle of 14 granite benches, a monument to the 14 women killed by a gunman in Montreal in 1989. It is December 6, Day Against Violence Against Women in Canada. The opening song is over, the drums have been carried to the center of the circle, and we begin our mourning dance. There are nine of us—Native and non-Native women together. We move slowly in a line across the circle, carrying a long black cloth over our heads, wailing our grief and anguish into the night sky. Four times we pass the center, moving to the four directions. We wail for the 63 missing and dead women from the Downtown Eastside; we wail for the sisters, daughters, mothers, friends who have died from or survived physical and sexual violence; we wail for the women of Afghanistan, for the women of Palestine, for the women on the streets of Vancouver who daily encounter economic and racist violence, we wail for ourselves.

We return to the center in silence, form a circle and gently, ever so tenderly, we put the cloth down on the ground, holding these women close to our heart. We move outward, singing the Women Warrior Song, a public song from the women of the Lil'wat Nation. The final round is sung without drums, and we raise our drums sticks in the air as a gesture of defiance and a promise to remember and honor the lives of these women.

This Mourning Dance was part of a program Alannah Earl Young and I facilitated with women from the Downtown Eastside Women's Centre in Vancouver between 2001 and 2003. The program was called *Restoring Sacred Vitality* and is an approach to repairing and restoring the body-spirits of women who have experienced extensive and ongoing violence. It teaches how to recover and *embody*—enact in the body in feeling, sensing, imagining, moving—the sacred interconnection between ourselves, all living beings and the land.

Vancouver is a large Canadian city on Coastal Salish Territory on the West Coast of Canada. Indigenous women in urban cores like Vancouver experience racist, sexist, and colonial violence daily. They come from diverse cultural, spiritual, and religious backgrounds; access to ceremony and connection to land and place is limited or nonexistent for many; and lack of affordable housing and cuts in social assistance rates mean they are always poor and living on the edge of crisis in terms of daily survival. Many are survivors of residential schools or children of survivors; many are the products of foster homes; in most of these cases they have experienced the transmission of intergenerational violence. The question we faced was what type of program would be most effective for this diverse and distinct population of Indigenous women?

In this chapter we will use the terms Indigenous, Native, Aboriginal, and First Nations interchangeably. There are many terms used to apply to "Indians" in Canada, many created through the Indian Act or in reaction to it. In Canada, the Indian Act served to disenfranchise more than 200,000 women and their descendants, none of whom are included in the "First Nations" who negotiate for title and land rights.[1] Because the women we work with use a wide range of terms to describe themselves we will also, but will foreground "Indigenous" as a term which connotes a relationship to land and which is recognized by all First Peoples at the level of the United Nations.

Over a three year period we developed an approach to regeneration and restoration from violence that centers on the body and draws on Indigenous Principles, that is, teachings from traditional Indigenous ways of knowing and acting in the world. By focusing on fostering a lived, felt sense of the sacredness of the body or *sacred vitality* and combining this with ceremony, traditional teachings, and community performance, we created a group process that restored participants' connection to themselves, their community, and the land. The restoration of a sense of sacredness of the body and of one's cultural identity fosters resilience and the ability to deal with adversity in creative rather than destructive ways.

It is important to stress here that there are a multitude of factors that impact the healing journey of any woman. This program made a small contribution. At minimum it allowed women to feel better about themselves during the time period of the groups. At best, it provided spiritual and somatic resources that increased participant's openness to further transformation. The core of this work is focused on accessing and balancing spiritual and body wisdom as a way of restoring relationships affected by violence. Our emphasis is on lifting up people's unique gifts and goodness. We don't have big dreams of *fixing* people, but rather we want to share what has helped us and the women with whom we have worked. The process we have developed addresses not only intimate violence but the violence of colonialism and racism.

Here, we first briefly consider our own locations and differences, describe where we work, why we adopted our approach and then describe what we do and give some examples of how we do it. We conclude with some reflections on how this process contributes to decolonization.

WHO ARE WE?

Alannah Young and Denise Nadeau developed the project together, while Denise did research on it and followed the participants closely for her dissertation for a Doctorate of Ministry. This chapter draws extensively on Denise's research and ongoing work in the area of embodied nonviolence. There are therefore two voices here—the *we* refers to our work and reflection together and the third person voice is that of Denise, who wrote this piece.

Alannah is Anishnabe and Cree from the Opaswayak Cree Nation, presently living in traditional Coast Salish Territory and working at the First Nations House of Learning at the University of British Columbia. She has worked with teachers from several Indigenous nations and these have shaped her Indigenous spiritual practice. Her work is informed by Indigenous Knowledges, nonviolence principles and critical race theory. She is currently involved with developing Indigenous leadership education that supports self-determined, decolonizing agendas. Denise is a European Canadian of French Irish heritage, raised in Quebec, with Mi'kmaq ancestry on her father's side. Her French ancestors intermarried with Mi'kmaq women and occupied Mi'kmaq territory on the Gaspé Peninsula. Her spirituality has been shaped by being raised a cradle-Catholic in Quebec, and more recently by feminist liberation and postcolonial Christian theology as well as antiracist feminism and the Catholic Worker movement. For many years she has worked alongside and participated in ceremony with both Native traditionalists and Native Christians, which has greatly influenced her religious worldview.

We came together because we both had an interest in exploring the body as a site for decolonization, based in our shared belief in the essential connection between body, land, and sovereignty. Decolonization of the body is a process whereby a person is able to recover their own voice and innate wisdom and experience their goodness and connection to land, culture, and community. It involves moving beyond and transforming learned ways of being that include the self-hatred and self-denial caused by racism and colonialism as well as behaviors that are based in reaction to oppression. The work of decolonizing the body is both deeply spiritual and political.

We have faced many challenges in working together, as a First Nations woman and a woman raised in white privilege, and as a traditional practitioner and a Christian. We have experienced the ongoing issue of transforming the dynamics of colonizer/colonized inherent in our relationship. Another challenge has been to create a constructive dialogue between our traditions as a model and approach to interreligious practice that can be helpful for women who come from many Nations and spiritual traditions.

In each of our groups there were usually a few women who still carried Christian injunctions against traditional Aboriginal spirituality. Some had been through residential schools; others were from Christian fundamentalist groups. Some combined Christian practices with traditional ones. Some had rejected Christianity completely. This meant that we had to find ways of being respectful of different traditions as we incorporated Indigenous Knowledges into the structure of the course.

Indigenous Knowledge is a concept that defies the Eurocentric need for definitions. At one level it refers to the teachings of different Indigenous peoples about their relationship to the land. The Royal Commission on Aboriginal Peoples sees it as "a cumulative body of knowledge and beliefs, handed down through generations by cultural transmission, about the relationship of living beings (including humans) with one another and their environment."[2] Indigenous Knowledges are both place and language specific, which is why we speak of them in the plural.

For Alannah, her intention has been to maintain this integrity of the teachings of oral traditions. This means to share them in a way that reflects how a tradition is connected to appropriate conditions, people, places, and times. One site of struggle is cultural appropriation, where knowledge is decontextualized from the land and community relationships. When the sources of knowledge aren't credited or acknowledged, profit and power is appropriated from First Nations peoples. Teaching how to respect ceremonies and protocols connected to place is a cocreative process that reflects and maintains equitable power dynamics. The appropriate protocol is to acknowledge historical relationships between peoples and land and identify ways that will demonstrate power sharing and enhance community vitality in accordance with the traditional teachings.

For Denise, her challenge has been to represent an anticolonial form of Christianity and only when this is appropriate. She affirms the role and responsibility of the Christian church in the genocide of Native peoples in North America. Her intention has been to find ways she can be accountable for the colonial history of which she is part, acknowledging both her complicity in and the benefits she has gained from it, as well as the integrity within the spiritual teachings of her own tradition that support nonviolence, compassion, justice, reparations, and interconnection.

WHERE WE WORK

Between 2001 and 2003 we piloted a program called *Still Movement: Restoring Sacred Vitality* with Native women in the Downtown Eastside of Vancouver. The program was held at the Downtown Eastside Women's Centre (DEWC), a women-only space. Two board members had approached us to do this because they wanted a program that would support aboriginal women's leadership and be an alternative to individual counseling, which few women accessed. They were concerned that there were not many resources that specifically addressed the needs of Native women in the inner city and that our sociopolitical focus offered an alternative to the therapeutic models available. The leaders of the Centre's healing circle, the only program there that was targeted at Native women, were also interested in our program because, as one said, "we want something more for the women. They are ready for a next stage."

We ran four groups over a two year period and the length of the groups varied. One course was once a week over 10 weeks with a one-day retreat outside the city; the second course ran for five weeks with two sessions a week and a one-day retreat. Participation ranged from 20 in one group to 7 in another, the latter in a training we offered which involved adding an explanation of our method so that the women could use some of the tools and the framework in their own work.

Participants were recruited by the leaders of the healing circle. The groups had a complex makeup, reflecting the reality of the urban aboriginal community. In one group, for example, there were two Nishga women, a Gitksa'an; a Cree woman from Saskatchewan, a woman of mixed Chinese and Native heritage, a mixed Cree and African-Canadian woman, a white woman who had married into and lived in Native communities in Northern Ontario for 20 years, a part Native Hawaiian; and two Coastal Salish women. The age range in all groups was from 35 to 60.

WHAT DOES HEALING MEAN?

The stated goal of the program was to support Native women's leadership development by affirming strengths and restoring connection through the use of ceremony, spiritual teachings and expressive arts therapies. Because most of the women we worked with were described by agencies and the media in terms of the extent of violence that they experienced (AIDS survivor, missing women, residential school survivor, etc.), we made it a point to not only avoid dominant representations of abused women, which reduces them to victims of violence, but to frame the program in terms of leadership training rather than healing from violence. This was connected to some concerns we had as to how the word *healing* was interpreted as applying to Native peoples by mainstream agencies in the inner city. Not only can *healing* be used to refer to a process that legitimates and maintains victim-oppressor positioning, but the colonial framing of the *healed* and the *not healed* has in many ways replaced the older distinction of the civilized and uncivilized. When we use the word healing we make it clear we are not pathologizing women's social suffering and that it has social, political, and spiritual dimensions.

Healing Initiatives and the Politics of Trauma

Many healing initiatives that address the problems of Native peoples, especially in inner-city areas, fail to link individual suffering to the broader psychosocial conditions in which most live. Common pastoral counseling, social work, and therapy approaches tend to focus on the negative aspects of people's behavior and pathologize the impacts of violence. In doing this they operate under what anthropologist Robert Paine termed a form of "welfare colonialism," which reflects the assumption that these populations need to be managed or changed and require help and guidance. This "non-demonstrative colonialism" is part of the ongoing relationship between First Nations peoples and the Canadian State, and it serves to veil the outright land grabs and assimilation policies of earlier colonialism.[3]

A significant example of these ongoing colonial dynamics in the healing industry is found in the language of trauma applied to Native communities and Native women. The extensive class, race, gender, and colonial violence that many Native women have experienced is lost in the diagnostic terminology of post-traumatic stress disorder (PTSD). This label is found in the American Psychiatric Society's *Diagnostic and Statistic Manual of Mental Disorders (DSM-IV)* and is applied to a wide range of physical and emotional responses. PTSD, like much trauma language, reduces suffering to a condition of medical pathology rather than a spiritual or moral problem caused by political violence. This *social suffering*—a term from medical anthropology—is transformed into individual cases of dysfunction.[4] The language of deficiency and dysfunction reduces to personality traits or syndromes behaviors that have emerged as survival or resistance responses to oppressive conditions.

Reframing Trauma and Healing

The term *psychosocial trauma* was created by the Salvadorean psychologist Ignacio Martin-Baro to describe the effects of routinized violence that Salvadoreans experienced during the ongoing civil war in the 1970s and 80s, a war where government forces were backed by the United States.[5] Rather than focusing on the individual, this concept of trauma gives primacy to the social network in which the human is embedded. Psychosocial trauma is trauma that is foreseeable and predictable; it affects an entire network of social relations. As long as dehumanizing social relations continue, the symptoms of trauma remain both in individuals and in communities. It is only in changing the social relations between colonizer and colonized that psychosocial trauma can be alleviated.

In applying the concept of psychosocial trauma to Native communities in North America, an additional dimension is added. Not only have social relations been dehumanized, but relations with the land and all living beings have been disrupted. Indigenous philosophies are based in cosmologies of relationships that include the interrelatedness of plants, animals, minerals, and humans. Multiple forms of colonial violence over generations have resulted in a spiritual disjuncture—a loss of connection with these relations. Ronald Niezen, in *Spirit Wars*, describes this as a "radical instability in the human relationship with the spirit world."[6] The many aspects of colonialism that attacked religious identity, many of which continue today in different forms, eroded communities' sense of their spiritual identity. For many, this spiritual dispossession was and is experienced in loss of awareness of connection to both those in their community and to the land.

Taiaiake Alfred, Mohawk traditionalist and a political scientist, suggests the word *regeneration* as an alternative to both recovery and healing. For him it is also a question of how a community identifies itself. "If you identify as victims then the best you can hope for is to be healed. Regeneration is about reconnection, acting out an identity where health, happiness, and harmony is a community goal."[7] We see the fostering of individual and communities' self-determination as essential to holistic health practices.

Joseph Gone, from the Gros Ventre Nation and professor of Psychology and Native American Studies at the University of Michigan, argues that the Western origins of modern therapy culture have contributed concepts for understanding forms of selfhood, emotion, social relations, and spirituality that are far removed and often at odds with enduring Indigenous knowledges and ways of being and perceiving the world.[8] In many Native societies the meaning of healing is not limited to discreet categories but involves the spirit, the human, and nonhuman worlds. Traditionally, healing was not distinguished "from the pursuit of strength that was the life focus of all adults," and it included the opportunity to enter spirit realms, engage with spirit powers and discover one's gifts.[9] Moreover, as Gone has noted, "healing in Native communities is modally understood to require access to sacred power."[10] When we use the word *healing*, and we do so selectively, we refer more to this understanding of healing that is common in traditional Native communities.

SACRED VITALITY AND VIOLENCE

The physiological impact of all forms of violence—be it intimate, sexist, racist, or colonial violence or the intersection of all these in the lives of Native women—is dissociation or disembodiment. Dissociation is "the state of being cut off from some aspect of one's process."[11] Unaware of one's inner responses, one is less able to perceive, sense, process, or respond to what is going on around oneself. Dissociation involves being unable to sense or process connection with other living beings, both human and nonhuman. The result is disconnection, which impacts individuals and entire communities that have experienced violence. The disconnected body-spirit (we use a hyphen between body and spirit because we understand the body and spirit as one, not separate) and community become devitalized, and dis-spirited—it is a body-spirit and community that has lost touch with its relations.

For Native women there are additional historical spiritual disconnections. While previously "our cultures promoted womanhood as a sacred identity, an identity that existed within a complex system of relations of societies that were based on balance," now through the process of a sexist and racist colonialism, Native women have lost their collective status as sacred.[12] At the individual level, when neither a woman's traditions nor her body is respected, this is played out in a loss of a sense of honor, lived out in the body-spirit.

The sense of the sacredness of the body is linked to the sense of sacredness of the land. Repairing disconnection involves recovering the body-spirit's sense of embodied relationship with land. This means restoring relationships with Earth as teacher and to one's place within the framework of relatives and natural teachers. It means restoring one's awareness of the sacredness of being a woman within this web of relationships. To do this requires recovering a *felt* sense of the body, which is becoming aware of the body in the present moment, and to see and experience it as sacred.

The term *sacred vitality*, refers to the feeling of energetic connection with one's own sacredness, with the Earth and with others in community, a feeling of being fully alive. This aliveness allows one to stand one's ground in experiencing one's rootedness in a web of relations. Not only does one recover a sense of one's own honor and dignity but also a sense of the honor and dignity of the web of relations. Sacred vitality supports transformation, affirms collective strength and sacredness in the face of oppression and creates new forms of power and nonviolent embodied ways of being in this world.

The fostering of sacred vitality is necessarily connected to an Indigenous Knowledges framework. Indigenous Knowledges include unique tribal customs, practices, and knowledge systems; environmental herbal, medicinal, spiritual knowledge; as well as ceremonies, songs, and dances. Indigenous Knowledges can also include contemporary forms of knowledge that may not have a pure traditional source or may be derived from a combination of contemporary sources. Indigenous Knowledge systems are ecologically centered and affirm the interrelationship between individuals, communities, and ecosystems. In transmitting Indigenous Knowledge through ceremonies, songs, and oral traditions we are teaching Indigenous theory, values, and cosmology, and providing an embodied connection to relations.

STILL MOVEMENT: HOW WE WORK

The program in the Downtown Eastside of Vancouver addressed the recovery of relations and of a sense of collective dignity through a combination of ceremony, bodywork, and expressive arts and was based on traditional cultural principles and values. The path to accessing sacred vitality is through restoring basic somatic (coming from the Greek word *soma*, meaning the living body) and spiritual resources that enable people to access their own internal knowledge, intuition, and vision, instead of looking for external validation from the colonial gaze.

We called the program "Still Movement," a title which combined the emphasis on the body, movement, and dance, with the sense of the sacred that can occur when one pays attention, often in stillness. While we played with the title a few times over the two years, this was the name that women kept using in the community. ("Hey, when is Still Movement going to happen again?" was a question we would be asked on the streets.) The program is constructed on two principles or spiritual values—the good life way and nonviolence—and has three phases: grounding in spirit, collective expressions of grief and lament, and affirming individual and collective strengths in performance and ceremony.

Principles: Nonviolence and the Good Life Way

The spiritual or cultural principles underlying the program are expressed through practice. The principle of nonviolence is expressed in the practice of nonjudgment and compassion for one's self and for others. It is lived out in an attitude of kindness toward oneself—there is nothing to fix, one just allows one's body-spirit to do what it needs to do at any particular moment. The emphasis on allowing with compassion, or acceptance, challenges years of self-hatred and judgment. We begin each session after a song, with a time of meditating on the breath as the Spirit within us and saying a short prayer that acknowledges our innate goodness. We practice compassion for self in many activities: a guided visualization that involves sending compassion and acceptance to specific parts of our body that have done so much for us over the years, or sending compassion if someone was experiencing physical or emotional pain through the breath to the part of the body holding the pain. Nonjudgment is introduced as a practice of nonviolence towards self and others, and includes challenging negative self-talk and being critical of others in the community.

The second principle, the Good Life Way, involves the consciousness of reciprocal relational responsibilities. Each Native culture has its own version of the Good Life Way: The Good Life Path or *Bimaadziwin* in Anishnabe; *Miyowicehtowin*—having good relations—for the Cree of the Northern prairies; *Sken-nen kowa*—maintaining peace between peoples—for the Iroquois; *Hozho*—walking in beauty, walking in a sacred manner, walking with a peaceful heart—for the Navajo. Common to these different versions of the Good Life Way are the lived values of relations, beauty, and balance. We reinforce the values of beauty, relations, and balance in practice through: the overall structure of the program, which followed the principle of balance by addressing the four parts of the self—the physical, spiritual, mental, and emotional dimensions. During each program we include a retreat day outside the inner city in which all participants have time to develop their spiritual and sensory relationships with the land. (By sensory we mean we encourage participants to use their sense of smell, taste, touch, hearing, and listening.)

Ceremonies, teachings, and prayers expand awareness of and make connections with all relations, reinforcing principles of beauty and balance. Indigenous song is a central part of every session, connecting participants to the land, ancestors, and all living relations. We encourage the development of a spiritual relationship with medicines and the ancestors. The medicines include the elements—earth, air, fire, water, animals, plants—and the relationship as one of giving and receiving.

In order to help participants develop a felt sense—i.e., an internal awareness of nonviolence and the Good Life Way—we teach a spiritual and physical practice of being in the present moment in the body. This is a Western approach called "embodiment practice," developed by Euro-American somatic therapist Susan Apoyshan, the principles of which are not in opposition to Indigenous Knowledge.[13] This practice involves consciously attending to sensations in the body and to the circulation of energy through the bodies and out into the environment. By increasing sensory awareness we can be more physically present in our bodies and aware of our relationship with others and the Earth. By gently allowing this process, participants can gradually overcome the sensations of numbness caused by violence and become aware of and slowly learn to tolerate feelings and sensations in the present. This restored ability to be in the present allows sensory engagement with and increases the effectiveness of traditional spiritual practices that involve the body's wisdom in the form of songs, dances, drumming, or using shakers, rattles, or medicines.

These foundational principles and embodiment practice are reinforced throughout the three phases of the program. The first, "Grounding in the Spirit/Gratitude" focuses on reaffirming a sense of each person's basic goodness and begins to develop the somatic resources for an embodied connection with her inner gifts. The second, "Transforming Anger, Cleansing and Lament" invokes traditions and practices of collective prayer and ceremony that address anger, grief, and loss." The third, "Celebrating Our Sacred Power/ Performing Community" involves somatic affirmation of individual and collective strengths or gifts, with some kind of performance and ritual collective action as a way of closing. Each phase and session includes spiritual teachings, somatic exercises (embodiment practice and resource development), creative expression activities (dance, movement, drawing, or writing around a theme), group dances, and ceremony.

Grounding in the Spirit/Gratitude: Examples

The first phase of the program involves building up resources so that participants begin to have a felt sense of their goodness. We begin this with the opening song, which acknowledges the traditional territory on which we are standing and begins the process of connecting to a positive sense of culture and history. We have several drums and rattles for group members. Alannah teaches Indigenous protocols about songs and then we sing the *George Family Song* to acknowledge the traditional and unceded territories of the Coast Salish peoples. The song is not only a reminder that the land is connected to a specific people but also a political statement about to whom the land belongs. We note that the land on which the Downtown Eastside is located was historically an intertribal gathering place for Coast Salish peoples and is rich with cultural spirituality. The George Family Song is a public song, which means it can be taught to others to sing in public places. We repeat this song every session, eventually getting each woman to lead it and encouraging them all to take singing leadership outside the group. After the group ended one Coastal Salish participant led the George Family Song in a public forum and she told us that she remembered that her uncle, who was related to the George family, had taught her the song many years before, thereby reclaiming her identity and a piece of her cultural history. With the same intention we close the group with another song, the "Women Warrior Song," a public song from the women of Mt. Currie (Lil'wat Nation).

For women who have been silenced in multiple ways singing is a culturally appropriate way of recovering voice. It reflects cultural self-esteem. We know how violent internalized racism is. Rather than introducing an intellectual analysis of the entire colonial historical dynamic, we are able to sing a song publicly and voice our sacred power in song as a way of restoring pride in where we come from. In doing this we are *re-membering*. This term plays on the image of re-ordering the members (as in bodily members), that is, creating a *counter memory* in the body of goodness, spirit, and interconnection. This involves both affirming sacred moments in one's past and acknowledging the sacredness of the self in the present. It includes reconnecting with spiritual and cultural traditions that have meaning for one's life now and re-membering the body's connection with Earth.

Singing is one way of reinhabiting the body, as is becoming aware of one's breath. Breath awareness fosters sensory awareness, which leads to a sense of body-mind integration. This is the ability to be fully *in* one's body and to be able to express and feel what occurs in daily life, an ability that has been lost through the experience of chronic violence, where we suppress our natural responses to survive. The process of recovery of awareness needs to be slow and gentle as often women experience much physical pain. We introduce gentle ways of waking up the body, with a "waking up the body dance," or a gentle self-touch, or contrasting movement and stillness, or identifying parts of the body where there is no pain and increasing awareness of that area to counterbalance areas of pain.

Two examples: One woman, who had described her body as being in con-stant pain, started moving cautiously in a "body-parts dance" and, as we in-troduced self-touch, slowly began to touch her arms, chest, and neck. At the end she commented on "just being allowed to touch myself. I had felt pain in my back, neck, spine, and arms, and then with the stillness and awareness it went away. Usually I just suffer, but the breathing also helped." Another woman spent most of the exercise touching her throat, later saying, "I got in touch by touching, I became aware of how much attention my throat needs and how much is stuck there."[14]

We teach *grounding,* a term that refers to an intentional connection with Earth at both a somatic and spiritual level. To be grounded is the ability to feel one's connection to the Earth, to gravity, to our center, the core flow of energy and spirit within our being. Somatically this means one does not get carried away and can integrate and allow strong feelings to move through and out one. To support the ability to ground we use activities that increase awareness of sensation in the legs and feet and sensing the body's energetic connection to the earth. It also involves an increasing awareness of the core of the body, the flow of energy from the top of the head to the pelvic floor. In feeling the connection to the ground though the feet and becoming aware of the sense of flow in the core, one becomes aware of oneself as having a center and boundaries, a critical element in equipping a person to resist violence. The practice of gratitude flows out of the experience of being grounded in the present moment as one becomes aware of the life, beauty, and diversity around us.

One example of a grounding activity we did was a "Legs Dance," which was done after increasing awareness of the feet though touch, stretching, and pushing with the feet. After the dance we asked participants to write a short poem. The two poems below are examples that express both aliveness and gratitude.

Legs

Alive, awakened, what a sensation.
You hold the weight of my body,
Sometimes it's heavy, some days
It's light, you complain but
Always to a deaf ear. I feel the connection
I feel the togetherness. You are part
Of me I never thought twice
About. Today I realize I am
As one, not a separateness.
My feet and toes feel alive,
Awakened because I have focused on them today
I've moved with them, I've danced with them
And realize I have a lot
To appreciate with my legs, feet and toes.
Today I am thankful for them![15]

What wonderful journeys my legs have taken me on:
Berry-picking, nut harvesting, walks in the woods
Dancing to all kinds of music
Walks in the park, with friends and alone.
Walks to work in all kinds of weather
The joy of warm mud oozing through my toes
Walking off my anger and frustration
Feeling good about
Comfortable fitting shoes[16]

One of the challenges we face is that many women are afraid to feel their bodies, often because when they do they become overwhelmed with emotions that are linked to past traumas. We do not want to retraumatize participants or provoke memories that make them feel bad, so a significant part of the early program work is facilitating what is called *resource development*. This term refers to providing tools to help contain the feelings that arise when women whose bodies have been numb for years start to *wake up*. We spend some time in the first few sessions developing either a *sacred container*, a *sacred place*, or an *animal helper*, who becomes a source of guidance or consolation. These activities create positive experiences in the body, creating a counter-memory of nonviolence and provide a place/space to contain strong feelings—both positive and negative.

Through a guided visualization process that incorporates focusing on body sensations, each woman first finds a resource within herself. She then draws and dances the resource to increase its strength and the bodily sensations associated with it. She keeps her drawing and we remind participants to go back to it and use their resources when they notice they are anxious or upset.

In one group the animal helpers were a fox, a tiger, a buffalo, two wolves, a horse, a bear, and a heron.

We also have activities that foster connection with ancestors and fore-mothers and affirm the legacies of the resilience, the creativity, and the strength of these women as a resource for us in the present. This *grounding in history* emphasizes gifts the ancestors have passed onto us or ways certain women in one's family have inspired or influenced one. For women who have been fostered out and may have little connection with their ancestry, we work at a metaphorical level and support them remembering strong women who have inspired them. We also do an activity where each person writes a list of all the circumstances, relationships, experiences, and qualities in their life they are grateful for. After everyone has written down their list or litany we invite them to dance or embody that graced gifted self and how it felt to be that self that is neither degraded or shamed but connected and sacred. This is both a re-membering and a reclamation of the sacred self.

Transforming Anger, Cleansing, and Lament

The second phase of the program addresses two things: the grief of the multiple deaths and losses that women have experienced throughout their lives, and the internalized oppression and self-hatred that is the result of being treated as inferior and of less value than those in the dominant society. The emotions of grief, pain, rage, and bitterness that are lodged in the body need to be acknowledged, honored, and completed, in the sense of being fully processed out of the body. The work of releasing and processing anger and grief is done both through preparatory somatic practices and the ceremonies of lament and cleansing.

Because much of the grief of loss is linked to the injustices of colonialism there is often anger that needs to be completed. However many participants feel uncomfortable with expressing anger, often for cultural reasons. Though we acknowledge that the process of anger needs to be completed in the body, we believe anger does not have a place in ceremony and can do damage to community. Therefore we focus on basic somatic tools that can help release or move anger through the body, as well as transform its energy. We explain that anger is a natural biological response to a violation of boundaries, as an animal which defends its territory when threatened. Anger that is unex-pressed can lead to rage and/or a turning in of anger on oneself.

We teach tools to release and transform anger in a series of activities that include: voice work; pushing (through the feet, eyes, head, and pelvic floor) so that one has a physical sense of inhabiting or taking space; grounding to help set limits and boundaries; and learning how to circulate energy out of one's endpoints—the head, feet, hands, tail, or pelvic floor. An example of how this was used to transform the impact of violence on the body is that of a woman who got in touch with a past violation and stayed with the process of circulating energy. She had a headache and sat in a chair, focusing on her face and belly and moving both her arms and legs, gradually in larger motions, as she continued to sit. Later she reported that, as she began to focus on the sensations of the headache, she followed them to her jaw and nose bone, a place where she had once been hit when attacked. She remembered that and felt the pain but continued to follow the sensations from the right side of her face through to her left palm "till the same dark energy left my palm and then out all four extremities."[17]

Traditional cleansing rituals can be adapted to address shame and internalized oppression. Cleansing plays a central role in traditional and contemporary Native healing and is seen as "eliminating or getting rid of bad energy, spirits, or emotions and includes outcomes such as elimination, purging, relieving pressure, and releasing emotions."[18] We use the terms *casting off* (from Christian imagery of casting out demons) and *cleansing* to describe the process of getting rid of or brushing off negative spirits and of purifying a person or space. The cleansing affects negative energies—such as negative feelings or self-concepts that have been generated through cultural stereotyping and injustice—that live in the body. To prepare for a cleansing ceremony we each share cultural teachings from our different traditions that involve cleansing. We speak about how casting out and cleansing makes more space within us for our sacred vitality.

While we do not consider it appropriate to describe in detail these cleansing ceremonies that drew from specific Native traditions, we can share some of the demons and spirits that were named and cast out in one ceremony which involved brushing with cedar. These were: disrespect, dirtiness, uncleanliness (like I wash and can never feel clean), injustice to the poor within the justice system (the injustice of having my daughter taken away), self-hatred, hatred of residential schools, unworthiness, and fear and self-doubt. As these were named and as we brushed each woman, several cried. One woman's left arm was trembling and she periodically shook the energy off. Another later shared how she felt "a lot of energy coming off everyone."[19]

We developed two approaches to lament—one individual, the other collective—for the expression of deep grief. The first involves each person finding the place in her body where she feels the most loss in that moment. She then moves through a creative expression sequence that involves exploring the sensations in her body, then drawing them, dancing them, and finally writing a poem about that loss. She shares this with one other person and then the whole group. We then close with a brief ritual and prayer of compassion for self and community. The second lament process is a collective lament, which involves song, voice (wailing), movement as a group carrying a black cloth together, and a ritual closing. We do these lament rituals during our one-day retreat outside the city, because this allows participants a full day to process their feelings and to feel and receive the support of the land, plant, and animal relations.

What is common to the cleansing and lament processes is that both bring to voice in the context of collective witnessing what has previously been silenced. By naming the pain and the injustices and then identifying with the suffering of the entire community, women assert and claim value for what has been lost by challenging the system that has publicly erased these values. In both the cleansing and lament rituals, the group members act as witnesses, mirroring pain and accepting the reality of the individual and collective history without diminishing, denying, or pretending a happy ending for either. The collective expression of rage and grief assumes moral power in the face of pain that has been unnameable when diffused in the individual stories. In assuming their agency, the women refuse to be made invisible. At the same time, the expression of grief in this ceremonial context allows individuals to let go and get on with their life in the present.

In the cleansing and lament rituals our purpose is to affirm steadfastness and resistance in suffering rather than relive memory or reinstate victimhood, in order that memory can be transformed as women allow themselves to feel and respond in ways they could not when frozen in the trauma. The anger, lament, and cleansing sessions allow for release of pain and the linking of individual suffering with that of the collective. One's suffering becomes transformed into a mark of identity within a historical and collective context. In self-identifying this suffering, rather than having it externally imposed, the pain becomes part of a legacy of steadfast resistance rather than impotence. It is then easier to move forward to celebrate who we are and who we are becoming as women who have the power to change and to make change—the next stage in the healing process.

Celebrating Our Warrior-Healer/Performing Community

The December 6 Mourning Dance described at the beginning of this chapter is an example of what we call "performing community," which is the culmination of the program. The decision to create a community performance occurs in the third phase of the course. We support women who celebrate their individual and collective strength in a collective creation and, if they wish, to perform it in the community. This performance allows them to bare public witness to past and present suffering and injustice and to embody a new vision of who they are and want to be. In the context of oppression, witnessing to and by one's peers becomes an antidote to being treated as an invisible object by an oppressor. For those who have been shamed publicly, public performance in one's own community is a way of reclaiming pride in one's identity.

As part of the process of embodying their strengths, participants first generate, through drawing and dance, their own understandings of being a warrior and healer and identify the role they would like to play in contributing to their community. They learn more somatic ways of connecting to each other in group dances and how to transmit nonviolent energy as a group. They choose whether to perform publicly or not, and we incorporate the group creation into a final ritual and ceremony of commitment and blessing.

In creating a performance the group actively makes meaning for itself and bares witness to both their individual and the group's sense of its power, sacredness, and connection. In order to distinguish the performance from a show or spectacle we create a sacred boundary around it with song and prayer, marking it as sacred time and space. The performance is generative because, in circumscribing itself in sacred time and space, it acknowledges and calls on other powers beyond the performers. It reminds us that we do not have to rely on just ourselves—that the Creator, spirits, and medicines can help us find the way back to harmony.

RESTORING SACRED VITALITY: STRENGTHS AND CHALLENGES

The process of decolonizing the body involves reversing the levels of disconnection in the body caused by daily racial, sexual, and colonial violence. It starts with the development of a felt sense of one's basic goodness and the sacredness of the body and its connection to land and relations. It moves to the completion, release, and transformation of the powerful emotions of grief, anger, sorrow, and bitterness and provides a cultural and spiritual context that supports moving on with one's life. It concludes with a third step, collectively embodying the identity of the group and collectively witnessing in performance for the community and for themselves. This allows a public statement of identity that is no longer determined by reaction to the colonizer's gaze. All three phases of this decolonization process, informed by the principles of nonviolence and the Good Life Way, create counter memories of connection and sacredness that gradually replace the body memories of violence. In highlighting individual and collective cultural resilience it supports each woman to move toward a self-determined agenda.

The Restoring Sacred Vitality program and pedagogy contains four elements that have been determined as critical for effectiveness as identified by an Ontario Aboriginal Healing and Wellness Strategy, launched in 1994 and completed in 2000. The "Strengthening the Journey" model of service is characterized by (1) an aboriginal circle of care, (2) finding balance, (3) integrated intervention (a combination of western and traditional approaches), and (4) supporting community development and empowerment.[20]

While addressing all of these elements in some way, our greatest challenge was the fact that our program was not connected to any coherent community development strategy, as well as the fact of the ongoing reality of violence that all the women faced when they left the program. A program like this can only be fully effective when it is part of a comprehensive decolonization program that includes sovereignty and community economic and social development that has the material, spiritual, and social needs of the entire community, including women and children, at its center.

The impact of the program on each woman certainly depends upon her negotiating many factors. For instance, as soon as she finishes the program she reenters an environment where she is often devalued. It is challenging to remember one's goodness when faced by a context of crises in one's family, the racism and sexism of day-to-day interactions, a housing shortage, no jobs, and one's ongoing vulnerability and exposure to violence as an Indigenous woman. As well, there is a sense of confusion about how colonialism and displacement are ongoing and current, not just a thing of the past. Despite such challenges, several of the women who took this program became involved in leadership in their communities or participated more in community activities. Others who were already doing this continued to do so in a more embodied way and were able to draw on ceremonial ways to assist them. Some still continued to have difficulties in getting out of situations that were harmful for them and the program's long-term impact was not immediately visible.

A critical factor in this approach to repairing the effects of racist and colonial violence is repetition and the development of a spiritual practice. It is the repetition of ceremonies, affirming traditional territories, affirming basic goodness and belonging, and using song, voice, and dance that works to restore women to wholeness. Like any kind of learning, this will be only one small piece in each person's journey to wellness. Each one takes what she/he can use and moves on, and maybe years later the teachings will be remembered and reinforced in other ways.

Decolonization of the body involves recovering the felt sense of connection with relations and reclaiming an identity that allows one to be self-defining and self-naming. In reexperiencing the distinct quality of aliveness in one's body—its sacred vitality—one can find one's own truth and resist and challenge imposed structures of thinking and being that have become incorporated in the body.

What sovereignty and self-determination mean for Indigenous women living off reserve and in urban centers—most of whom do not have access to band resources or a traditional land base—is a question that will be determined by these women in the future. When the sense of one's connection is restored, it is easier to challenge racism, sexism, and colonialism from a sense of one's worth and collective power. The Salish woman who was able to use the support of the group to challenge the prohibition of her use of sage in her meetings for Native seniors in a mixed race seniors center; the Cree counselor who confronted a social worker who was trying to apprehend a young woman's baby; or the Gitksan women who taught us her clan's warrior dance so that we could perform it at the Women's Valentine Day Memorial

March, all show us women engaging in everyday acts of resistance from which a new collective understanding of the "freedom to be who one is" will slowly emerge.

NOTES

1. See Bonita Lawrence, *"Real" Indians and Others: Mixed-Blood Urban Native Peoples and Indigenous Nationhood* (Vancouver: UBC Press, 2004) for how Indigenous women were and continue to be denied their aboriginal rights.

2. "Royal Commission on Aboriginal Peoples: Bridging the Cultural Divide. A Report on Aboriginal Peoples and Criminal Justice in Canada" (Ottawa: Canada Communication Group, 1996), Vol. 4, 454.

3. Robert Paine, "The Nursery Game: Colonizer and Colonized in the Canadian Artic," *Etudes Inuit Studies* 1 (1977): 5–32.

4. Arthur Kleinman, Veena Das, and Margaret Lock, eds., *Social Suffering* (Berkeley: University of California Press, 1997).

5. Ignacio Martin-Baro, *Writings for a Liberation Psychology*, ed. Adrianne Aaron and Shawn Corne (Cambridge, MA: Harvard University Press, 1994).

6. Ronald Niezen, *Spirit Wars: Native North American Religions in the Age of Nation Building* (Berkeley: University of California Press, 2000), 35.

7. Gerald Taiaiake Alfred, "The First Nations Leadership Crisis," lecture sponsored by The First Nations House of Learning, University of British Columbia, Vancouver, Canada, February 7, 2003.

8. Joseph Gone, "Indian Mental Health Service Delivery: Persistent Challenges and Future Prospects," in *Culturally Diverse Mental Health: The Challenges of Research and Resistance*, ed. Jeffrey Scott Mio and Gayle Y Iwamasa (New York: Brunner-Routledge, 2003), 218–19.

9. Mary-Ellen Kelm, *Colonizing Bodies: Aboriginal Health and Healing in British Columbia, 1900–50* (Vancouver: UBC Press, 1998), 99.

10. Gone, "Indian Mental Health," 220.

11. Susan Apoyshan, *Body-Mind Psychotherapy: Principles, Techniques, and Practical Applications* (New York: W.W. Norton and Co., 2004), 226.

12. Kim Anderson, *Recognition of Being: Reconstructing Native Womanhood* (Toronto: Second Story Press, 2000), 57.

13. Apoyshan, *Body-Mind Psychotherapy*.

14. Denise Nadeau, "Restoring Sacred Vitality: Reconnection and Regeneration with Women Who Suffer Routinized Violence," unpublished Doctor of Ministry thesis, San Francisco Theological Seminary, 2003, 139.

15. Poem courtesy of Carol Martin.

16. Nadeau, "Restoring Sacred Vitality," 141. Verse by Phillipa Ryan—poem courtesy of Phillipa Ryan.

17. Nadeau, "Restoring Sacred Vitality," 172.

18. Rod McCormick, "Healing through Interdependence: The Role of Connection in First Nations Healing Practices," *Canadian Journal of Counselling* 31 (1997), 184.

19. Nadeau, "Restoring Sacred Vitality," 187.

20. *Aboriginal Healing and Wellness Strategy: Longitudinal Study Phase I* (Toronto: Centre for Applied Social Research, Faculty of Social Work, University of Toronto, 2000).

BIBLIOGRAPHY

Alfred, Gerald Taiaiake. "The First Nations Leadership Crisis." Lecture sponsored by The First Nations House of Learning, University of British Columbia, Vancouver, Canada, February 7, 2003.

Anderson, Kim. *Recognition of Being: Reconstructing Native Womanhood.* Toronto: Second Story Press, 2000.

Apoyshan, Susan. *Natural Intelligence: Body Mind Integration and Human Development.* Baltimore: Williams and Wilkins, 1999.

Apoyshan, Susan. *Body-Mind Psychotherapy: Principles, Techniques, and Practical Applications.* New York: W.W. Norton and Co., 2004.

Battiste, Marie, and James (Sa'ke'j) Youngblood Henderson. *Protecting Indigenous Knowledge and Heritage: A Global Challenge.* Saskatoon, Canada: Purwich Publishing Ltd., 2000.

Dyck, Noel. *What Is the Indian "Problem": Tutelage and Resistance in Canadian Indian Administration.* St. John's, Newfoundland: Memorial University Press, 1991.

Gone, Joseph. "Indian Mental Health Service Delivery: Persistent Challenges and Future Prospects." In *Culturally Diverse Mental Health: The Challenges of Research and Resistance,* edited by Jeffrey Scott Mio and Gayle Y Iwamasa, 211–29. New York: Brunner-Routledge, 2003.

HeavyRunner, Iris, and S. J. Morris. *Traditional Native Culture and Resilience.* College of Education and Human Development, University of Minnesota. Vol. 5, No. 1.

Kelm, Mary-Ellen. *Colonizing Bodies: Aboriginal Health and Healing in British Columbia 1900–50.* Vancouver, B.C.: UBC Press, 2001.

Kleinman, Arthur, with Robert Desjarlais. "Violence, Culture and the Politics of Trauma." In *Writing at the Margin: Discourse Between Anthropology and Medicine,* edited by Arthur Kleinman, 173–89. Berkeley: University of California Press, 1995.

Kleinman, Arthur, Veena Das, and Margaret Lock, eds. *Social Suffering.* Berkeley: University of California Press, 1997.

Martin-Baro, Ignacio. *Writings for a Liberation Psychology,* edited by Adrianne Aaro and Shawn Corne. Cambridge, MA: Harvard University Press, 1994.

McCormick, Rod. "Healing through Interdependence: The Role of Connection in First Nations Healing Practices." *Canadian Journal of Counselling* 31, no. 3 (1997): 172–85.

Nadeau, Denise. "Restoring Sacred Vitality: Reconnection and Regeneration with Women Who Suffer Routinized Violence." Unpublished Doctor of Ministry thesis, San Francisco Theological Seminary, 2003.

Niezen, Ronald. *Spirit Wars: Native North American Religions in the Age of Nation Building.* Berkeley: University of California Press, 2000.

Paine, Robert. "The Nursery Game: Colonizer and Colonized in the Canadian Artic." *Etudes Inuit Studies* 1, no. 1 (1977): 5–32.

CHAPTER 7

※

Healing Generations in the South Puget Sound

Suzanne J. Crawford O'Brien

Healthy relationships are the basis of healthy communities.
—*South Puget Intertribal Planning Agency*[1]

When Congress passed the Indian Self-Determination Education and Assistance Act in 1975, it was a landmark legislative move, that would transform Native health care in the United States. The act instructed the Bureau of Indian Affairs and the Indian Health Service to begin turning over management of services to tribal governments. In the last 20 years that process has accelerated as more and more communities have moved toward local governance of social services. The result has been a radical transformation in medical care for Native people, as they have moved to take control and direction of their local health care needs,[2] and implement culturally relevant care that incorporates indigenous culture and spirituality within health and wellness programs.[3] This chapter provides a case study of one such program: the South Puget Intertribal Planning Agency (SPIPA) and its Women's Wellness Program. A cooperative effort of five South Puget tribes, SPIPA's Women's Wellness Program addresses Native women's health concerns, with services such as cervical and breast cancer screening, assistance and counseling for sexual or domestic violence, and publications that celebrate indigenous culture and educate Native women about health care issues. The South Puget Intertribal Planning Agency itself collaborates with South Puget tribal governments to facilitate events and programs such as drug and alcohol counseling, vocational rehabilitation, and food distribution services.

The South Puget Intertribal Planning Agency's approaches to health and wellness, while in many ways quite contemporary, maintain a very traditional view of the embodied subject and what it means to be a healthy self. Through a historically and culturally contextual analysis of SPIPA's annual Intertribal Intergenerational Women and Girls' Gathering, this chapter explores what it means to be a healthy embodied self for Native women in the South Puget Sound. What emerges is a view of the embodied subject consistent with tradition: healthy individuals need healthy communities, and healthy communities need individuals with working identities, identities defined by reciprocal relationships between human, ecological, and spiritual communities.

CULTURAL CONTEXT: INDIGENOUS COAST SALISH VIEWS OF HEALTH AND HEALING

In order to fully understand the significance of SPIPA's work as a contemporary expression of a traditional view of a relational self, it is necessary to consider the historical and cultural background of these South Puget Sound communities. It is useful, for instance, to briefly reflect upon what we know of indigenous religious and healing practices in the region, and how these help to frame views of the nature of the self, the body, and illness.[4] Earliest written accounts attest to religious traditions that emphasized relatedness as an essential quality of strength and health. Illness was attributed to an inability or failure to embody one's proper identity within community. This might be caused by alienating one's own spirit powers, or the result of being injured by another person's spirit power.

Spirit powers, as well as any ritual or ceremonial activity associated with them, were frequently referred to as *tamanawis* (various spellings) in nineteenth-century literature, borrowing a general term from the Chinook trade jargon to refer to a wide variety of distinct spiritual beings and practices. In his work with the Skokomish Twana, William Elmendorf described ways of procuring spirit powers through vision quests, ritual purification, and through inheritance.[5] Establishing a relationship with spirit powers endowed individuals with certain strengths and abilities—abilities that would become an integral part of their identity in community.[6] As Smith notes,

> a strong tie [was] felt to exist between individual and power: people were strong because of their power and strong people got more or stronger powers...Pride, gruffness, a fondness for berries, any such personality differences, were connected with certain animal or bird powers or inanimate objects in nature...Other traits, such as the ability to remain a long while under water, to be a good hunter or wood worker, were likewise related to similar capacities of animals or birds. These often had specific reference to economic pursuits.[7]

Relationships with spirit powers, according to these ethnographies, endowed individuals with their working identity—the gifts and strengths that they could bring to their communities. Those with wolf power were excellent hunters, tree power might enable you to be "attractive and a good singer," and gifted "to lead on social occasions," while someone with snake power may be unpleasant, and antisocial.[8] Elmendorf argues: "In this culture all human success and failure, skill and mediocrity, received their explanation in terms of personal relations or lack of relations with supernatural beings."[9] Hence, one's *working identity*—who you were or ought to be within community—was intrinsically bound up within these spiritual relationships.[10] Maintaining spiritual relationships was to enable oneself to fulfill one's obligations. Breaking such relationships could well incur the loss of personal identity and responsibility. Elmendorf noted one example of this when a Twana healer told him:

> I've discovered that woman's tamanawis way up the mountain—(Mt. Rainier). Now this woman's power has got mad at her because she never came to the mountain to pick berries. Her power was (a berry-picking power), it belongs to that mountain, and the purpose of that power is pick berries. And that (power) got mad at that woman because she never went to the mountain to pick berries. That's the food of that power—berries. And now he had left that woman and made her sick.[11]

Failing to fulfill the particular vocation that the power implied, or failing to annually renew the relationship during winter spirit dances could alienate one's spirit power and could result in illness. As Smith noted, "Failure to meet the ceremonial requirements of one's power caused a friction, which resulted in the illness or ultimate death of the human who was thus stubborn in refusal. Weakness of the body through fatigue or physical illness might cause the power to become detached or dislodged, a state, again, which involved illness and ultimate death if the power could not be recovered."[12] What is important here is this: personal identity and wellness in Coast Salish culture were inherently entwined. The loss of one was tied to the other. Identity, one's vocational role in one's community, depended on a healthy relationship with one's spirit power.

An emphasis on relationships as definitive of the self can be seen within disease etiologies of the Puget Sound as well. A healthy self existed within a network of relationships, and illness often signified a breakdown in those social relationships. According to early ethnographies of the region, illness could be caused by several things. First, spirit sickness was often an indication that one's relationships with spirit powers may be compromised and in need of attention. Secondly, as one observer noted, illness could stem from disease-causing power that had been sent out "in an invisible manner," by "wicked medicine men."[13] Such instances have been described as a "mental concentration of 'hate'" sent out by an angry person. Or, finally, illness could result from one's soul wandering away or being abducted by the dead.[14] Throughout the Northwest, a common belief was that each individual was comprised of a number of souls that might be stolen or wander from the body and become lost. Excessive grief or trauma, contact with the dead, offending a spirit-power, or inappropriate thoughts or actions could result in such soul loss.[15] If the lost soul was not recovered, death could result. As Reverend

Myron Eells, Congregationalist missionary to the South Puget Sound in the late nineteenth century, noted: "Sometimes before a person dies, it may be months, it is supposed that a spirit comes from the spirit world and carries away the spirit of the person, after which the person wastes away or dies suddenly. If it is discovered that this has been done, and there are those who profess to do it, then they attempt to get the spirit back by a *tamanous* [sic], and if it is done the person will live."[16] A consistent theme throughout historical texts was the importance of healthy relationships for the maintenance of a healthy self. Broken relationships with spirit powers, offense to other human beings, or unhealthy ties to the dead might all result in illness and/or soul loss. If illness was understood as an expression of compromised human or spiritual relationships, healing was frequently comprised of activities geared toward renewing, restoring, or negotiating those relationships.

What is important to briefly point out is that ruptured relationships led to the dissolution of the self. A part of the self was lost, and as a result individuals suffered spiritually, emotionally, and physically. Soul loss was, literally, an inability to be one's self. In brief, the embodied self could wander, be lost, be recovered, and be defined by a complex web of reciprocal relationships with human communities, spiritual communities, and ecological communities. The embodied subject was porous and relational. A loss of a working identity (to be who you are meant to be within community) could result in illness.

Given such harmful effects of interpersonal, intertribal, or interspiritual conflict, negotiating and maintaining relationships were core means of preventing illness. Acting with generosity, respect, and kindness was, in a sense, preventative medicine. When illness occurred, and human or spiritual relationships needed to be mended, healing performances by medicine men and women gave flesh to conflict, and embodied relational restoration. Indeed, healing practices were often perceived as most effective when they were communal and familial affairs—drawing upon the strength of collective expression, and demanding that (perhaps fragmented) members of the community come together to facilitate renewal.[17] Winter spirit dances reflected this focus on collective support for and engagement with the individual, serving as spaces for healing, for reaffirming relationships with spirit powers, and for strengthening familial and communal bonds.[18] Nineteenth-century disease etiologies and healing practices were means for expressing and restoring compromised relationships within and between communities.[19] Within this complex network of relationships the health of the individual and community, and of the flesh and spirit were inseparable. A healthy self was not individual, but what McKim Marriot has described as *dividual,* or defined by connection rather than separation.[20] Such a view reflects Arthur Kleinman's assertion that some indigenous modes of embodiment present a body that acts as "an open system linking social relations to the self, a vital balance of interrelated elements in a holistic cosmos."[21]

HISTORICAL CONTEXT: COAST SALISH
HEALING IN TRANSITION

These views of healing and illness were severely challenged by the importation of new diseases and ways of seeing the world introduced by colonialism.[22] From the 1770s to the 1850s Native peoples of the Pacific Northwest were confronted with waves of smallpox, measles, tuberculosis, malaria, meningitis, influenza, mumps, dysentery, syphilis, and gonorrhea, and it is estimated their populations dropped by approximately 88 percent during that time.[23] It was within this context of epidemic illness that the first missionaries arrived in the Pacific Northwest. Early Christian missions had relatively little success in securing converts, a failure they attributed to rampant disease and the persistence of indigenous healers.[24] While other forms of religious practice had faded, missionaries noted, traditional healers were the most resilient. Missionaries' influence would grow, however, after 1855 with the establishment of reservations, when church leaders joined with reservation agents to suppress traditional religions, healers, and healing practices. But even after the establishment of reservations, missionaries continued to be frustrated by their parishioners' resistance against abandoning traditional modes of healing.

Reverend Myron Eells, a reservation-era missionary in the South Puget Sound, argued that traditional healers posed the greatest challenge to conversion. As he wrote, "This kind of *tamahnous* has more power over the Indian mind than any other. The others have reference in a general way to religion, and are partly practiced to wile away the time in the winter, or to call people together for a social time; but this has reference to their lives. It is material and intensely practical."[25] Eells' preaching and theology was unable to compete with such indigenous healing traditions, traditions that met their "material, and intensely practical" needs.[26]

Conversion to Euro-American modes of medical care was problematic in this early reservation era for other reasons as well. In part, this was because Euro-American medicine was hugely inadequate at the time, relying on methods such as bloodletting and medicines such as mercury that were as likely to sicken as to cure. But Euro-American medicine was also problematic, because it reflected a worldview wherein individual health was independent of relationships, and in which physical, emotional, and spiritual health were distinct categories of experience.

The Indian Shaker Church: Christian Faith, Native Healing

Throughout the following decades, Native people of the South Puget Sound created ways of engaging with Euro-American culture, religions, and medicines on their own terms, in ways that maintained indigenous views of the self, of illness, of healing, and what it means to have a working identity. One profoundly important historical example of this was the religious movement that became known as the Indian Shaker Church. The Shaker Church arose in the 1880s, when most Native communities had been moved to reservations. In this context, their traditional political, social, economic, and spiritual structures had all been profoundly challenged. Though many of the previous epidemics such as smallpox had subsided, people struggled with new epidemics including alcoholism, poverty, and despair. Euro-American officials on the reservations were actively suppressing traditional religious practice, and the people were looking for hope.

In 1882, Squaxin Island tribal member John Slocum (Squi'sacht'uhn) was near death. Slocum died, spent three days in heaven, and in the midst of his own funeral, awoke, and issued a prophetic message to his people announcing that they had been called to found an Indian Church. A year later he once again became ill. While praying for him his wife, Mary Thompson Slocum, was filled with the spirit and began to shake. As she shook over him, he was cured. As one church elder later described the event: "There she felt something come down from above, and flow over her body. It felt hot, and she began to tremble all over." Slocum soon fully recovered.[27] This *shake*, as it was soon referred to, became a predominant feature of the new faith, and soon many others were experiencing this healing power. Within a few decades the movement spread throughout the Pacific Northwest, from British Columbia to Northern California, and east to the Columbia Plateau, becoming one of the most important indigenous religious movements of the region.

The Shaker Church was distinctly Christian, with its reverence for a monotheistic yet triune God, and praise for Jesus and the Holy Spirit. Shakers prayed, used the cross, and took up lives of sobriety, responsibility, and modesty. Some Shakers used the Bible, though most found it unnecessary as they had direct access to God through their prayers and the shake.[28] Within this context, the Church maintained traditional ways of viewing the self, illness, and healing. This continuity was at least partially responsible for the large number of medicine men and women who converted to the Shaker Church. As Reverend Eells noted: "About this time, an order came from the Indian department to stop all medicine men from practicing their incantations over the sick...And then the medicine men almost entirely joined the Shakers, as their style was more nearly in accordance with the old than with the religion of the Bible."[29] The movement became quickly successful, evidenced by Reverend Eells when he wrote in 1894 of declining numbers in his own church, explaining that the Shakers had "taken the larger share" of his parishioners.[30]

The Shaker Church was immediately compelling for so many Native people because it shared key elements of indigenous worldview. While its external expression and much of its belief system differed, the Shakers shared a fundamental view of the self as relational, and of health and well-being as dependent upon properly maintaining and negotiating those relationships. As H. G. Barnett illustrated, the primary emphasis of the early Shaker Church was healing. The techniques employed in healing services mirrored those that had been used by medicine men and women for centuries. Further, just as previous cultural traditions had emphasized a relationship with a personal spirit power as a source of meaning, purpose, and vocation, Shakers emphasized the vital importance of a personal relationship with the Holy Spirit, which empowered people to live meaningful, healthy lives. Each person had his or her individual *shake*, a manifestation of the spirit unique to that person.[31] The Shaker Church, likewise, emphasized the indigenous ethos of collective survival—that kinship and community were central to life. This stood in sharp contrast to Eells' mission, which emphasized individual salvation, even at the cost of alienating one's family or community. By contrast, the Church placed a strong emphasis on caring for family and community, helping tribal members spiritually (through prayer, healing, guidance, and memorializing the dead) and materially (through the distribution of food, financial assistance, and other needs). Shakers continued a cultural tradition of caring for others as a spiritual obligation.[32] Indeed, some felt that "a failure of charity within the congregation or the family (might) spoil the harmony that mobilizes the Spirit to cure the sick."[33]

The manner in which the movement spread—most often by word of mouth through extended families—reflects this emphasis on relationality as well. Indeed, one important contribution the Shaker Church brought to Coast Salish spirituality was the way in which it expanded this circle of interconnectedness beyond the local tribal community. The Indian Shaker Church was seen as a church for Indians—all Indians. It was not the spiritual practice of a single community, but rather a movement that could unite diverse tribal communities—from British Columbia to Northern California—within a wider family of faith. By expanding the circle of relationality within a postcolonial context, the Indian Shaker Church gave Native people an important tool for collective survival—if they were to survive, they must do so together. As various scholars have asserted, Shakers succeeded where non-native missions had failed because they reimaged Christianity in a way that meshed with indigenous worldviews. Shakers brought Christianity in line with indigenous notions of the embodied self, of what it meant to be a healthy person with a working identity—a person shaped by kinship and community. Shakers supplied religious practices with healing as a central feature, as well as practices that met "material, intensely practical," and spiritual needs.

The Shaker Church remains one of the most important indigenous religious organizations in the Pacific Northwest, with Shaker churches or elders being found on most reservations throughout the region. In the contemporary era, the Shaker Church exists alongside a vibrant revival of Coast Salish spirit dancing, which has grown exponentially since the 1970s. Pamela Amoss and Crisca Bierwert, among others, have ably written about this phenomenon.

As Amoss and Bierwert describe, contemporary longhouse spirit dancing centers on all-night ceremonies that take place during the winter months. Here, those who have been initiated into the tradition sing their spirit songs, and dance to honor their spirit powers. What is immediately evident in both Amoss and Bierwert's accounts is the central role of *healing* in contemporary spirit dancing (many dancers come to the movement out a desire for personal healing), of *community* (the tradition is built upon and works to reinforce relationships), and *meeting material needs* (the gatherings are arenas for feeding others, distributing resources, and supporting those in need).[34]

What the Shaker Church and the revival of Longhouse Spirit Dancing attest to is the ability of Native communities of Puget Sound draw upon rich traditions that creatively respond to cultural change. Within these degrees of change and adaptation, what has remained consistent are views of the embodied self. The embodied self is working, healthy, and functional when it is fulfilling its role within a network of relationships: with spirit-powers (or with the Holy Spirit), with the human community, with the ancestral community, and with the natural world. Breaks in relationships have tangible results: illness and soul loss. Healing requires restoring the soul, restoring identity, and returning individuals to their place in community.

CONTEMPORARY APPROACHES TO HEALING: SPIPA AND THE WOMEN'S WELLNESS PROGRAM

This historical and cultural background is necessary for understanding the significance of SPIPA's work, and in particular the work of its Women's Wellness Program. Here one can see a contemporary example of cultural adaptation—incorporating elements of non-Native culture—but doing so in ways that maintain a culturally continuous sense of the embodied subject, and what it means to be well. This organization stands as a striking example of the remarkable achievements that can be made when health care is controlled and directed by local tribal communities, rather than national bureaucracies. The South Puget Intertribal Planning Agency and their Women's Wellness Program have constructed culturally relevant modes of care that have been effective, and hold great promise for the future. What makes their approach so effective, I would suggest, is that it draws upon a sense of the embodied self continuous with the past, one in which health and wellness are defined by maintaining a working identity within community. This working identity is defined by relationships—with the human, spiritual, and ecological worlds.

Those seeking to develop culturally relevant modes of care for Native people in South Puget Sound face a variety of challenges, not the least of which is the spiritual diversity in the region. Some Native people identify with the Indian Shaker Church, others with the Longhouse spirit dancing traditions. Others are devout members of various Christian denominations, while others mirror the religious make-up of the Pacific Northwest more generally, in which a majority of people identify as "spiritual" but are not affiliated with any particular religious group. Additionally, while most tribal communities in the region are predominately Coast Salish, each differs significantly, with particular histories, cultures, and practices. Given this, how could SPIPA construct programs that would be culturally relevant? The success of their programs attests to their ability to do just this: identify the core values, ways of seeing the self and the world, and notions of health and wellness that are shared by the groups in question. For that reason, it makes an ideal case study.

The focus here is an annual Intertribal Intergenerational Women and Girls' Gathering facilitated by SPIPA's Women's Wellness Program, and the ways in which this event demonstrates a view of the embodied subject and wellness that is consistent with tradition. This particular event takes place at a 4-H camp located in the South Puget Sound, in a quiet setting that allows space for reflection and relaxation, walks around a lake, and swimming and canoeing. The three-day event is filled with classes focusing on traditional crafts (basketry, beading, drum making, rawhide rattles, etc.). Other events draw upon traditional spiritual and cultural activities such as talking circles, drumming circles, storytelling, a sweat lodge, and a giveaway ceremony, while elders discuss traditional spirituality and the role of ceremony in life and healing. At the same time, workshops and speakers address important issues for women's wellness (diabetes care and prevention, HIV/AIDS, domestic violence, cancer screening and prevention, etc.), and there are opportunities for free biomedical care (diabetes screening, mammograms, and pap smears). Many women have their annual exams at the Gathering, exams they would not likely have otherwise. Simultaneous to all this, holistic care practitioners are also a very popular addition, providing free massage, reiki, reflexology, as well as yoga and *tai q'i* classes by the lake. The incorporation of biomedicine and eastern practices such as yoga and reiki certainly shows the influence of outside cultures. Despite this, however, what emerges is a view of the self and what it means to be healthy that is consistent with earlier cultural traditions.

SPIPA's efforts demonstrate a culturally continuous view of the embodied subject. Here, a healthy self is *porous, dividual*,[35] defined by relationships with human, spiritual, and ecological communities. To be healthy is to have a working identity, that is, to fulfill your obligations to your community, and to do so by honoring your particular gifts and strengths. At the heart of SPIPA's programs and activities is this concern: creating and enabling a spirit of interrelatedness. As a document published by SPIPA explains, "Healthy relationships are the basis of healthy communities."[36] To be healthy is to exist in proper relationship to human, ecological, and ancestral communities, and to live within that web of relatedness requires a sense of one's calling, the gifts that one brings to that community.

Defining "Traditional" in a Nontraditional World

The women who plan the annual Gathering as well as the various Women's Wellness Program's events seek to do things in a way that is "traditional," and that is culturally relevant. But what did these women mean by *traditional*? Is it *traditional* to do beadwork when beads were only introduced in the last 150 years? Is it *traditional* to have a sweat lodge run in a Lakota style? When this question was posed to various women, a common sense emerged that "traditional" activities drew upon a continuous cultural heritage, a heritage shared with their ancestors. This included oral traditions, arts, recipes, and wisdom. However, this could also include elements of their heritage that had been modified or adapted to meet contemporary needs and concerns.

Further, "traditional" culture was seen as holding a wealth of resources for recovering a healthy life. "Traditional" was often used in a manner synonymous with "healthy." Take for example an article published by the Women's Wellness Program in 2001. In this piece Alysha Waters of the Native Foods Project argues:

> Only a hundred and fifty years ago, the ancestors of this region were the healthiest of any group of peoples living upon the earth. Cancer was very rare and diabetes and heart disease were virtually unknown. For thousands of years Pacific Northwest tribes had food production systems in place that sustained healthy communities. These food systems were rich in tradition and ceremony while connecting integrally to trade, commerce, and sound environmental practices...The health and nutrition of Indian peoples has been greatly affected by the destruction of the sustainable Native American food production systems...it is imperative to return to a diet similar to a traditional one.[37]

Many South Puget tribal publications point to higher rates of diabetes, heart disease, and cancer among contemporary Native women as evidence that, "today's Native women don't live the healthy lifestyle of the ancestors."[38] Diabetes is described as being, "like the measles or small pox, it is yet another western culture disease that we must develop resistance to if our culture is to survive. The once active lifestyle of our ancestors has been lost to modern conveniences, a sedentary lifestyle, and a high fat diet."[39]

Other women explained that "traditional activities" might look quite different than similar activities undertaken hundreds of years before, but that the spirit, intent, and philosophy behind them may well be the same. One example described to me included a craft designed to bring traditional beliefs to bear upon contemporary problems. During a retreat for Native American youth, young people were educated about safer sex, and the importance of caring for their bodies and communities. Elders met with the young people, teaching them beadwork, basketry, and leatherwork. One project in particular involved making medicine bags. After cutting and sewing the leather pouches, the young people designed and beaded images onto them. The medicine bags differed from historic practice in one important way: they were designed to act as condom carriers. Bringing practices, philosophies, and ethics of their heritage to bear upon a very contemporary problem, these medicine bags serve as a moving example of the adaptability of tradition. With these medicine bags around their necks, it was explained to me, young people have a stronger sense of who they are, and what their responsibilities are to their communities and to themselves.

The annual Women and Girls' Gatherings likewise demonstrate this malleable understanding of tradition. The Gathering has as its stated goal to present women with "traditional and alternative modes of healing." A SPIPA staff member and one of the founding organizers of the event explained to me that "traditional" could include all "first peoples medicine." As she defined it, "first peoples medicine" needn't be limited to the tribes in the immediate region, but can encompass practices of other indigenous peoples that share a common sense of healing as restoring to wholeness the "person within community."[40] Given this, the Gathering includes its striking list of alternative practitioners: massage therapists, *qi'gong* instructors, Reiki practitioners, acupuncturists, and reflexologists. These practitioners are always popular attractions, and women are eager to have time with them. During the first gathering I attended as a volunteer, my task was to keep track of appointments with these practitioners, and make sure elders found their way there at the appointed time. The task was delightful, affording me the opportunity to chat with women as I drove them, in an electric golf cart, from the lake to the field up above the lodge where tipis and a yurt had been erected, and where the massage therapists and reiki practitioners were at work. The women were collectively thrilled with the opportunity to try something new, to pamper themselves a bit, and to feel cared for. To my surprise, they saw no great discrepancy between massage and a sweat lodge. While it was certainly clear to them that each came from a different cultural background and meant different things, it was also a common response that they both served a very "traditional" function—helping women be healthy so that they could care for their children and communities.

The Importance of Interrelatedness

The guiding principle behind the Women's Wellness Program and its efforts is the notion of a healthy self as one that exists within a network of relationships. When an individual knows where they stand within this relational network, they have a strong sense of purpose, a clear sense of identity, and the courage and strength to be the person their community needs them to be. It is repeatedly emphasized that the solution to many of the physical, emotional, and social illnesses facing them is a strong community. And strong communities, it is argued, require strong women. A giveaway ceremony, which takes up much of the final day of the Gathering, is an excellent illustration of this value placed upon reciprocity and community. Hundreds of items, many handmade, are brought to the Gathering to be given away. Beginning with elders, women are invited to select an item. This continues, until, by the end of the day, everyone goes home loaded with gifts and food. One participant later described the event, saying, "the idea is to redistribute the goods amongst our friends and family, which is a very traditional concept many times lost in the throws of consumerism and capitalism. This redistribution of goods echoes the values of reciprocity and balance so ideal to traditional Native culture."[41] While distinct, the giveaway is clearly recognizable as sharing elements of a traditional potlatch. Potlatches—formal giveaways prevalent throughout the Northwest with the purpose of honoring elders, thanking people, establishing relationships, and honoring achievements—share much in common with this event. Here, elders are honored, achievements and contributions are recognized, and importantly, relationships are affirmed.

The emphasis on community and interrelatedness as a source of healing was likewise apparent within a talking circle that occurred at the 2004 Gathering. The talking circle had been introduced as a place for women to reflect on cancer survival, but the event quickly shifted its focus. Rather than discussing individual struggles with cancer, the women immediately turned to a discussion on the health of their communities and families. They talked about coping with the death of loved ones, particularly children, and their fears concerning the drugs, alcohol, and violence in their communities. As women shared very personal stories, other women reached out in support and encouragement. It is striking that even in those contexts intentionally set aside for women to reflect upon their individual ailments, those *personal* ailments were immediately conceptualized within a context of *community* and extended family and of the need for the entire community to be whole and well.

And certainly, this emphasis on interdependency and responsibility within community is a central focus of many activities and speakers at the annual Gatherings. Caring for one's own health, it is argued, is important because of one's obligations to others. A newsletter distributed at one year's Gathering displayed this notion well. The image shows several granddaughters, laughing with their grandmother—an elder from one of the South Puget tribes. The caption of the photo reads: "Don't have time for a mammogram? If not for yourself, then who? Remember: early detection saves lives."[42] The message the image suggests is significant: women's responsibilities to others imply a responsibility to care for themselves. It is a dual message: women are intrinsically valuable, but they are also defined by their relationships to others. Such values appear to have a powerful impact on women. In comments written by various women at the conclusion of the 2004 Gathering, one woman noted that the event, "taught me to take better care of my body and the world." One woman said that the weekend encouraged her "to regard my body as a unique gift." Others had a renewed desire to "meditate, contemplate, and apply the recognition of my body as a creation of unique design," and that the Gathering "made me aware of how important it is to be a strong politically active Native woman."[43] Such comments clearly reflect a view that communal and individual health are profoundly interconnected.

A Working Identity: Healing Communities

This sense of a self that is interdependent with community leads these women to link their own health and wellness to their ability to help heal their communities. The Women and Girls' Gathering emphasizes what are seen as women's special gifts and unique roles within their communities. As one woman noted, the weekend reminded her of "the importance of teaching my daughters that women are so important, and that womanhood should be celebrated." Another woman wrote that she was "now determined to be a strong elder," so that she could provide leadership and guidance for younger women in her community. Another woman reflected on the important place women have as healers and caretakers, and her renewed desire "to help my sisters, mother, grandmother, and nieces engage in preventative breast care," and to "reach out to women in my life and insist on prevention and early screening." One woman perhaps best summed up this ethos when she wrote that she had a renewed desire to "take care of myself, not just for me, but also for my family."[44] Such perspectives reflect a cultural ethos within which the healthy self is conceived as one engaged in a working identity—fully embodying who they are meant to be, fulfilling their obligations, and sharing their strengths within community.

This sense of an embodied subject that is inherently interconnected with community is clear. Individual health and wellness is inseparable from communal wellness. It is a reciprocal process: women can only nurture their community if their community in turn nurtures them. This is what helps to make the annual Women and Girls' Gathering such an important event: here women are cared for and can care for each other. One woman recovering from breast cancer expressed this well when she wrote: "Part of the medicine is having people say to you, 'You look good.' Or, 'It's so good to see you.' Or 'You are welcome here.'"[45] During a talking circle, a woman who had recently moved to the region described the challenges she had been facing without her family nearby, and expressed her appreciation for the welcome she had received. Many women noted that these few days where women could be with women provided them the opportunity to share grief, fears, and concerns, and to offer each other much needed support and encouragement.[46]

Further illustrating a sense of a healthy self that is inherently relational, many women over the years have noted that the power of this Gathering lies in the space it provides for women to come together and build relationships.[47] Women noted that they valued "getting to know women from other tribes," experiencing "love and caring" from other women, "the joy of female bonding," and enjoying the "connection of women" at the Gathering. Other women said that renewing friendships reminded them of "the power of being a woman," and "the similarities between women from different tribes." One woman said that the Gathering gave her a chance to meet other "women of power," and thereby "regain a sense of my own power, and strength." The weekend inspired a sense of "collective empowerment." One woman pointed to the healing that can occur when "we all come together and teach each other what we know."[48]

Healing the Relationship with Place

Another important element of this notion of an inherently relational embodied subject is that the healthy self is seen as being interconnected not only with the human community, but the more-than-human community as well. In this case, Native women of the South Puget Sound point to the importance of renewing a connection with their ancestral landbase. An example of this can be found within a workshop at the 2002 Gathering, when women met to make traditional herbal teas. As the women learned about the plants' various medicinal values, they combined and bagged the teas to be given away at the Giveaway ceremony. A similar example can be seen at the 2001 Gathering, when a local elder taught the women about a variety of plants, their uses, and their spiritual importance. The workshop was held in a large room overlooking the lake, while just behind us other women were gathered, learning how to weave baskets. As the speaker explained, having a relationship with the earth and the plants that it provides is an important part of wellness.

> [Traditionally] we were so connected with Mother Earth, Nature...A lot of our young people are getting away from it, from our culture, our traditions. If you really want to know about medicine, you have to look at yourself. What do you want? It's about spirituality. As you walk on Mother Earth, do so with a prayer...The key to these medicinal plants is prayer....Spirituality is the most important thing. All of these plants have a spirit. That's the medicine. Prayer. Listening. Take a look at nature. Enjoy its spirit and your connection with it...It's their *spirit* that makes them effective. It's the relationship with the plant that makes them work.[49]

As this woman makes clear, the strength of working with plants, particularly as a spiritual and healing practice, is the relationship that you build with the plant, and with the place in which it grows. Such ideas reflect the understanding that *health* is a *relational condition*, where wellness is maintained through the cultivation and honoring of relationships with place.

One woman with whom I spoke helped to illustrate this notion well. She explained to me that she often feels "kind of hollow when I'm around other Indian women, women who know who they are and where they came from." This woman had grown up away from her Native roots, was not connected to her tribal community, and knew very little about her own cultural background. She explained that she envied the women she saw with their strong sense of identity and community. But, she also noted that she genuinely appreciated coming to this Gathering because of "the openness here, the welcome." She explained that she had been most struck by the workshop on the spirituality of working with plants. She had begun to realize that even if she could not have a relationship with her tribal community, which was geographically far removed, she could have a relationship with her ancestors through the land and the plants. As she explained:

> These sessions, what people are talking about, let's me know that I can reach a sense of my Indian identity through spirit, through prayer. What she was saying about Devil's Club [a plant indigenous to the Pacific Northwest] really got me, because I was just out hiking with my friend, and I saw that plant, I really saw it for the first time, and I said, "Wow! What is that!?" And my friend said, look, it's all over the place—you've seen that plant a million times before. But it was like I saw it for the first time, like it *wanted* me to see it. I was just so excited about it, it was so beautiful, so amazing, those full leaves, and the spines, so intricate. And then she [the session leader] started talking about that plant, and I realized it was the same one. I really felt like there was an important connection there, you know?[50]

The notion that plants have spirit and a sentient awareness, and that they can act as a living tie to one's heritage and ancestry, enabled this woman to regain a sense of connectedness and relationality with the land, her heritage, and her indigenous identity.

Another example of this can be cited in a publication by SPIPA's Women's Wellness program, in which a Squaxin Island tribal member recalled her family's plant gathering heritage. For this woman, gathering plants remained a sensual, tactile way of maintaining her relationship to her ancestors and the land on which they lived. The very smell and feel of plants are an expression of the connections between herself and her ancestors.

> Memories of my grandmother, Annie Jackson Krise, and grand-aunt Elvina are easily awakened by the sight, smell, touch and taste of traditional plants. I remember as a child being taught about the importance of traditional plants, which ones were used for medicinal purposes, and which ones were used for food...I still gather food and medicines from the forest....Every time I pick a berry, I remember my ancestors. Every time I smell yarrow, I remember my

grandmother. Every time I drink Indian tea, I remember my uncle. The activity of gathering keeps these memories alive.[51]

For these women, plants act as sentient, powerful reminders of their interconnectedness with the landscape and their ancestors. They convey a sense of a healthy self, a working identity that is inherently relational.

Healing the Spirit, Honoring the Ancestors

For many women who plan, facilitate, and attend the annual Gathering, its success lies in its emphasis on spirituality. During a planning meeting for the 2004 session, one woman explained that she wanted to see a continued "emphasis on spirituality and ceremony...because wellness is about having healthy communities, not just individuals. And to get healthy communities, you need spirituality and ceremony."[52] Spirituality is central, many have emphasized, to giving women a strong sense of purpose, strength, and identity. And indeed, during a service-learning internship with the Women's Wellness Program, my student Megan MacDonald noted, "The women of SPIPA have a deep understanding of this relationship [between spirituality and wellness], and are excited to have an underlying spiritual theme at the Gathering."[53] As another woman explained, "there is more than one dimension to things— (there is) a way to be connected to our traditions—through spirituality, and such spirituality is the key to wellness."[54] Various publications, events, and activities at SPIPA emphasize this sense of spirituality as a means for renewing relationships with community, land, ancestors, and the Creator. As one article in the Squaxin Island tribal newspaper argues, engaging with cultural traditions is a way of maintaining a spiritual connection with the ancestors: "Through articulation of our values, we realize a relationship with our ancestors."[55] Wellness and healing are facilitated by maintaining this spiritual connection with the ancestors.

Throughout the years I have volunteered with these Gatherings, women repeatedly testify to the healing and renewing power of reconnecting with their heritage, and regaining a sense of interconnectedness with their ancestors. One woman, for instance, expressed hope that her son had gone to live with his uncle to learn their cultural ways, and was certain this would help him recover from alcoholism. Another woman tearfully discussed the impact connecting with her cultural heritage had had upon her vocation as a health-care provider. Another woman shared how rediscovering her indigenous spirituality had helped her recover from the grief of losing her child, and had given her new strengths and gifts to bring to her community. In conversation after conversation, women make clear that regaining a life engaged with their cultural heritage, in which they cultivate relationships with communities, landscape, and ancestors, holds the keys to wellness, healing, and collective renewal. For these women healing is a process of recovery that enables them to reclaim their working identity, and their sense of vocation and purpose within their communities. Healing enables women to become stronger, and so work to heal the wider network of relations within which they live.

This was powerfully illustrated by a story told during a talent show that took place on the final evening of the 2001 Gathering. The story was told by a young woman, and acted out by young children, all dressed in powwow regalia or the woven cedar hats, shawls, and button blankets traditional to the Northwest Coast. Mount Rainer, as the story went, had once been a beautiful woman. She had decided to leave her husband, Mount Adams, because he was having an affair with her sister, Mount St. Helens. She fled, taking her baby and her dowry with her. When Mount Adams discovered she had gone, he erupted in fury. Afraid for her safety, Mount Rainier dropped her hairpins as she ran, and each hairpin turned into another peak of the Cascade mountain range separating her from Mount Adams. As she traveled, she sought to lighten her load, and dropped pieces of her dowry along the way: sockeye salmon, plants, and berries. Wherever she dropped them, they flourished, explaining why salmon, medicinal plants, and a wide variety of berries can be found in the mountain ranges between Mount Adams and Mount Rainier. After telling the story, the young woman explained its significance. The story, she said, has to do with the process of healing, of letting go, and of learning from the journey.

> We can be injured by things that happen to us in life...In this story, it is injury caused by men. But this story explains that when we let go of pain, that that grief brings life. We don't just leave it behind, but the grief and pain and loss give birth to new life, to good things. Her pain is why we have the Sockeye, and the berries, and medicine. The story is about healing, and why it's important. We seek it in different ways, in Church, in the Longhouse, the Smokehouse, the Shaker Church, the Sweat lodge, but we need to let go of those hurts, in order for them to turn into something new, to grow into healthy things, that will bring life to other people. Healing is moving on, and it benefits others, the whole community, when you do it.[56]

CONCLUSIONS

The story embodies what the founders of the Women and Girls' Gathering had set forth as their mission: that women would leave "with new skills, renewed with spirit and in strength."[57] The story further supports a view of the embodied subject that is inherently relational, and a sense that when people are well, when they are fully able to claim their working identity, they are best able to bring life and healing to their communities. This is *traditional* healing: women coming together to help each other achieve wellness, strength, and cultural identity.

The Intertribal Intergenerational Women and Girls' Gathering and its approach to healing embodies the cultural creativity and adaptability of the region, as well as, importantly, its emphasis on wellness and healing as essentially relational activities. Illness (frequently if not always) emerges from a breach in relationships—whether human, ecological, or spiritual, and healing more often than not centers on negotiating and restoring these relationships. Changing expressions of healing—from vision quests, to the Indian Shaker Church, to the revival of spirit dancing, to intertribal events such as the Women and Girls' Gathering, may all look very different, but they share several important features. They share in a common sense of the embodied subject as one that is defined by a complex web of relationships. They share a sense of health as dependent upon the ability of an individual to embody her working identity, honoring her position within that web of relationships, and contributing to the well-being of her community. They share a sense of the fundamentally reciprocal nature of individual and community—that the wellness of one depends on the wellness of the other.

Whether a ceremony to retrieve a lost soul in the nineteenth century, yoga by Panhandle Lake, or attending a Shaker healing service, the understanding of the self and of what it means to be healthy remains continuous. The *diseases* may have changed, but the *illnesses* remain very similar: broken relationships, soul loss, loss of identity and community. These illnesses can contribute to physical manifestations—diseases such as diabetes, heart disease, alcoholism, cancer—that biomedicine works to cure. But healing illnesses requires engaging with a culturally continuous sense of the embodied subject, of what it means to be healthy, and remembering the "patient" is fundamentally a person-within-community.

NOTES

1. *South Puget Intertribal Planning Agency Annual Report* (1999): 13. Data for this chapter is drawn from ethnographic observations conducted during volunteer work with SPIPA's Women's Wellness Program from 2001 to 2006, and from publications and documents produced by SPIPA, the Women's Wellness Program, and the five tribes themselves. Great thanks are due to all the volunteers and staff at SPIPA for their support and assistance with this project.

2. Everett R. Rhoades, ed., *American Indian Health: Innovations in Heath Care, Promotion and Policy* (Baltimore, MD: The Johns Hopkins University Press, 2000): 89.

3. See, for example, Ethan Nebelkopf and Mary Phillips, eds., *Healing and Mental Health for Native Americans: Speaking in Red* (Lanham, MD: Alta Mira Press, 2004), which discusses a wide array of community-directed programs. These include the Friendship House Healing Center in San Francisco; the Healthy Nations Initiative, which is funding a variety of tribal programs; Yup'ik and Cup'ik community-centered substance abuse programs; and Native Circle, a holistic HIV/AIDS mental health program. The Diné Nation has, in many ways, been at the forefront of this effort. For an excellent history of contemporary efforts, see Wade Davies, *Healing Ways: Navajo*

Health Care in the Twentieth Century (Albuquerque: University of New Mexico Press, 2001).

4. Readers interested in a more in-depth discussion of traditional Coast Salish views of healing and the body should consult Pamela Amoss, *Coast Salish Spirit Dancing: The Survival of an Ancestral Religion* (Seattle: University of Washington Press, 1978); Crisca Bierwert, *Brushed by Cedar, Living by the River: Coast Salish Figures of Power* (Tucson: University of Arizona Press, 2000); and Jay Miller, *Lushootseed Culture and the Shamanic Odyssey: An Anchored Radiance* (Lincoln: University of Nebraska Press, 1999).

5. William W. Elmendorf and A. L. Kroeber, *Twana Culture* (Pullman: Washington State University Press, 1992), 182, 492. Tweddell notes that Snohomish youths sought such spirit powers in the high country, near Lake Getchel and what is now Stevens Pass. See Colin E. Tweddell, "The Snohomish Indian People," *Coast Salish and Western Washington Indians, vol II* (New York: Garland Publishing, 1974), 551; Melville Jacobs, Leo J. Frachtenberg, and Albert S. Gatschet, *Kalapuya Texts: University of Washington Publications in Anthropology 11* (Seattle: University of Washington Press, 1945): 346–47; Marian Smith, *The Puyallup-Nisqually*, Columbia University Contributions to Anthropology 32 (New York: Columbia University Press, 1940), 58. Elmendorf notes that "when a person dies his power does not go with him to the country of the dead. It has always followed him around like a dog, and after he dies it is just like a lost dog. Sometimes the power will just forget its dead owner, but sometimes it wants to belong to someone and it comes and hangs around a relative or a descendent of its dead owner. This makes the person it chooses sick, until a doctor can treat him and find out what is the matter and bring the power to him. Then he has to show that power at a power dance," William W. Elmendorf, *Twana Narratives: Native Historical Accounts of a Coast Salish Culture* (Seattle: University of Washington Press, 1993), 191. Elmendorf also notes, "when a power that belonged to a dead ancestor comes to a person or wants to come to him, that makes the person sick. Then a doctor comes and diagnoses the case and brings the power to that person, so he can show it and use it and then he gets well" (p. 190). Smith shares this view that powers could be inherited from deceased relatives: "But the power said, 'Don't kill me. I used to belong to your uncle...I belong to you," Smith, *The Puyallup-Nisqually*, 84.

6. For another example of a similar Guardian Spirit tradition, see Jean-Guy Goulet, *Ways of Knowing: Experience, Knowledge, and Power among the Dene Tha* (Lincoln: University of Nebraska Press, 1998).

7. Smith, *The Puyallup-Nisqually*, 57, 59.

8. Ibid., 68–75; Elmendorf and Kroeber, *Twana Culture*, 488; Elmendorf, *Twana Narratives*, 169.

9. Elmendorf and Kroeber, *Twana Culture*, 480–81.

10. For discussion of the notion of *working identity* within indigenous healing practices, see Jerome Levi, "The Embodiment of a Working Identity: Power and Process in Raramuri Ritual Healing," *American Indian Culture and Research Journal* 23, no. 3 (1998): 13–46.

11. Elmendorf and Kroeber, *Twana Culture*, 17.

12. Smith, *The Puyallup-Nisqually*, 60.

13. Myron Eells, *Indians of Washington Territory* (Washington, DC: Smithsonian Anthropological Papers, 1884), 675.

14. Elmendorf and Kroeber, *Twana Culture*, 506–7.

15. See Wayne Suttles, *Coast Salish Essays* (Seattle: University of Washington Press, 1987); Amoss, *Coast Salish Spirit Dancing*; and Robert Boyd, *People of the Dalles: The Indians of Wascopam Mission* (Lincoln: University of Nebraska Press, 1996), 80. See also Elmendorf and Kroeber, *Twana Culture*, 516. Smith notes that the elderly, the sick, and small children, those lacking power and a clear sense of self-identity, are particularly vulnerable to soul loss (*The Puyallup-Nisqually*, 86).

16. Eells, *Indians of Washington Territory*, 677.

17. Elmendorf, *Twana Narratives*, 221; Elmendorf and Kroeber, *Twana Culture*, 505.

18. See Stephen Dow Beckham, Kathryn Anne Toepel, and Rick Minor, "Native American Religious Practices and Uses in Western Oregon," *University of Oregon Anthropological Papers* 31 (Eugene: University of Oregon Press, 1984); Boyd, *People of the Dalles*; and Robert Boyd, *The Coming of the Spirit of Pestilence: Introduced Infectious Diseases and Population Decline Among Northwest Coast Indians, 1774–1874* (Seattle: University of Washington Press, 1999). See also Elizabeth Jacobs and Melville Jacobs, *Nehalem Tillamook Tales*, *University of Oregon Monographs, Studies in Anthropology* 5 (Eugene: University of Oregon Press, 1959); Melville Jacobs, "Coos Narrative and Ethnologic Texts," *University of Washington Publications in Anthropology* 8, no. 1 (1939); Melville Jacobs, "Coos Myth Texts," *University of Washington Publications in Anthropology* 8 (1940): 127–260; Melville Jacobs, *Content and Style of an Oral Literature: Clackamas Chinook Myths and Tales* (Chicago: University of Chicago Press, 1959); Melville Jacobs, "Indications of Mental Illness Among Pre-Contact Indians of the Northwest States," *Pacific Northwest Quarterly* 50, no. 2 (April 1960): 2–15; Jacobs, Frachtenberg, and Gatschet, *Kalapuya Texts*; Bierwert, *Brushed by Cedar*; and Suttles, *Coast Salish Essays*.

19. John Scouler records an instance regarding the death of Futilifum, a Chinook warrior: "As the case was obviously hopeless it was judged improper to give any active medicine. Before he died he vomited an entire bulb of the phalangium esculentum (camas)...After Futilifum's death it was recollected that six months previously, while in good health, he had eaten a quantity of camas at the house of a Kowlitch (Cowlitz) chief who was famed for his skill in medicine. The superstitious fancy of the Indians immediately took fire; they believed that their favorite warrior F. had been charmed to death by the Kowlitch chief; while their resentments were yet warm a party was sent off and unfortunately succeeded in shooting the devoted chief." John Scouler, "Journal of a Voyage to N.W. America," *Oregon Historical Quarterly* 6 (1935): 278–79.

20. For a similar discussion of Navajo traditions, see Maureen Trudelle-Schwarz, *Molded in the Image of Changing Woman: Navajo Views on the Human Body and Personhood* (Tucson: University of Arizona Press, 1997); and, among the Dene Tha, see Goulet, *Ways of Knowing*.

21. Arthur Kleinman, *The Illness Narratives* (New York: Basic Books, 1988), 11.

22. See for example, Boyd, *Coming of the Spirit*; Robert Ruby and John Brown, *The Chinook Indians: Traders of the Lower Columbia River* (Norman: University of Oklahoma Press, 1976); Tzvetan Todorov, *The Conquest of America: The Question of the Other* (New York: Harper and Row, 1984); Clifford Trafzer, *Death Stalks the Yakama: Epidemiological Transitions and Mortality on the Yakama Indian Reservation, 1888–1964* (East Lansing: University of Michigan Press, 1997); Leslie Scott, "Indian Diseases as

Aids to Pacific Northwest Settlement," *Oregon Historical Quarterly* 29 (1928): 144–61; and George Guilmet, Robert Boyd, David Whited, and Nile Thompson, "The Legacy of Introduced Disease: The Southern Coast Salish," *American Indian Culture and Research Journal* 15 (1991): 1–32.

23. Boyd, *Coming of the Spirit*, 34. Reverend Parker noted in 1835 that "since the year 1829, probably 7/8 if not as doctor McLoughlin believes, 9/10 have been swept away by disease, principally by fever and ague." Rev. Samuel Parker, *Journal of an Exploring Tour Beyond the Rocky Mountains, in the Years 1835–1937* (Ithaca, New York: Mack, Andrus and Woodruff, 1840), 188. William Fraser Tolmie noted much the same devastation on the Columbia in the late 1830s: "On its lower bank, just opposite to Coffin Island, is the site of an Indian village, which a few years ago contained two or three hundred inhabitants, but at present only its superior verdure distinguished the spot from the surrounding country. Intermittent fever which has almost depopulated the Columbia River of its aborigines, committed its fullest ravages and nearly exterminated the villagers, the few survivors deserting a spot where the pestilence seemed most terribly to wreck its vengeance." William Fraser Tolmie, *The Journals of William Fraser Tolmie, Physician and Fur Trader* (Vancouver, B.C.: Mitchell Press, 1963), 183. It is significant that the spread of disease was in large part reflective of the new emerging economy: trade systems surrounding cattle and oysters facilitated the spread of measles and smallpox in the mid nineteenth century. It is no small irony that contemporary illnesses among Native communities are also due to economic demands: from oyster farming on Willapa Bay to Uranium mining in the Southwest.

24. Helen Neilson, "Focus on the Chehalis Indians 1800–1900," unpublished Master's thesis, Pacific Lutheran University, 77–78; and George Pierre Castile, ed., *The Indians of Puget Sound: The Notebooks of Myron Eells* (Seattle: University of Washington Press, 1985), 29.

25. Castile, *Indians of Puget Sound*, 409.

26. Reverend Modeste Demers appeared to share this view: "Everywhere we meet the same obstacles which always retard the conversion of the Indians, namely: polygamy, their adherence to the customs of their ancestors and, still more, to *tamanawas*, the name given to the medicines they prepare for the sick." Clarence B. Bagley, *Early Catholic Missions in Old Oregon, and Travels Over the Rocky Mountains in 1845–6*, Vol. 1 (Seattle: Lowman and Hanford Company, 1932), 83–84.

27. Chehalis Silas Heck in H. G. Barnett, *Indian Shakers: A Messianic Cult of the Pacific Northwest* (Carbondale: Southern Illinois University Press, 1972), 25.

28. For further information, see Barnett, *Indian Shakers*, and James Mooney, *The Ghost Dance Religion and the Sioux Outbreak of 1890* (Washington, DC: Bureau of American Ethnology, 1896), 748, 750.

29. Mooney, *Ghost Dance Religion*, 749.

30. Myron Eells, "S'kokomish Agency, Washington," *The American Missionary* 48, no. 4 (April 1894): 167.

31. See Barnett, *Indian Shakers*, 149–50. Barnett suggests that, in contrast to later Pentecostal traditions, the Congregationalist modes of worship available to Coast Salish people in the late nineteenth century failed to supply this same sense of a personal engagement with a powerful spiritual presence. Eells himself makes reference to this possibility, equating Shaker practices with the rambunctious worship of Holiness churches found elsewhere in the country.

32. Eells notes as well that, "Parental and filial love are quite strong, and the poor are generally cared for by their relatives and friends," *Indians of Washington Territory*, 615.

33. Amoss, *Coast Salish Spirit Dancing*, 638

34. See Crisca Bierwert, *Brushed By Cedar*, and Amoss, *Coast Salish Spirit Dancing*.

35. See Barbara Holdrege, for a discussion of his notion of "dividual" bodies. Barbara Holdrege, "Body Connections: Hindu Discourses of the Body and the Study of Religion," *International Journal of Hindu Studies* 2, no. 3 (1998): 341–86.

36. *South Puget Intertribal Planning Agency Annual Report* (Shelton, WA: South Puget Intertribal Planning Agency, 1999), 13.

37. Alysha Waters, "Native American Food Production Systems/A Historic Perspective/Their Link to Healthy Communities," *Native Women's Wellness Newsletter* (Summer 2001): 6–7. In 2002, an article in *Intertribal News* reported that the Nisqually Community Garden was planting a crop of camas, "an important historical crop... second only to salmon." The garden is part of a series of Traditional Food and Food Systems Workshops that took place among the Skokomish, Nisqually, Chehalis, and Squaxin Island in 2001 and 2002, emphasizing the intergenerational exchange of knowledge about plants and traditional foods.

38. *South Puget Intertribal News* (February–March 2006), 6

39. Ibid., 11.

40. Personal communication, field notes, November 12, 2000. This raises the interesting question of cultural appropriation, and how it may differ from cultural context to cultural context. While many of the Native women present would protest the appropriation or theft of Native traditions by non-natives, they nonetheless do not see an ethical dilemma in borrowing elements of biomedicine or other "first peoples" medicines. In my opinion, these are indeed two different issues, because of the power differential inherent in the colonial (or neo-colonial) context. The appropriation of a colonized peoples' culture by the colonizer is an expression of hegemony made possible by their position of power. The integration of elements of the colonizers' culture by the colonized, on the other hand, is an act of survival, a creative response to a loss of power.

41. Megan MacDonald, field notes, Summer 2004.

42. *Native Women's Wellness Newsletter* (Winter 2000–2001), 8.

43. SPIPA's Women and Girls' Gathering, annual report, 2004.

44. Quotations taken from evaluation forms completed at conclusion of 2004 Women and Girls' Gathering, used by permission.

45. Genny Rogers, "Sharing the Message at Home: Genny Rogers Shares How She Took Charge of Her Cancer Treatment—And Saved Her Breasts," *Native Women's Wellness* (Fall 2002): 5.

46. Field notes, July 30, 2004.

47. Field notes, August 1, 2004.

48. *South Puget Intertribal Planning Agency's Intertribal Intergenerational Women and Girls' Gathering, Annual Report* (Shelton, WA: South Puget Intertribal Planning Agency, 2004).

49. Field notes, August 30, 2001.

50. Field notes, August 30, 2001.

51. Charlene Krise, "Memories of Gathering," *Native Women's Wellness Newsletter* (Summer 2001): 1–3.

52. Field notes, Nisqually Tribal Center, May 2004.

53. Megan MacDonald, field notes, Summer 2004.

54. *South Puget Intertribal Planning Agency's Intertribal Intergenerational Women and Girls' Gathering, Annual Report.*

55. Barbara Whitener, "Language Program," *Klah'Che'Min* (August 2001): 9.

56. Field notes, "Talent Show, Women and Girls' Gathering, Panhandle Lake, August 18, 2001."

57. *South Puget Intertribal News*, 2.

BIBLIOGRAPHY

Amoss, Pamela. *Coast Salish Spirit Dancing: The Survival of an Ancestral Religion*. Seattle: University of Washington Press, 1978.

Bagley, Clarence B. *Early Catholic Missions in Old Oregon, and Travels over the Rocky Mountains in 1845–6*, Vol. 1. Seattle: Lowman and Hanford Company, 1932.

Barnett, H. G. *Indian Shakers: A Messianic Cult of the Pacific Northwest*. Carbondale: Southern Illinois University Press, 1972.

Bierwert, Crisca. *Brushed by Cedar, Living by the River: Coast Salish Figures of Power*. Tucson: University of Arizona Press, 2000.

Boyd, Robert. *The Coming of the Spirit of Pestilence: Introduced Infectious Diseases and Population Decline among Northwest Coast Indians, 1774–1874*. Seattle: University of Washington Press, 1999.

Boyd, Robert. *People of the Dalles: The Indians of Wascopam Mission*. Lincoln: University of Nebraska Press, 1996.

Castile, George Pierre, ed. *The Indians of Puget Sound: The Notebooks of Myron Eells*. Seattle: University of Washington Press, 1985.

Davies, Wade. *Healing Ways: Navajo Health Care in the Twentieth Century*. Albuquerque: University of New Mexico Press, 2001.

Dow Beckham, Stephen, Kathryn Anne Toepel, and Rick Minor. "Native American Religious Practices and Uses in Western Oregon." *University of Oregon Anthropological Papers* 31 (1984): 1–144.

Eells, Myron. *Indians of Washington Territory*. Washington, DC: Smithsonian Anthropological Papers, 1884.

Eells, Myron. "S'kokomish Agency, Washington." *The American Missionary* 48, no. 4 (April 1894).

Elmendorf, William W. *Twana Narratives: Native Historical Accounts of a Coast Salish Culture*. Seattle: University of Washington Press, 1993.

Elmendorf William W., and A. L. Kroeber. *Twana Culture*. Pullman: Washington State University Press, 1992.

Goulet, Jean-Guy. *Ways of Knowing: Experience, Knowledge, and Power Among the Dene Tha*. Lincoln: University of Nebraska Press, 1998.

Guilmet, George, Robert Boyd, David Whited, and Nile Thompson. "The Legacy of Introduced Disease: The Southern Coast Salish." *American Indian Culture and Research Journal* 15 (1991): 1–32.

Holdrege, Barbara. "Body Connections: Hindu Discourses of the Body and the Study of Religion." *International Journal of Hindu Studies* 2, no. 3 (1998): 341–86.

Jacobs, Elizabeth, and Melville Jacobs. *Nehalem Tillamook Tales: University of Oregon Monographs, Studies in Anthropology 5*. Eugene: University of Oregon Press, 1959.

Jacobs, Melville. "Coos Narrative and Ethnologic Texts." *University of Washington Publications in Anthropology* 8, no. 1 (1939).

Jacobs, Melville. "Coos Myth Texts." *University of Washington Publications in Anthropology* 8 (1940): 127–260.

Jacobs, Melville. *Content and Style of an Oral Literature: Clackamas Chinook Myths and Tales*. Chicago: University of Chicago Press, 1959.

Jacobs, Melville. "Indications of Mental Illness Among Pre-Contact Indians of the Northwest States." *Pacific Northwest Quarterly* 50, no. 2 (April 1960): 49–54.

Jacobs, Melville, Leo J. Frachtenberg, and Albert S. Gatschet. *Kalapuya Texts: University of Washington Publications in Anthropology 11*. Seattle: University of Washington Press, 1945.

Kleinman, Arthur. *The Illness Narratives*. New York: Basic Books, 1988.

Krise, Charlene. "Memories of Gathering." *Native Women's Wellness Newsletter* (Summer 2001): 3.

Levi, Jerome. "The Embodiment of a Working Identity: Power and Process in Raramuri Ritual Healing." *American Indian Culture and Research Journal* 23, no. 3 (1999): 13–39.

Miller, Jay. *Lushootseed Culture and the Shamanic Odyssey: An Anchored Radiance*. Lincoln: University of Nebraska Press, 1999.

Mooney, James. *The Ghost Dance Religion and the Sioux Outbreak of 1890*. Washington, DC: Bureau of American Ethnology, 1896.

Native Women's Wellness Newsletter. Shelton, WA: South Puget Intertribal Planning Agency, Winter 2000–2001.

Nebelkopf, Ethan, and Mary Phillips, eds. *Healing and Mental Health for Native Americans: Speaking in Red*. Lanham, MD: Alta Mira Press, 2004.

Neilson, Helen. "Focus on the Chehalis Indians 1800–1900." Unpublished Master's thesis, Tacoma, WA, Pacific Lutheran University, 1970.

Parker, Samuel. *Journal of an Exploring Tour Beyond the Rocky Mountains, in the Years 1835–1837*. Ithaca, NY: Published by the Author, Mack, Andrus, & Woodruff, Printers, 1840.

Rhoades, Everett R., ed. *American Indian Health: Innovations in Heath Care, Promotion and Policy*. Baltimore, MD: The Johns Hopkins University Press, 2000.

Rogers, Genny. "Sharing the Message at Home: Genny Rogers Shares How She Took Charge of Her Cancer Treatment—And Saved Her Breasts." *Native Women's Wellness* (Fall 2002): 5.

Ruby, Robert, and John Brown. *The Chinook Indians: Traders of the Lower Columbia River*. Norman: University of Oklahoma Press, 1976.

Scott, Leslie. "Indian Diseases as Aids to Pacific Northwest Settlement." *Oregon Historical Quarterly* 29 (1928): 144–61.

Scouler, John. "Journal of a Voyage to N.W. America." *Oregon Historical Quarterly* 6 (1935): 276–87.

Smith, Marian. *The Puyallup-Nisqually.* Columbia University Contributions to Anthropology 32. New York: Columbia University Press, 1940.

South Puget Intertribal News. Shelton, WA: South Puget Intertribal Planning Agency, February–March, 2006.

South Puget Intertribal Planning Agency Annual Report. Shelton, WA: South Puget Intertribal Planning Agency, 1999.

South Puget Intertribal Planning Agency's Intertribal Intergenerational Women and Girls' Gathering, Annual Report. Shelton, WA: South Puget Intertribal Planning Agency, 2004.

Suttles, Wayne. *Coast Salish Essays.* Seattle: University of Washington Press, 1987.

Thom, Brian David. *Coast Salish Senses of Place: Dwelling, Meaning, Property and Territory in the Coast Salish World.* Unpublished Doctoral dissertation, Montreal, Canada, McGill University, 2005.

Todorov, Tzvetan. *The Conquest of America: The Question of the Other.* New York: Harper and Row, 1984.

Tolmie, William Fraser. *The Journals of William Fraser Tolmie, Physician and Fur Trader.* Vancouver, B.C.: Mitchell Press, 1963.

Trafzer, Clifford. *Death Stalks the Yakama: Epidemiological Transitions and Mortality on the Yakama Indian Reservation, 1888–1964.* East Lansing: University of Michigan Press, 1997.

Trudelle-Schwarz, Maureen. *Molded in the Image of Changing Woman: Navajo Views on the Human Body and Personhood.* Tucson: University of Arizona Press, 1997.

Tweddell, Colin E. "The Snohomish Indian People." *Coast Salish and Western Washington Indians,* vol. *II.* New York: Garland Publishing, 1974.

Waters, Alysha. "Native American Food Production Systems/A Historic Perspective/Their Link to Healthy Communities." *Native Women's Wellness Newsletter* (Summer 2001): 6–7.

Whitener, Barbara. "Language Program." *Klah'Che'Min* (August 2001): 9.

PART IV

———— ✠ ————

Healing through Narrative and Storytelling

CHAPTER 8

———— ❖ ————

"The Stories Are Very Powerful": A Native American Perspective on Health, Illness, and Narrative

Eva Marie Garroutte and Kathleen Delores Westcott

In his seminal work *The Illness Narratives*, physician-anthropologist Arthur Kleinman[1] indicted modern medicine as a serious failure. In both medical training and health-care delivery, he asserted, doctors maintained a reductionist preoccupation with *disease*, or the objectively measurable changes in the body's biological structure or functioning. At the same time, they stubbornly overlooked *illness*, or the patient's subjective experience of symptoms and suffering. Kleinman charged that narrowly focused physicians left patients to struggle—alone and often to the further detriment of their health—to make sense of threatening medical events and the deterioration implied by many chronic conditions.

As a corrective, Kleinman prescribed greater attention to the patients' lived experiences, accessible through their stories. He invited health professionals into the narrative processes by which patients invest illness with meaning. In this way, he argued, doctors could do more than assist in the restoration of physical function—a goal that was not always realistic. By collaborating to help patients re-story their lives, physicians could help them become, in an even more meaningful sense, whole.

This early work accompanied an explosion of research. Much of it emanated from the social sciences and humanities, taking up issues in narrative analysis applied to the discourses of health and illness.[2] Another body of research emerged from the health professions.[3] Work from these diverse sources is united by careful attention to the narratives of patients, often conceived as "wounded storytellers"[4] whose injuries invest them with a special authority to answer the previously unquestioned "voice of medicine" with their own "voice of the life world."[5]

Contributors to these burgeoning fields of inquiry agree that good medical care is grounded not only in providers' scientific expertise but also in their "narrative competence," meaning their "ability to listen to the narratives of patients, grasp and honor their meanings, and respond to their stories."[6] Advocates of a narrative approach argue that health professionals who attend to patients' stories are more likely to diagnose accurately, prescribe appropriately, and craft a mutually acceptable treatment plan.[7]

Recent work argues that attention to patient narratives may be especially important in the medical care of racial and ethnic minorities, whose health perspectives may be most unfamiliar to their providers and least often heard.[8] Native Americans are a rapidly growing racial population[9] in which there are significant barriers to the sharing of patient narratives. Many health-care providers have limited (or no) exposure to Native American people, while cultural norms and historical experiences often combine to encourage reticence in this patient population.[10] Native Americans may be particularly reluctant to discuss fundamental health knowledge, beliefs, and behaviors with caregivers because these are frequently informed by narratives with sacred or mythic elements and interwoven with ceremonial practices.[11] This chapter experiments with developing a new methodology for the collection and presentation of research data. Our approach focuses on the preparation of a long segment of interview material. In it, a Native American teacher and healer describes the ways that conventional healthcare has failed to take account of her distinctive values as an Anishnaabe woman.[12] Her narrative, which features a traditional Native American story embedded within a personal story, allows her to draw out the culturally located meanings of her medical situation, to contrast her own perspectives with those of her healthcare providers, and to explain the consequences of cultural knowledge for her medical decisions. The contrast highlights themes that commonly appear in Native American narratives of health and illness, including the importance of physical and spiritual relationships and the active role of narrative in creating relationships. We then examine the broad implications of the story for interactions between healthcare providers, researchers, and Native American people, with attention to the challenges and opportunities that may attend encounters with such narratives.

WHAT WE DID

This section discusses the methodology informing the coauthors' collaboration, and the intellectual context in which our efforts make sense. It will be of interest to students of culture and narrative and to those who seek to understand strategies for delivering healthcare to diverse populations; it is also of special concern to scholars who are interested in new models for a distinctively American Indian (or indigenous) scholarship. It may have less appeal to the general reader, who may wish to skim or skip ahead to the subheading labeled "Interview Material."

A New Theoretical Direction

The theoretical perspective of "Radical Indigenism" proposes new types of research relationships between the academy and Native American communities, guided by individuals who have commitments in both camps. At the heart of this perspective is an approach that takes the philosophies of knowledge carried by indigenous peoples seriously. It challenges researchers and health practitioners to risk encountering the claims of their research participants or patients not merely as colorful or interesting beliefs to be approached as curiosities or construed within foreign intellectual frameworks. Instead, Radical Indigenism asks non-Native people to grant the possibility that, even while the philosophies underlying indigenous encounters with the world may proceed from assumptions that differ from scientific ones, they may nevertheless include tools for the generation of knowledge. Radical Indigenism has been more fully described elsewhere as a theoretical perspective.[13] This chapter undertakes an exercise in developing a practical model for realizing its goals in research related to Native American healthcare.

At the heart of our experimental methodology is the presentation of a long segment of transcribed text in which a Native American speaker describes and comments upon issues in medical interaction. Unlike alternative approaches to medical discourse,[14] a strategy guided by Radical Indigenism does not make narratives the object of analytic scrutiny in order to reveal something beyond themselves—the genres they embody, the underlying power structures they presuppose, the mechanisms by which they persuade, or the like. Although professional academics value such questions, ordinary Native American people seldom (in our experience) view them as especially relevant to daily concerns. They tell their stories not to invite their dissection, classification, and reconstruction within academic categories, but because they have something to say. Accordingly, our goal is to allow a Native American patient to fully express her perspectives and values *in a way that can be heard* by powerful institutions with which she interacts around issues of health.

The Coauthors' Collaboration

The coauthors of this chapter have been friends and colleagues for about 15 years. In 2001, Kathleen Westcott suffered a traumatic brain injury and consequently entered a program of rehabilitative therapy. Her experiences prompted her to think deeply about the ways that her own commitments to, and assumptions about, recovery and wellness contrasted with those of conventional health-care professionals. She approached Eva Garroutte to invite research collaboration. We began this work by distinguishing two roles for the project, which we labeled the *facilitator* (Garroutte) and the *interlocutor* (Westcott). We felt these terms implied a better balance of responsibilities than alternatives such as *researcher* and *participant*. We then defined duties and attached them to the two roles, drawing in part upon participatory action research in their formulation.[15] Duties shared between the facilitator and interlocutor included the following: to participate in preparatory conversations to define general topics for discussion, to take part in a subsequent series of interviews, to study interview transcripts and identify themes to be prioritized for publication, to select portions of interview material to illuminate these themes, and to work iteratively with chapter drafts to ensure completeness, clarity, and accuracy.

The *facilitator* accepted primary responsibility to formulate framing questions to focus the interviews around defined themes and to write the sections of the chapter that would position the selected material within relevant literature and describe the methodology. Her central goal was to represent ideas and perspectives important to her as a professional sociologist. The *interlocutor* accepted primary responsibility for reflecting in advance of the interviews on the topics we had defined and for articulating ideas and experiences. She also had the responsibility to amend and finalize the interview material so that it accurately reflected her views while, as she specified, "communicating teaching in the telling." Her central goal was to represent perspectives important to her as a Native American and a recipient of health services.

Data Collection

Data collection consisted of three audiotaped, semi-structured interviews that were conducted by telephone between March and April 2005, with a total duration of about six hours. The style of the interviews drew on the research perspective proposed in Holstein and Gubrium's influential monograph, *The Active Interview*.[16] This perspective, which develops earlier work by Mishler,[17] challenges previous understandings of interview research that constituted the subject as a "vessel of answers" and the interview conversation as a "pipeline" for conveying them. By contrast, Holstein and Gubrium argue for the interview as a collaborative venture, a unique product of interaction between specific individuals.[18] The general point of interviews understood in this way "is to engage respondents in meaningful talk about their everyday worlds in terms that derive from the circumstances of lived experience."[19] As an *active* interview, our discussion was loosely guided by the framing questions but was then allowed to unfold naturally to accommodate additional themes. We also modified this perspective to accommodate norms we agreed were respectful of values we hold as Native American people. These modifications included, for instance, allowances for appropriate ceremonial observance before, after, and (in one case noted below) during the interviews.

Analytic Procedures

All interviews were audiotaped and fully transcribed, after which the co-authors worked conjointly with the transcripts to select a segment of material to be presented in the "Interview Material" section of our chapter. Since this iterative process of editing and refinement was at the center of our methodological experiment, we formally specified its guiding principles. They included:

1. To preserve the unique power of oral discourse. People speak differently than they write, and while our goal was to create a written text, we hoped to reproduce, as much as possible, the experience of conversation with a Native American patient. We agreed that both parties could propose changes to the selected interview text to be presented in the Interview Material section but that the facilitator should focus mainly on suggestions for restructuring the order of ideas to enhance clarity. Both authors attempted to minimize other changes, striving for amendment more than revision. We especially avoided altering the respondents' originally spoken words except where absolutely necessary to communicate intended meanings. This meant retaining the original, conversational form of the narrative—including repetitions, tense shifts, grammatical and syntactical creativity, stylistic devices such as contractions and incomplete sentences, and other common features of spontaneous speech.

2. To share narrative power. Methods of narrative interviewing and analysis, of which the method we propose here is a species, typically try to foster "communicative equality" with research participants.[20] Facilitator and interlocutor agreed that appropriate power sharing implied that each should receive an equal opportunity to express her perspective. This meant a radical departure from conventional analytic methods, which commonly disassemble respondents' discourses, presenting only snippets that may serve as little more than proof texts for authorial arguments.[21] Instead, we reserved approximately half of the chapter text for the "Interview Material" section. Moreover, we agreed that the interlocutor should be allowed to present ideas in this section without interruption, just as the facilitator was allowed to do in other sections. This meant that the facilitator's comments, questions, and prompts were edited out of the interview segment, which then read as a seamless, continuous text.[22] The coauthors consented to resolve differences of opinion about chapter drafts through consensus whenever possible but specified that the facilitator's comments on the "Interview Material" section were fundamentally advisory; the final authority over the interview material rested with the interlocutor. The reverse was true for other sections of the chapter.

3. To respect indigenous epistemological assumptions, meaning assumptions about how *knowledge* is defined and sought, and how claims to it are justified.[23] Readers may be inclined to classify our efforts in this chapter (together, perhaps, with qualitative analyses more generally) as closer to *art* than to *science*. In this, we are untroubled because we embrace an epistemological principle common to numerous indigenous cultures, including traditions with which the interlocutor has personal familiarity and training. This principle recognizes artistic engagement as both a sacred activity and a strategy for generating knowledge: "a way of prayerful work."[24] In this view, the creative process is much more than invention, however skillful. It is a rigorous

method of inquiry by which the seeker may encounter the fundamental, if unseen, nature of things; explore their relationships in self-transforming ways; and draw the resulting knowledge into physical form.[25] As corollary to our decision in favor of this epistemological assumption, we chose *beauty* as a central evaluative criterion. In our framing, preparation and presentation of results, we set out to create a narrative that not only communicated accurately but also in a way that compelled an aesthetic sensibility.[26]

The following material was selected from a series of three interviews that invited the interlocutor to discuss her experiences in receiving healthcare from a conventional provider, like a doctor or a nurse. It conveys the interlocutor's ideas and perspectives in her own words.

INTERVIEW MATERIAL

In the past, I've made it a point *not* to seek health care from an ordinary "Western" [allopathic] medical practitioner. A big part of my unwillingness to use conventional care is that health care providers often have a very different view of illness, in general, than I do. I can give you an example from my own experience of having suffered a traumatic brain injury at work a couple of years ago. When I went to the doctor, the first thing he wanted to do was to give me antidepressants. I was told that this is a standard treatment for such an injury. But I refused to take the drugs. And the doctor yelled at me, "You just don't want to get better!"

Of course, that wasn't the case. As a Native person, it is my belief that there is no injury and no illness that happens by chance. Instead, illness is regarded as a *teacher,* and it is my responsibility to find the guidance in it. In relation to that perspective, taking prescription drugs is a major conflict for me. I've been given stories by elders to live with and work with my entire life. One of these stories taught me about what we lose if we rely heavily on prescription drugs, or addictive substances, to manage the symptoms of illness quickly—thereby suppressing the "voice" of the illness instead of going through the experience and considering it as a teacher. When we don't come into relationship with the illness as student-to-teacher, we lose a lot. The stories I've been given are very powerful stories. I can tell one about illness. It actually has to do with relationships between illness, suffering, and loss and teaches about how illness can be a catalyst for a creative response to human suffering. But I need to go offer tobacco first.

Pause. The interlocutor exits the house, completes ceremonial observance, and returns to conversation.

This story was originally given to me by an elder whose name is Ignatia Broker. I just now went out and offered tobacco with the understanding that the story is a living being. It's alive. So it's important to follow the principle of reciprocity: by giving a gift and asking the story to impart itself to us in a way that will help us gain insight and knowledge, and perhaps even wisdom. Ignatia gave this story for that purpose.

I'm not the only person Ignatia shared this story with. Another version of it is published by the Indian Elementary Curriculum Development Project of the Minneapolis (Minnesota) Public Schools. However, if you compared them, you would notice a distinction between my version and the published version. The differences are the result of my walking with this story for 25 years. Ignatia told me this story would teach me and guide me in my work; this story and my life have become interwoven. The story and myself have established a lasting relationship. So I've made an offering to the story. I consider the offering a form of food. This is a way that I express gratitude to Ignatia and to the story. So, let's just begin. I'm going to tell a really simplified version. (The following indentation signals a transition from the interlocutor's "ordinary" speech about her own experiences to an Anishnaabe story.)

This story takes place among the Anishnaabe people of the Great Lakes region, many hundreds of years ago. It begins at a time of year when the snow is melted and the rivers are running. It's a story about a young woman in her early 30s, her husband, her children, and her village. This young woman and her husband were looked upon by their people as very admirable because the bond of marriage between them was pure. It was joyous and effortless—their friendship, their intimacy as a couple, their pleasure in being parents, their regard for the older generation, their responsibility toward the elders and toward their community.

In this particular season, which was early to mid-spring, the husband prepared to go on a fishing trip with other men from their village. They set off early in the morning. His wife continued with the day, gathering firewood, tending their children, preparing meals. It was maple sugaring time, so those activities were also taking place. The day went on with bright sun. There was a warming wind and high hopes for a new year. There was a lot of gratitude among the people for having made it through the winter, for the food stores having lasted long enough.

At the end of the day, the men returned in their canoes to the river's edge where the village was newly established. But there was a heaviness in their bodies as they got out of the canoes. The women came to the edge of the river to help unload the day's catch. It then became apparent that there was somebody missing. The young woman who is the subject of this story realized very quickly that her husband hadn't returned. She heard the story about how he had been pulled under the current and drowned. It was an unusual event. No one could save him.

Her grief began as everyone expected it to, and followed its normal course through all of the ritual and ceremonial procedures: through the burial, through the giveaway, through the cutting of her hair, through one year of carrying her husband's personal bundle. In all these traditional ways, she observed his absence for an entire year. But in this story, the year passed, and the woman was as deeply in grief as at the first moment of learning about the loss of her husband. She had taken care of her children for that entire year and met all her ceremonial responsibilities. But the whole time she felt that she'd walked about quite numb. So after the year-end feast that would usually have ended her year of mourning, she left the village. She walked away, walking into the woods, where she found a particular tree that she felt drawn to. She sat down with her back to the tree, isolating herself. She stayed there season upon season: through spring, through summer, through fall and through winter. The people of the village took care of her children. They kept her wood stores up, gathered her food. They brought small offerings out to her. When the weather got cold, she would return to her lodge to sleep and later return to the tree, speaking to no one.

Of course, after a time, the elders of the community were deeply concerned. So they came together and they inquired among each other, "What are we witnessing here?" What they learned was that this woman was acting in her own purity and goodness, her own ability. The elders acknowledged among each other, "She's thinking. She's thinking on our behalf. She is working on this carefully within her heart. This wouldn't be happening if there weren't something coming our way that we need to be prepared for. She's been called to go out and to learn about it." The elders continued, "We have to support her as though she's in a prolonged search for guidance, for communion. We may not even be alive when whatever it is she's seeking to prepare us for occurs." But they were excited to simply back this woman and support her. They reminded the people in the village to keep up what they were already doing. They realized that there was great purpose in her behavior and that they must uphold her well.

A second year passed. It came to be about mid-June. The woman was still sitting there against this tree. And one day, early in the morning, she heard somebody speaking to her, which was very unusual. This hadn't occurred for this entire time. She hears a voice, she looks around, but she really can't see anybody. She eases her body back against the same tree—then she hears the voice again. Only this time she not only hears the sound of the voice but she feels the vibration of the voice, pulsating through her spine. She realizes the tree is talking to her.

Now, anyone listening to the story will understand the tree isn't audibly talking. Instead, their minds have become one, the mind of the woman and the mind of the tree. There's a communion occurring here. The woman and the tree are sharing the energy of thought. And the tree is saying, "My granddaughter, I've held you all these months. I've come to know you well. I've come to know your devotion to your people and the strong bond that you carry with your husband. I know that you've lost your will to live and that your desire to drop your body and cross over to join your husband is strong. At the same time, your desire to be of some use to your people is also strong, and it has always been there. You've always connected this desire with your marriage. But I've come to know you well, Granddaughter, and to love you well. I want you to stand. I want you to stand tall, turn around and face me." Which the woman does.

The tree continues, "I'm going to show you something about myself. I'm going to share my own self with you by giving you some of my own skin. First, I am going to teach you how to strike my skin." She does that. The woman strikes the skin—the bark of the tree—and she strikes it in a particular way causing the skin to just flip right off! Then this blessed tree says, "I am giving you the skin of my very being and I'm going to teach you to cut it in a certain way.... I'm going to teach you to go to some of the other ones in the Plant Nation in these woods. You will gather basswood for sewing and willow for framing.... You will continue to gather my skin for the body of these baskets that I'm going to teach you to make. They'll be fine and strong, and they'll have great beauty."

So for several days, the woman and the tree worked together closely. The first birch bark baskets emerge out of their work. They are glistening in the sun—golden, radiant, functional, beautiful. Then the woman sits. She looks at what they've done. She sighs at the beauty of it, feeling the joy alive in her heart again. The tree speaks to her again through her mind saying, "My grand-daughter, do you notice that your will to live has returned to you out of your own dignity, your own integrity, out of your desire to help your people, and your willingness to stay alive? You've learned a new skill and you're learning to come into relationship with me, in a manner not unlike your relationship with your husband. Now, I want you to go back to your people. When you have returned to your people, I want you to give these baskets to them as a gift, so that their life will be more beautiful, and a little easier. As you continue to make them, they will continue to provide for you the way your husband once did, and you will continue to live in good relationship with all life.[27] You will be able to care for your children."

So the woman picked up three baskets. She walked back to the village. She was quite radiant but also very humble and grateful. It was the elders that saw her coming first. They stood together to greet her and to welcome her back. And the moment they saw the baskets, without really even knowing the use that they would have and the ease that they would bring, they saw the beauty of them, and their hearts filled with understanding. The woman told the story about the gift she'd been given, and how she'd been restored with the will to live: how she'd been brought back into relationship through knowledge and skill to a purposeful life. She continued to make the baskets. She taught her children how to make them. The tree had given her the way to make offerings and the songs to sing—everything that was necessary to do this work in a sacred way. She passed all this on, and it continues to be passed on to this day. Mii'iw.[28]

Ignatia gave me that story and I told it over and over, eventually under-standing something very important about grieving: about the courage to grieve deeply, to not back off from it, whether it comes from loss, or trauma, or illness. Working as an art therapist, I have told that story many times in different settings, including different kinds of training situations for therapists and social workers, or health-care providers. In those contexts, I would ask my listeners these questions: "What would happen if someone today isolated herself in this way, if she went into her grief that deeply? What are some of the things that would occur?"

The people would very quickly respond that she would have been charged with neglecting her children, and those children would have probably been placed into foster care. Maybe a health-care provider or social services agency would place her on a suicide watch so that she could not become a danger to herself. The woman would have been diagnosed, probably with depression. And she would probably have been treated for this mental illness with prescription medication.

So then I would ask, "What would we have lost the moment that this woman was put on medication?" Most of the time somebody would answer, "We would have lost the relationship between her and that tree. Then we would have lost the teaching regarding how to make birch bark baskets." People would observe that, by taking medications to make herself feel better, by suppressing the so-called feels bad symptoms of her loss, she would presumably have recovered according to some timetable imposed from outside herself. She would have then sacrificed very important teachings about the relationships between suffering, sacred knowledge, the natural world, creative process, and healing.

All these outcomes are true, but the story doesn't even end there. In our own time—the time of our grandmothers, our mothers, and ourselves—many other Anishnaabe women have lost their husbands and their partners with whom they had children. They have lost them through the effects of genocide, poverty, colonization, alcoholism, depression, and despair. Having not yet found a purposeful life in our present-day circumstances, many Native American men in our communities have drifted off or become unable to provide for their women or their children. Then one day I walked into a souvenir store up in Bemidji, Minnesota. This is close to Red Lake, Leech Lake, and White Earth Reservations. There was an island running down the middle of the store, covered with birch bark baskets. I asked, "Where did they come from?" And the clerk said, "Oh, they came from a woman named Josephine Ryan." Later, Josephine told me that she goes around to all the community centers in the area, teaching the Native women to make the baskets. Then she gathers the baskets that they make and she sells them for the women. She takes the money back to them so that they can stay at home on the reservation, raising their children without going into the towns to find work.

Josephine understands her connections to this story about the first birch bark baskets, which of course she knows well. As I continued to think about this story, I began to understand it much more deeply. I understood what had been given at that time long ago—what had been anticipated by those elders who supported the woman. That woman's courage and her stubborn willingness to go into her grief *that* deeply—those qualities brought her people a gift that became a very, very critical gift *many hundreds of years later*. If she had avoided the depth of her suffering, through prescription medication or some other means—such as quickly seeking another partner, using alcohol, or obsessively working—the Anishnaabe people would have also lost the relationship between Josephine Ryan and all the single mothers in our communities today. Anishnaabe mothers would be without the dignity and the skill that would give them the extra dollars that would help them stay at home in their community and continue to live as Native women, close to their relatives, rather than leave and go into town for a job.

I've often thought over the years that this is a very, very good teaching story. It has relevance to my feelings about psychotropic drugs especially—because they very clearly affect our ability to listen to the unseen world, to commune, to become of one mind with other forms of life besides human life. They distort that ability. But really, I am inclined not to take *any* medication, and for a similar reason. I want to be sure that I don't miss what an illness is trying to teach me by sidestepping it through symptom management. If I miss meeting the teacher in the illness, there can be consequences for me—and even for all the people who have gone before me and for all those who are yet to be born.

Instead of relying solely on drugs to treat illnesses once I have them, my ideal health strategy is to take measures to avoid becoming ill. One thing that is distinctive about Native American medical treatment is that it tends to be preventative, rather than crisis oriented. Treatment does not so much address the symptomatic state; rather, treatment focuses on the vitality and right relationship of the individual. Native American medicine is greatly concerned with helping people be in a vital relationship with the natural world in traditional ways, so that we remain healthy. I try to observe those teachings.

Of course, even using such preventive measures, sometimes I still get sick, and then there are *times* when I choose to take prescription drugs. But I think very carefully before I make that decision. First, I try to understand what the illness might have to teach me. It's stories like the one I just told that have affected my perspective about this. I have experienced some very serious illnesses and injuries in my life, most recently the brain injury that I mentioned before. But in a challenging—at times overwhelming—set of life circumstances, stories like this one are my rudder. With each illness, with each loss, I hold myself to the principles taught within this story. These principles contribute to a cohesiveness of logic—of purposeful, creative living—that makes it possible for me to *endure*, for starters, then to learn through creative process, then to share what I have received. So you see, through these stories, life is made new.

I think it would be rare today for a doctor to encounter the perspective that I've just described, particularly to have it articulated by a patient. But I do know elders that hold to that perspective. They also take Western prescription medication when it seems wise to do so. But they will still follow with traditional forms of treatment, employing plant, animal, and mineral medicines, and ceremonial process. Like me, they turn to our traditional stories to receive knowledge, insight, healing, and guidance in this process.

UNPACKING THE STORY

The material presented in the "Interview Material" section reveal one patient's distinctive and richly developed narrative that describes her own experiences related to health and health care, grounds them in a cultural context that blends sacred teachings with knowledge of the natural and spiritual worlds, and shows the consequences of that foundation for specific medical decisions. This narrative also provides many insights for those concerned about the health and health care of Native American people, and the linkages of those domains to cultural expressions of religion or spirituality.

On the one hand, the literature that has developed Kleinman's concept of "illness narrative" suggests that the interlocutor's story is not unique. The central theme of *illness as teacher* corresponds closely to the *quest story*, a genre that Arthur Frank's typology distinguishes as the most common among published illness stories and that includes a seventeenth-century account by John Donne and a nineteenth-century one by Friedrich Nietzsche.[29]

In contrast to *restitution stories,* in which the plot tracks the sufferer's expeditious return to a "good as new" condition, the quest story recounts a journey. It portrays illness as a vehicle by which the sufferer travels toward insight and returns to bear witness. The quest story acknowledges the need to mourn the losses that illness imposes but nevertheless insists that suffering is ultimately redeemed. These genre-typical ideas feature strongly in the interlocutor's narrative. Health-care providers who recognize such similarities may conclude that Native American ideas about health and sickness are not altogether foreign.

At the same time as it shares features with other *quest stories,* the interlocutor's narrative also displays culturally distinctive themes. One theme deserves particular mention because, while it is not universal among Native American peoples, some version of it recurs with sufficient regularity across tribes for it to be considered strongly characteristic.[30] This is the idea that individual health conditions and decisions do not implicate individuals exclusively; rather, individual suffering has personal *and* societal consequences. Its appropriate resolution requires active engagement by an entire community and contributes, in turn, to the ability of communities to survive and to thrive in tightly woven webs of interrelationship.

Nor are such relationships limited in the ways non-Native listeners might assume. During our review of interview transcripts, the interlocutor underscored the extensiveness of the relationships bearing upon the individual's health. As she noted,

This story is about how a woman who lived a long time ago, placed herself into a relationship with a being in the natural world. And it's a story about how she placed herself into a relationship with Anishnaabe women who are alive today. *And* it's a story about how she placed herself into a relationship with her ancestors. Because the tree is present in this story *as* an ancestor. It functions there as human ancestors also do—as literally a teacher and healer. That tree is part of a community of relationships that joins together human and other beings in a way that cuts across time—and ultimately resides within Gitchi Manitou, the Kind-Hearted Great Mystery.

It is important to notice that, far from simply enumerating possible relationships, the interlocutor's story also allows for their creation. Through narrativization itself the interlocutor *experiences* relationship. For example, she first experiences relationship with a plant being in the form of the tobacco offered before the storytelling can proceed. She then experiences relationship with a story that is explicitly understood as a living being. And she experiences relationship with a community of ancestors—from the woman of whom the story is told, to the individual who gifted the interlocutor with the story, to many unknown others who carried it for generations. Thus, things literally get done in the process of telling the story in a traditional manner, and they get done within a community that links together both human and other-than-human actors as well as the temporal domains of past, present, and future. One can hope that if health professionals understand the distinctive place that stories may assume in Native cultures—their literal, active role in creating and maintaining relationships that are conducive to healing—then they might be more interested in hearing them.

The interlocutor's discussion of the many interrelationships through which the individual's health decisions reverberate brings up an even more fundamental point. Kleinman astutely observed that individual illness narratives often revealed a great deal not only about the sufferer but about the larger societal context. He explicitly linked "putative physical disease" to societal ills such as political oppression and economic hardship; he simultaneously observed that conventional, biomedical constructions of sickness systematically deflect attention from anything but individual, physical concerns. In this way, exclusively biomedical models serve the interests of states in maintaining current sociopolitical arrangements and obscure any need for interventions that might allow those wounded by them to heal.

Nevertheless, Kleinman concluded that few patients grasp such realities: "The chronically ill are caught up with the sheer exigency of their problems."[31] Yet the expansive perspective that our interlocutor describes, one that expressly takes in the huge number of relationships—personal, societal, spiritual, and intergenerational—through which the individuals' illness ramifies, may provide an unusually broad basis for Native American perspectives. As she observed,

The dominant society has been in relationships of colonization, dispossession, and exploitation with American Indian people for the last 500 years. The effects have not gone away. *All* interactions between peoples, between communities, between humans and the natural world—they continue to be horribly distorted as part of the natural chain of consequences. And then the doctor wants to talk about *why I have a headache?* One reason, I think, that Native Americans get such a bad deal from Western medicine is that medicine *doesn't see the storyline*. Colonization has affected Native Americans in every way, including our health. It's *still* affecting all of us as individuals and as peoples.

Such remarks suggest that providers may be surprised how much *insight* Native American patients have into the sociohistorical dynamics surrounding their health circumstances. These perceptions explode the frame of biomedical models of sickness and may be uncomfortable for non-Native listeners to hear. But those who would follow the *narrative turn* of contemporary health-care delivery and social science should be prepared for the possibility that Native patients grasp that the effects of colonization are inscribed onto bodies.

Those who hope to elicit patient narratives should also realize that conventional terminology may frame discussions in ways that Native patients find unacceptable. For example, while the interlocutor granted the utility of placing her story in conversation with the scholarly literature on *illness narratives*, she urged health-care professionals away from this terminology in discussion with Native patients or interview respondents. Although Kleinman's work has given this term a central and unquestioned place in the researcher's lexicon, she feared it might alienate Native patients:

> This is my experience of stories in traditional contexts. Any story about adversity that occurs in life is held within a larger story—a story that reveals the abiding nature of balance and of the ultimate wellness of the cosmos. I think a common perspective among Native Americans would be: "Why would *any* story be an '*illness* narrative'?" To call something that discredits it instantly. Stories like mine are "*wellness* narratives."

Health professionals wishing to interact with Native patients around their stories need to consider the language of their requests, noticing how terminology is laden with assumptions. They may need to try various ways of inviting patients into conversations about health and to be sensitive to the larger implications of conventional ways of framing questions.

Such observations lead to remarks concerning the virtue of what might be called epistemological humility. While many researchers follow Kleinman in urging healthcare providers to listen to patients' stories, others express anxiety that the narrative turn in health research and medical training might compromise both scholarship and care. Patients, they point out, are not immune to false beliefs or error. For this reason, scholars such as Gabriel argue that patients' illness narratives "must be treated with the same skepticism and suspicion with which we approach all other sources of authoritative knowledge...understanding them, comparing them, privileging those which deserve to be privileged and silencing those that deserve to be silenced, questioning them, testing them, and qualifying them."[32]

While we do not deny the fundamental point that American Indian patients can (like anyone else) be wrong, evaluative injunctions such as this one imply that provider and patient share basic assumptions about what is real, what can be known, and how. Our data strongly suggest that this may not be the case when providers interact with Native American patients. Consistent with our emphasis on the perspective of Radical Indigenism, we contend it would be a mistake for health-care providers simply to dismiss the interlocutor's distinctive assumptions—about, for instance, the knowledge-generating relationships that are possible with the natural world—as obviously flawed or necessitating external testing, reconstruction, or suppression.

We suggest that the typical health-care provider is not in a good position to evaluate claims that compete with those of their own biomedical models of sickness until they learn a great deal about the cultural-intellectual contexts in which such claims take root. This position likewise implies that health professionals appropriately refrain from using knowledge gleaned from patients' stories to control them or persuade them of the superior truth of the biomedical model. A recent publication from the Institute of Medicine, entitled *Health Literacy: A Prescription to End Confusion,* makes clear that this remains a common goal among many medical practitioners.

This publication argues that "to be health literate in America means having the cognitive capacity to comprehend the Western biomedical perspective."[33] It then explores strategies for disseminating this version of health literacy throughout the population. While the authors of *Health Literacy* urge care providers to adapt their communication to patient perspectives, they warn that the "adequacy of [the patient's health literacy]...is affected by culture."[34] There is little subsequent suggestion that allopathic providers might learn anything from the alternative, culturally grounded models for seeking and acting on health knowledge that patients may bring to the medical encounter. The central task for medical practitioners, in this view, seems only to find some way to work around such cultural obstacles with good-natured tolerance.

While we certainly do not urge rejection of the biomedical model, our perspective informed by Radical Indigenism encourages openness to other definitions and sources of health knowledge. We encourage providers to allow at least the *possibility* that they and their culturally distinctive patients might learn *from each other,* exchanging knowledge born of different assumptions and rationalities, as they move toward mutually acceptable therapeutic plans.

We close with some reasons that the medical interview may nevertheless not constitute, for Native American patients, a setting that easily allows for the narrative exchange that Kleinman and his intellectual successors rightly urge health-care professionals to facilitate. The typical medical encounter is brief, averaging only about 15 minutes,[35] while the interlocutor's narrative is long. Although some major themes might have been communicated more quickly, the narrative is not just a package of information that can be stripped down to bullet points. It is a complex performance with multiple parts, including ritual observance that requires the gathering of particular ceremonial objects and access to a setting separate from the interview context. Failing to accommodate the needs of this narrative would have changed it dramatically and probably silenced the speaker. Moreover, the interlocutor's remarks involve cultural and spiritual traditions that many Native American people treat as privileged information to be shared only with trusted others. Doctors who would involve their Native American patients in cross-cultural exchange may have to meet them outside usual professional contexts; there is often no substitute for community engagement.[36]

Naturally, there are limitations to the analysis we undertake. The "Interview Material" section summarizes the opinions and health-care experiences of one Anishnaabe woman. Ideas about health and illness vary greatly from tribe to tribe and even person to person; physicians should not stereotype Native American patients by generalizing our results to all of them. Still, we hope that the narrative we present will sensitize readers to some general features that may distinguish a Native American patient's health perspectives.

Our experimental methodology, which explores novel strategies for collecting, analyzing, and presenting data, imposes another limitation. These strategies make it unlikely that strict scientific evaluative criteria are satisfied. This observation, however, does not distinguish our project from other types of narrative analysis, which have argued that conventional standards such as reliability and validity should be replaced or significantly redefined in relation to this type of work.[37] Moreover, our analysis should be judged in terms of the criteria we specified as relevant for the inquiry: its success in honoring the power of oral communication, distributing narrative power equitably, and privileging creative process as a means of knowledge acquisition.

CONCLUSION

In conclusion, we have applied the theoretical perspective of Radical Indigenism to guide the analysis of a patient's narrative about health and illness. In so doing, the authors hope to alert health-care providers to the possibility that a Native American patient's apparent "non-adherence" to some or all elements of a treatment plan may have complex origins that should not be neglected in decisions about care. We encourage health professionals to seek greater familiarity with the cultures of their Native American patients in respectful ways, while appreciating the challenges of achieving it.

NOTES

Manuscript preparation was supported by a Mentored Research Scientist Development Award (1K01AG022434–01A2) from the National Institute on Aging to Eva Garroutte. The authors are grateful to Drs. Catherine Riessman and Sharlene Hesse-Biber for insightful comment on early versions.

1. Arthur Kleinman, *The Illness Narratives: Suffering, Healing, and the Human Condition* (New York: Basic Books, 1988).

2. See, for example, Lynn M. Harter, Phyllis M. Japp, Christina S. Beck, eds., *Narratives, Health, and Healing: Communication Theory, Research, and Practice* (Mahwah, NJ: Lawrence Erlbaum Assoc., 2005); Brian Hurwitz, Trisha Greenhalgh, and Vieda Skultans, *Narrative Research in Health and Illness* (Malden, MA: Blackwell Publishing, 2004); S. Kay Toombs, *The Meaning of Illness: A Phenomenological Account of the Different Perspectives of Physician and Patient* (Boston: Kluwer Academic Publishers, 1992). Reviews in Susan E. Bell, "Experiencing Illness in/and Narrative," in *Handbook of Medical Sociology*, 5th ed., ed. Chloe E. Bird, Peter Conrad, and Allen M. Fremont (Upper Saddle River, NJ: Prentice Hall, 2000),184–99; Lars-Christer Heydén, "Illness and Narrative," *Sociology of Health and Illness* 19, no. 1 (1997): 48–69; Vieda Skultans, "Narrative, Illness and the Body," *Anthropology and Medicine* 7, no. 1 (2000): 5–13.

3. E.g., Glyn Elwyn and Richard Gwyn, "Stories We Hear and Stories We Tell: Analyzing Talk in Clinical Practice," *British Medical Journal* 318 (1999): 186, 187–88; Trisha Greenhalgh, "Narrative Based Medicine in an Evidence Based World," *British Medical Journal* 318 (1999): 323–25. Reviews in Rita Charon, "Narrative Medicine: A Model for Empathy, Reflection, Profession, and Trust," *Journal of the American Medical Association* 286, no. 15 (2001): 1897–1902; Rita Charon, *Narrative Medicine: Honoring the Stories of Illness* (New York: Oxford University Press, 2006).

4. Arthur W. Frank, "The Standpoint of Storyteller," *Qualitative Health Research* 10, no. 3 (2000): 354–65; Arthur W. Frank, *The Wounded Storyteller: Body, Illness, and Ethics* (Chicago: University of Chicago, 1995).

5. Elliot George Mishler, *The Discourse of Medicine: Dialectics of Medical Interviews* (Norwood, NJ: Ablex Publishing Corporation, 1984).

6. Charon, "Narrative Medicine," 1897.

7. Jack A. Clark and Elliot G. Mishler, "Attending to Patients' Stories: Reframing the Clinical Task," *Sociology of Health and Illness* 14, no. 3 (1992): 344–72.

8. J. E. Carrillo, A. R. Green, and J. R. Betancourt, "Cross-cultural Primary Care: A Patient-based Approach," *Annals of Internal Medicine* 130, no. 10 (May 18, 1999): 829–34; Carmen R. Green, "Unequal Burdens and Unheard Voices: Whose Pain? Whose Narratives?" in *Narrative, Pain, and Suffering*, ed. Daniel B. Carr, John D. Loeser, and David B. Morris, *Progress in Pain Research and Management* 34 (Seattle, WA: IASP Press, 2005): 195–214; M. Kagawa-Singer and S. Kassim-Lakha, "A Strategy to Reduce Cross-cultural Miscommunication and Increase the Likelihood of Improving Health Outcomes," *Academic Medicine* 78, no. 6 (2003): 577–87.

9. U.S. Census Bureau, *Statistical Abstract of the United States*, Section 2: Vital Statistics (2003). Available at:. Retrieved January 16, 2006.

10. Ann Garwick, "What Do Providers Need to Know about American Indian Culture? Recommendations from Urban Indian Family Caregivers," *Families, Systems & Health: The Journal of Collaborative Family Health Care* 18, no. 2 (2000): 177–90; Raymond Reid and Everett R. Rhoades, "Cultural Considerations in Providing Care to American Indians," in *American Indian Health: Innovations in Health Care, Promotion, and Policy*, ed. Everett R. Rhoades (Baltimore: Johns Hopkins University Press, 2000); Len Kelly and Judith Belle Brown, "Listening to Native Patients. Changes in Physicians' Understanding and Behaviour," *Canadian Family Physician* 48 (2002): 1645–52.

11. Wynne Dubray and Adelle Sanders, "Interactions between American Indian Ethnicity and Health Care." *Journal of Health and Social Policy* 10, no. 4 (1999): 67–84.

12. The Anishnaabe are a northeastern, Algonquian-speaking people also known by band names including Ojibwe/Ojibwa/Ojibway/Chippewa. Tribal creation stories relate that the Anishnaabe have inhabited this continent from the earliest time of its creation through a vision of Gitchi Manitou, the Great Mystery. Anishnaabe, who follow traditional teachings, are responsible for discovering Gitchi Manitou through interaction with his creations in the natural world and to imitate his selflessness and generosity. They are called to follow the Great Mystery in applying their unique talents in an ongoing and intentional creative process, "continu[ing] the work put into motion by the Creator." Basil Johnston, *The Manitous: The Spiritual World of the Ojibwe* (St. Paul: Minnesota Historical Society Press, 2001): 3.

13. Eva Marie Garroutte, *Real Indians: Identity and the Survival of Native America* (Berkeley: University of California Press, 2003).

14. Reviews in Richard Gwyn, *Communicating Health and Illness* (London: Sage Publications, 2002): 27–81.

15. William Foote Whyte, ed., *Participatory Action Research* (Newbury Park, CA: Sage Publications, 1991).

16. James A. Holstein and Jaber F. Gubrium, "The Active Interview," in *Qualitative Research Methods*, Vol. 37 (Thousand Oaks, CA: Sage, 1995).

17. Elliot G. Mishler, *Research Interviewing: Context and Narrative* (Cambridge, MA: Harvard University Press, 1986).

18. See further Lars-Christer Heydén, "Illness and Narrative," *Sociology of Health and Illness* 19, no. 1 (1997): 48–69.

19. Holstein and Gubrium, "The Active Interview," 77.

20. Catherine Kohler Riessman, "Narrative Interviewing," in *The Sage Encyclopedia of the Social Sciences*, Vol. 2, ed. Michael S. Lewis-Beck, Alan Bryman, and Tim Futing Liao (Thousand Oaks, CA: Sage, 2004): 710.

21. Catherine Kohler Riessman and Lee Quinney, "Narrative in Social Work: A Critical Review," *Qualitative Social Work* 4, no. 4 (2005): 391–412; Catherine Kohler Riessman, "A Short Story about Long Stories," *Journal of Narrative and Life History* 7, nos. 1–4 (1997): 155–58.

22. We find partial precedent for this methodological strategy in the "direct scribing" method proposed by Martin, in which she uses transcribed interviews to facilitate young people in creating written accounts of their lives. Fay E. Martin, "Tales of

Transition: Self-narrative and Direct Scribing in Exploring Care-leaving," *Child and Family Social Work* 3, no. 1 (1998): 1–12.

23. See, for example, John Greco, "Introduction: What Is Epistemology?" in *The Blackwell Guide to Epistemology*, ed. John Greco and Ernest Sosa (Malden, MA: Blackwell Publishing, 1999): 1–31.

24. Gregory A. Cajete, *Look to the Mountain: An Ecology of Indigenous Education* (Durango, CO: Kivaki, 1994), 157.

25. Calvin Luther Martin, *The Way of the Human Being* (New Haven, CT: Yale University Press, 1999), 134ff.

26. The work of Religious Studies scholar Joseph Epes Brown helps expand our idea of beauty as a criterion of evaluation in American Indian philosophies. While recognizing that the artistic expressions of particular tribal peoples are tied to distinctive cultural ideas and values, Brown nevertheless identifies aesthetic themes that commonly reappear across even very diverse tribal contexts. Among these, he suggests, is the idea that beauty is not only a property of the created object. Instead, aesthetic determinations may also depend heavily upon the nature of the *creative process*. These include the integrity of the guiding ritual procedures and the far-reaching complex of *relationships* that the artistic journey invokes and nourishes. Joseph Epes Brown with Emily Cousins, *Teaching Spirits: Understanding Native American Religious Traditions* (New York: Oxford University Press, 2001): 63–66.

The interlocutor's own perspectives as an Anishnaabe woman likewise link ideas about beauty to ideas about ceremonial responsibility and about relationship. As she observed in our discussions for this article: "There is a 'place' within each living being—not just humans—that is at all times in harmony, 'of one mind,' with the whole of creation. This 'place' is eternal, inviolable, unconditionally loving. It is not dependent on form. Often, we come to it through sacred, ritual discipline. When we are sitting in this 'place'—when we are of one mind with the eternal truths that endure even when there is no form—then the things we draw into form are beautiful."

Following, the authors present a storytelling approach that engages similar ideas about the qualities of an aesthetic form, the creator's responsibilities to that form, and understandings about ceremonial responsibility and relationship as aspects of a creative process that gives birth to beauty. We encourage readers to watch for and evaluate the success with which the distinctive aesthetic principles we have described are honored in this effort.

27. "To live in good relationship with all life" is an English translation of the Anishnaabe term *bimaadizinwin*, which is notably difficult to translate. The interlocutor suggests that a looser interpretation might be "to live life to the fullest." Spielman attempts a more elaborate interpretation when he observes that *bimaadizinwin* implies outcomes such as "living a long, fruitful life in communion with family, community, other-than-human persons, the environment, the Creator, and the spirit world—and the responsibility of using the gifts that we are given in the best way that we can." Roger Spielman, *"You're So Fat! Exploring Ojibwe Discourse"* (Toronto, ON: University of Toronto Press, 1998), 160.

28. *Mii'iw* is the Anishnaabe word for ending a story or concluding one's remarks. It may be translated, "This is what I have to say." The subsequent indentation signals the break between the Anishnaabe story and the interlocutor's "ordinary" speech.

29. Frank, *The Wounded Storyteller*, 116.

30. Erwin H. Ackerknecht, "Introduction: An interview with Erwin H. Ackerknecht," in *Medicine and Ethnology: Selected Essays*, ed. H. H. Walser and H. M. Koelbing (Baltimore: The Johns Hopkins University Press, 1971): 17–29.

31. Kleinman, *The Illness Narratives*, 119.

32. Yiannis Gabriel, "The Voice of Experience and the Voice of the Expert—Can They Speak to Each Other?, in *Narrative Research in Health and Illness*, ed. Brian Hurwitz, Patricia Greenhalgh, and Vieda Skultans (Malden, MA: Blackwell Publishing, 2004), 183.

33. Lynn Nielsen, Alison M. Panzer, and David A Kindig, eds. *Health Literacy: A Prescription to End Confusion* (Washington, DC: National Academies Press, 2004), 117. Available at: www.nap.edu.

34. Ibid., 32.

35. Jozien M. Bensing, Debra L. Roter, and Robert L. Hulsman, "Communication Patterns of Primary Care Physicians in the United States and Netherlands," *Journal of General Internal Medicine* 18 (2003): 335–42.

36. Kelly and Brown, "Listening to Native Patients"; Reid and Rhoades, "Cultural Considerations in Providing Care."

37. Holstein and Gubrium, "The Active Interview."

BIBLIOGRAPHY

Ackerknecht, Erwin H. "Introduction: An Interview with Erwin H. Ackerknecht." In *Medicine and Ethnology: Selected Essays*, edited by H. H. Walser and H. M. Koelbing, 17–29. Baltimore: Johns Hopkins University Press, 1971.

Bell, Susan E. "Experiencing Illness in/and Narrative." In *Handbook of Medical Sociology*, 5th ed., edited by Chloe E. Bird, Peter Conrad, and Allen M. Fremont, 184–99. Upper Saddle River, NJ: Prentice Hall, 2000.

Bensing, Jozien M., Debra L. Roter, and Robert L. Hulsman. "Communication Patterns of Primary Care Physicians in the United Sates and Netherlands." *Journal of General Internal Medicine* 18 (2003): 335–42.

Brown, Joseph Epes, with Emily Cousins. *Teaching Spirits: Understanding Native American Religious Traditions*. New York: Oxford University Press, 2001.

Cajete, Gregory A. *Look to the Mountain: Ecology of Indigenous Education*. Durango, CO: Kivaki, 1994.

Carrillo, J. E., A. R. Green, and J. R. Betancourt. "Cross-cultural Primary Care: A Patient-based Approach." *Annals of Internal Medicine* 130, no. 10 (May 18, 1999): 829–34.

Charon, Rita. "Narrative Medicine: A Model for Empathy, Reflection, Profession, and Trust," *Journal of the American Medical Association* 286, no. 15 (2001): 1897–1902.

Charon, Rita. *Narrative Medicine: Honoring the Stories of Illness*. New York: Oxford University Press, 2006.

Clark, Jack A., and Elliot G. Mishler. "Attending to Patients' Stories: Reframing the Clinical Task." *Sociology of Health and Illness* 14, no. 3 (1992): 344–72.

Dubray, Wynne, and Adelle Sanders. "Interactions between American Indian Ethnicity and Health Care." *Journal of Health and Social Policy* 10, no. 4 (1999): 67–84.

Elwyn, Glyn, and Richard Gwyn. "Stories We Hear and Stories We Tell: Analyzing Talk in Clinical Practice." *British Medical Journal* 318 (1999): 186–88.

Frank, Arthur W. "The Standpoint of Storyteller." *Qualitative Health Research* 10, no. 3 (2000): 354–65.

Frank, Arthur W. *The Wounded Storyteller: Body, Illness, and Ethics.* Chicago: University of Chicago Press, 1995.

Gabriel, Yiannis. "The Voice of Experience and the Voice of the Expert—Can They Speak to Each Other? In *Narrative Research in Health and Illness,* edited by Brian Hurwitz, Patricia Greenhalgh, and Vieda Skultans. Malden, MA: Blackwell Publishing, 2004.

Garroutte, Eva Marie. *Real Indians: Identity and the Survival of Native America.* Berkeley: University of California Press, 2003.

Garwick, Ann. "What Do Providers Need to Know about American Indian Culture? Recommendations from Urban Indian Family Caregivers. *Families, Systems & Health: The Journal of Collaborative Family Health Care* 18, no. 2 (2000): 177–90.

Greco, John. "Introduction: What Is Epistemology?" In *The Blackwell Guide to Epistemology,* edited by John Greco and Ernest Sosa, 1–31. Malden, MA: Blackwell Publishing, 1999.

Green, Carmen R. "Unequal Burdens and Unheard Voices: Whose Pain? Whose Narratives?" In *Narrative, Pain, and Suffering,* edited by Daniel B. Carr, John D. Loeser and David B. Morris, 195–214. Progress in Pain Research and Management, no. 34. Seattle, WA: IASP Press, 2005.

Greenhalgh, Trisha. "Narrative Based Medicine in an Evidence Based World." *British Medical Journal* 318 (1999): 323–25.

Gwyn, Richard. *Communicating Health and Illness.* London: Sage Publications, 2002.

Harter, Lynn M., Phyllis M. Japp, and Christina S. Beck, eds. *Narratives, Health, and Healing: Communication Theory, Research, and Practice.* Mahwah, NJ: Lawrence Erlbaum Assoc., 2005.

Heydén, Lars-Christer. "Illness and Narrative." *Sociology of Health and Illness* 19, no. 1 (1997): 48–69.

Holstein, James A., and Jaber F. Gubrium. "The Active Interview." In *Qualitative Research Methods.* Vol. 37. Thousand Oaks, CA: Sage, 1995.

Hurwitz, Brian, Trisha Greenhalgh, and Vieda Skultans. *Narrative Research in Health and Illness.* Malden, MA: Blackwell Publishing, 2004.

Johnston, Basil. *The Manitous: The Spiritual World of the Ojibwe.* St. Paul: Minnesota Historical Society Press, 2001.

Kagawa-Singer, M., and S. Kassim-Lakha. "A Strategy to Reduce Cross-cultural Miscommunication and Increase the Likelihood of Improving Health Outcomes." *Academic Medicine* 78, no. 6 (2003): 577–87.

Kelly, Len, and Judith Belle Brown. "Listening to Native Patients. Changes in Physicians' Understanding and Behaviour." *Canadian Family Physician* 48 (2002): 1645–52.

Kleinman, Arthur. *The Illness Narratives: Suffering, Healing, and the Human Condition.* New York: Basic Books, 1988.

Kohler Riessman, Catherine. "A Short Story about Long Stories." *Journal of Narrative and Life History* 7, nos. 1–4 (1997): 155–58.

Kohler Riessman, Catherine. "Narrative Interviewing." In *The Sage Encyclopedia of the Social Sciences,* 710, edited by Michael S. Lewis-Beck, Alan Bryman, and Tim Futing Liao. Vol. 2. Thousand Oaks, CA: Sage, 2004.

Kohler Riessman, Catherine, and Lee Quinney. "Narrative in Social Work: A Critical Review." *Qualitative Social Work* 4, no. 4 (2005): 391–412.

Martin, Calvin Luther. *The Way of the Human Being.* New Haven, CT: Yale University Press, 1999.

Martin, Fay E. "Tales of Transition: Self-Narrative and Direct Scribing in Exploring Care-Leaving." *Child and Family Social Work* 3, no. 1 (1998): 1–12.

Mishler, Elliot G. *The Discourse of Medicine: Dialectics of Medical Interviews.* Norwood, NJ: Ablex Publishing Corporation, 1984.

Mishler, Elliot G. *Research Interviewing: Context and Narrative.* Cambridge, MA: Harvard University Press, 1986.

Nielsen, Lynn, Alison M. Panzer, and David A Kindig, eds. *Health Literacy: A Prescription to End Confusion.* Washington, DC: National Academies Press, 2004.

Reid, Raymond, and Everett R. Rhoades. "Cultural Considerations in Providing Care to American Indians." In *American Indian Health: Innovations in Health Care, Promotion, and Policy,* ed. Everett Rhoades. Baltimore: Johns Hopkins University Press, 2000.

Skultans, Vieda. "Narrative, Illness and the Body," *Anthropology and Medicine* 7, no. 1 (2000): 5–13.

Spielman, Roger. *"You're So Fat! Exploring Ojibwe Discourse."* Toronto: University of Toronto Press, 1998.

Toombs, S. Kay. *The Meaning of Illness: A Phenomenological Account of the Different Perspectives of Physician and Patient.* Boston: Kluwer Academic Publishers, 1992.

U.S. Census Bureau. "Statistical Abstract of the United States." Section 2: Vital Statistics (2003). Available at http:// www.census.gov/prod/www/ststistical-abstract-2001_2005.html (accessed March 21, 2008).

Whyte, William Foote, ed. *Participatory Action Research.* Newbury Park, CA: Sage Publications, 1991.

CHAPTER 9

—— ❖ ——

If All These Great Stories Were Told, Great Stories Will Come!

Rodney Frey, with Thomas Yellowtail and Cliff SiJohn

Upon retelling the last of a series of his most cherished stories from the Buffalo Days, Tom Yellowtail, a Crow elder, turned to me and shared the following words that have resonated ever since. "If all these great stories were told, great stories will come!" His favorite was that of Burnt Face, which along with others, he wanted recorded so future generations would always remember.[1] All my professional life has been involved with facilitating the telling of the stories of other people, certainly in collaboration, and hopefully appropriately and respectfully. Prominent among the stories of others have been those of Tom Yellowtail and Cliff SiJohn, a Coeur d'Alene elder.

The Crow refer to the act of storytelling with the expression, *baaeechichiwaau*, literally meaning, "retelling one's own." As with many tribes, the Crow adhere to the importance of retelling—to one's elders, family, and friends—those experiences that have been personally transformative and life changing. In this chapter I will be repositioning myself, indeed "retelling one's own" story. This would certainly be a new role for me, entered into with some degree of reluctance and with a great degree of humility. Should I retell my own story? Is it appropriate? Could it be of any value to others? But in re-listening to Burnt Face, the answers were provided. It is a retelling, in fact, only made possible by the story-gifts Tom, Cliff and others have so generously facilitated for me. Retold here will be Tom's *Burnt Face*, along with other great stories, as I have lived them through my own healing journey. Joining our stories will be those of Cliff. And let us see what great stories may come.

As with so many elders, in the storytelling of Tom Yellowtail and Cliff SiJohn, lessons are to be discovered by the listener with effort, embedded within the story. They are seldom made explicit by the teller. The lessons gained may, in fact, differ from listener to listener. In accord with a storytelling session, this essay will unfold as story, the voices of three tellers interwoven within its distinct pedagogy.

As we considered the best way to convey the meaning within our voices, both Tom and Cliff elected to format their segments reflective of the oral nuance of their telling. To reflect a sense of the dynamic rhythm in their words, we have italicized voiced inflections and stresses, and added a series of dot ellipses to approximate the duration of pauses, from brief (two dot) to longer (three dot and four dot). Paragraph demarcations reflect the critical segments selected for this presentation. My text formatting lacks these oral nuance considerations. The edited segments of Tom's *Burnt Face* are based upon a 1993 audio recorded transcription and a conversation we had at that time on the use of the oral nuance format. His words appear below under "Into the Fire" and immediately follow the subheadings of our unfolding story. Cliff's words are transcribed from two short segments of a 1997 recording we did together and from a 2006 recorded conversation I had with Cliff. To begin to appreciate and access something of the power of storytelling, the reader is encouraged to become a listener. Have someone read the words aloud to you. A great story is to be experienced as it is told. We begin with Tom Yellowtail.

Into the Fire

In the *days* when they *still*...move about the country...the *territory* where the Crow Indians...roam...about...moving from one place to another...is this area...comprising...the rivers...the Little Bighorn...the Bighorn...the Yellowstone River...*and the* Missouri River...and the Indians...would follow some of these rivers...move about every few days, *from way down there* next to the North Dakota border line...on up this way toward these Bighorn Mountains....

In the evening...in the camp...the children...would play...build a bonfire or something like that...and play...and this one night they *did* build a bonfire...and they were chasing each other around playing games....and a young lad of about the age of this boy here now...I'd say the lad was probably...was probably about ten years old....they were all playing around this bonfire...chasing each other...and while they were playing like that...chasing each other... some were standing back and others would be chasing around each other... and *somebody*....gave a push to this one boy as he was going...the fire over here...and when he got pushed he *fell into* that...into that bonfire which burned him pretty bad...before they rescued him...pulled him out...but he was burned already...pretty bad...into the bonfire...the *big fire* he fell into....

And...that accident happened so the...the other children all quit playing...for one of them got hurt...and...the child was taken to his...camp... his parent's camp...and they took care of him...

And the next few days...the *sores* started from that *burn*...on his *face*.... and he was *burned* so...so much that...his face had to...sores were on and finally come to...to *heal* as *scabs*....and...he would still try to play with his other friends...yet...but his face was *disfigured then* after these...sores had healed...and tightened up and his face was...*disfigured*...

We never know when we might get pushed into a bonfire. In December 2005, I was diagnosed with third-stage Hodgkin's lymphoma. I was a fit 55, or so I thought, happily married with a wonderful family, professionally successful, and about to begin a most unanticipated journey that threatened it all. I blamed no one. In fact, I felt no anger. But it could not be ignored. The cancer had to be acknowledged and dealt with. Based upon my particular staging, a protocol of 6 cycles of 12 chemotherapy treatments lasting some 6 months and involving a recipe of ABVD (chemotherapy) drugs was prescribed. I put my faith in my doctors, with the chemo and all the biomedical treatments they offered. In turn, I looked after my body as best I could, trying to eat well and continue my morning runs, until I couldn't, then power walks through the nearby arboretum. When I could, I fly-fished the local reservoirs and rivers: "for therapy," I told my wife. But the question lurked—is there something else I should do?

Solitary Journey

And the other kids would make fun of him...*"ahh...look at him...look at his funny...ugly face!"*...and all that....and that made the boy...*ashamed*...he felt ashamed the way the other kids would make fun of him...an ugly face....

So...he didn't like that and he wanted to leave camp...be away from... staying in camp....so...he...he got bedding and...and things to stay away from the camp....*when the camp move about*...he'd travel along the side of them...I'd say probably a half a mile away from them or so...and he doesn't come into camp for he is *ashamed*...of what the other kids would make fun of him...when they look at him....and...so he stayed that way...his parents would try to bring him back and he won't do it....he has his bedding...he stays there and they bring food for him...and he's sad and he doesn't come back into the camp...to play with the other...his friends...other children....

Whether by choice or being somehow marked by the big "C," I certainly felt out of the norm, differentiated from my students, colleagues, and family as my hair thinned and fatigue overcame me. On campus I was greeted by concern, by those willing to engage me, or by silence by those, perhaps, not sure how to engage. As my once thick eyebrows vanished, so too it seemed did my recognition: I was traveling incognito! Though I cut back on many of my faculty responsibilities, I deliberately chose not to "stay away from camp," continuing my full teaching load and work with my graduate students. Nevertheless, in so many ways, it is indeed a solitary journey.

Taking to the Mountains

And...*as the camp move about*...moving about...toward the Bighorn Mountains....and *he*...he had in mind...as they were approaching the Bighorn Mountains...he thought to himself...*"now* when we get to this Bighorn

Mountains...I'll...I'll quit staying alone...with my people...my parents...
my parents are among the group in that camp....*I'll leave* them when we get to
these mountains...and take the mountains...and go up somewhere and fast..."

A short time after being diagnosed I was having lunch with Cliff SiJohn,
sharing the situation with him. His words helped initiate the critical path in
my journey, my taking to the mountains. Cliff emphasized the importance of
appreciating the distinct, though interrelated, processes of both the *exterior
healing* and the *inner healing*. "Listen with your heart," he said. While putting
my full faith in my oncologist, my surgeon, my family physician, my nurses—
for the external healing, I would need to attend to my inner healing as well.
But in what ways? Where within should I look?

It was 1974. I had just completed my masters degree in anthropology, and
was offered an opportunity to conduct my first ethnographic research, sponsored by the Crow Tribe of Montana. I was to assemble an introductory paper
that presented "traditional" Crow perspectives on the causes and treatments
of illness. It would be used to help Indian Health Service physicians better
communicate with and deliver health care to their Crow patients. Among
the elders, it was suggested I interview Tom Yellowtail.

I remember our first meeting. The sun was gazing down into the Lodge,
and Tom Yellowtail was dressed in his Sundance regalia, offering prayers with
the hundred or so other Sundancers. He was the medicine man running the
Dance. I was absolutely unfamiliar with the form of intense prayer I was now
observing. Held during the height of the summer, Sundancers give of themselves for the welfare of family members, dancing and fasting from food and
water for the three and sometimes four days of the Dance. On occasion, a
dancer might "take a hard fall," as he or she received a vision and "medicine."[2] After the Dance, Tom invited me to his home for a visit and to learn
more about his Sundance ways, a learning that would continue for years to
come.

The next summer I was again at the Yellowtail Sundance, along with my
wife and six-month old son, Matt. We came early so I could assist the dancers
with the hard work of setting up the Sundance Lodge. We would be going
to the mountains and bringing back the 12 lodgepole pine poles, used as the
overhead rafters, cutting and bringing back the cottonwood "Center Tree,"
and constructing the lodge itself. My wife and I didn't see much of our son
that first afternoon, as Matt was placed in a beautifully beaded cradle board
and carried around to the various tipi and wall-tent camps by his many new,
adoring "grandmothers." I also remember standing at the Lodge door as the
dancers, with their Eagle-bone whistles blowing to the beat of the drum,
charged the Center Tree and danced back from it. I was beginning to appreciate the personal stories and sacrifices of these dancers. Just then, tears filled
my eyes, my knees buckled as I sat down crying uncontrollably.

During the winter of 1976, Matt suddenly became very ill. I was a desperate parent, reaching out to the only way that seemed to offer any hope for my ailing son. As we drove to the hospital, I pledged to give of myself in prayer, going without food and water, for a three day fast for my son's recovery. At his welcoming and under his guidance, Tom Yellowtail helped me with that fast and much more. Over the next months and years I would receive a number of very special gifts, including the health of my son, as well as an introduction to Tom's favorite story—*Burnt Face*—along with an appreciation of something all together unexpected that happens in the act of telling the stories. As Cliff SiJohn explains:

> When you *tell* a story…it goes *far beyond* being a…myth or a…entertainment…it has to do with how you walk *this life* the Creator has given you…and *that life* is pointed in a certain way because of the First People *who come alive* in the story…and who can *swirl around you*…as the Turtle is saying his thing or as the Chipmunk is saying something…they swirl around you and you feel that Indian medicine so strong…because there is a *significant feeling* about being so close to the Animal People…*they are the ones who taught us to live.*… this is Chipmunk talking to you…this Coyote talking to you.…this is the Elk talking to you…and the Deer and the Eagle…and this is the *Hawk* what he said…of how to live our lives.…so…when we're telling the stories…when it comes through *the heart* and out of the mouth…the heart then cleanses it to make it *pure*…that *the power* of the Animal People…is still here.… *all these things*…suddenly come *alive*…and they're just as *alive* as they were a thousand years ago…that these were the First People…they were the ones who *led us* to the lives we have right now.…

Timing can be most intriguing. In the early fall of 2005, I had Cliff down to campus as a guest speaker in my freshmen, year-long World Religions course. Over 200 students from other sections of this course attended. We gathered on a grassy hillside, as the sun began to set and a hawk circled above. Cliff spoke of his family's ways, but what he wanted most to emphasize for these students was the importance of "strapping on their cedar-bark baskets" and "going to the mountains to gather huckleberries." It would be hard work going up to those mountains and searching for, and finding, the right berry patches; then picking those berries with care, not harming the bushes, keeping those berries safe, and storing them to be used later—to nourish and feed others and themselves. "Cherish those berries." During the year ahead, it would be these most valuable berries that would be added to each student's basket, as lessons, teachings, insights, all special "gifts." As if speaking to each student individually, Cliff charged them to listen with their hearts and minds to what their teachers would be offering. It will be hard work, but these gifts of berries, unique for each student, would come to nourish them, and in times of challenge, help protect them.

Around the same time as Cliff's visit to my class, Valerie Jackson, one of Tom Yellowtail's granddaughters, contacted me needing to "hear my grandpa's voice again." Tom had passed on "to the other side camp" in November 1993. But Tom's *Burnt Face* would again be "retold." With an internet search, Valerie had found the web page on Tom and Susie Yellowtail I developed for my students. On that page was a streaming, audio segment of Tom's *Burnt Face* story, recorded in the summer before his passing. Valerie felt this particular healing story would be of immense help for her own son who was beginning a treatment program for his methamphetamine addiction. I made a compact disk of Tom's entire telling of the *Burnt Face* story lasting over 40 minutes and sent it to her.

With these two serendipitous crossings, I was reintroduced to a young lad's journey and took a hard look into my own berry basket, revisiting my gifts of 30 years ago. As I listened carefully to Tom Yellowtail's words, they revealed themselves in ways seemingly all together new, fresh, and poignant, and in ways that spoke directly to something I was about to begin. Reflecting into my own basket of berry gifts, it would be this "great story" that would chart the path of inner healing Cliff had asked me to consider and engage, and on which other gifts of berries would be placed and applied. As I would give voice to *Burnt Face* with my heart and through my actions, Burnt Face comes alive and swirls around me. With Burnt Face, I would attempt not only to make sense of my situation, but make my own story actively engage and plot its unfolding. And together we take to the mountains. As I had done for my son some 30 years ago, I would now do for myself.

Preparing for the Journey

So...he told his parents...to make him several pairs of moccasins...and to prepare when the men go *hunting* and making jerky...to save up...plenty of jerky... to take with him when he leaves...when they get to the mountains...and quite a few extra pairs of moccasins...and enough...enough clothing to...to leave the camp...the camp could go on and he'd take to the mountains...and fast somewhere...."I'll go do that...if I return...if I'm lucky to do my fasting...and I may return to my people....if not...if something happens to me...why that...that'll be it...that'll be alright"....he *knew* those conditions...but he decided he's going to *leave* the camp...they can go on...and he would...he would *leave* the camp and take to the mountains and fast somewhere....

So...the parents prepared all those extra pairs of moccasins for him...*things he would need* for him to get along with...and the jerky...for the food...so he could spend quite a few days...quite awhile...before he...would return to his people....he wanted to do that fasting....*so*...*alright*...he was determined to do that fasting....

So...they got to the mountains...and he bid his folks goodbye for awhile... other friends..."now you folks go on and I'll...I'll take these mountains and I'll find a place where I'll fast...for quite awhile"....*so* he left the camp and he took to the mountains and went south…along the mountain range…kept on…traveling…into Wyoming…kept traveling south and finally he come to a place…*"I believe this is a good place"*…where the present Medicine Wheel is now.…he come to that place…look things over the country…*"right here is where I will…fast!"*.…

Soon family and friends were making jerky and extra moccasins. When Rob Moran, my "elder bro," a Turtle Mountain Chippewa, first heard the news he immediately drove over some 350 miles from his Warm Springs, Oregon home, to offer prayers, salmon from the Deschutes River, and much needed laughter. In my backyard, the Sweat rocks were heated and we entered the Little Lodge. Rob tied strips of blue and white cloth to the overhead saplings supporting the Lodge's coverings, renewing its connection with the Sundance Lodge and to the two Flags of the Center Tree. With his medicine things laid out before us and the burning of cedar, Rob asked the Creator to watch over his "younger bro," and all those in need of help. Each week thereafter, Rob called and sent e-mails, offering a joke or a story, an update on the family, and his concerns.

A short time later Josiah Pinkham, a close Nez Perce friend, had me down to his home just south of Lapwai for a "Healing Sweat" and a meal of traditional foods. Joined by two elders and his brother, it was a powerful Sweat of prayers, sharing, and heart talk. As Josiah said, "we wanted you to know that we would be there with you for your entire journey." One of the elders, Leroy Seth, shared even more, "a little bonus," he said with a smile. As he sat next to me in the darkened Lodge, the steam thick in the air, Leroy began to swoon and became listless. Once outside and clearheaded, he told us that while in the Lodge he "heard a song, coming from near the fire pit, sung by the Little People or maybe Children!" He went on to relate how he had felt and shouldered some of my challenges, a "gift to you." After the meal, Josiah presented me with a beautiful Pendleton blanket, while his wife, D'Lisa, gave me a candle in a dragonfly holder and a supply of *qhasqhs,* a medicine root used in the Sweat Lodge. I had brought with me my Buffalo Skull, wrapped in a black blanket, a blanket Leroy had given me a couple of years prior as part of his give away. I presented it to Josiah. In the days leading up to the Sweat, it had come to me that the Skull should now belong to Josiah. I had received it many years before from Joseph Epes Brown,[3] when I taught his courses for him during a sabbatical. With the Sweat being so critical in the preparation for any journey, Cliff offers the following thoughts on its significance and use, and of the potential of being "reborn." As Cliff explains:

We have the Sweat House…the Sweat Lodge…was *given* to us by the Creator.…the way I was taught…and practice is that the Sweat Lodge is the *womb*…of the Mother…Earth…and when we go in…we go in…*naked*…we go into that…*dome* that is made up of…*cedar sticks*…we go into that...*womb* that is dressed on the floor...with cedar boughs and up into the bow...is stuck different medicine things...tied a little something...sister's hair...mother's hair...father's...something *significant* to you...

You go in there to *pray* to the Creator...for...many different things...but never *specifically* about..."oh...I want this...oh...I want that...bring this to me...bring me money...bring me women"....that's not the purpose...you go in there pray for *good things* to happen to your people...for the old people... for their pain to *go away*...so they have an easy time this winter...you go in there to pray *to take* the borrowed things that we now have and *learned* from a different society...jealousy and greed...hatred...for each other...we pray to the *Amotqn*...to the Creator...in this womb...of Mother Earth...

And the things that are inside of you come out...in the form of *sweat*... comes onto your body...and the hotter you have those rocks...the rocks come *alive*...and the more water you put on them...make heat and you *suffer*... suffer for your people...suffer for your *mother*...suffer for your father...suffer for your *grandma*...who had no doctor when she had children...*suffer* for that umbilical cord that connects us...*all the way*...generation to generation to generation to generation...suffer...for the people....

It is to help you...open up...your spirit...so it can gain the power...of the Animal world...and you can *rejuvenate* yourself....*re*...*charge* yourself...to *heal yourself* from the inside...just like you crawl inside the womb...of the Mother Earth...you also crawl inside yourself...and *all of those things* that have been...keeping you *out of balance*...will come out in the form of *sweat*...and when you crawl out...you are weak...you go and take cold water...throw it on yourself...*hard*...from the top of your head clear down...you *rub* yourself...rub that sweat so it goes into the water...onto the ground...and *all* those things in your heart that have been hurting...all those poisons in your body that come out...that water will take that *away* into the ground...into the creeks...into the rivers...take it away from you...

That's...the *power*...of the Animal world...*the power* of the Jump Dance is in everyone of those Sweat Lodges...the Sweat Lodge was given to us by the Creator to help us find the way to heal ourselves...*find* our way to clear our minds...in a clean pure way...to separate ourselves *from the sweat* that keeps us out of balance...so that whatever was troubling us is gone....this is what that *womb* will do...when you come out you are reborn again...clean like a baby... and we have to do that many times...because of the *pitifulness* of our lives...

On campus, two friends and colleagues—one Yaqui and "adopted" Shoshone-Bannock, and the other Nez Perce—brought gifts. Ed Galindo smudged my office and me with cedar and prayer, leaving me with a supply of cedar and advice—eat lots of meat and drink four liters of water daily. I left him with a small Eagle feather I had been gifted many years ago. Sarah Penney, along with her dad and some of the Native students, gave me a basket of "healing," including traditional gifts—a fishing hook, sweetgrass, mountain tea, and cous root her family had collected. As Cliff explains, such things, like cedar, are gifts to the people, given a long time ago.

Cedar...came to our people...in a *dream* to some medicine people...the people were sick and they *couldn't do* anything for them...and so during this one *particular night* ...these Animal People...First People came to them...and there was *Blue Jay*...and there was *Hawk*...and there was *Badger*...and they came to the people and said "we want *to show* you something"...so they took these people out of this tipi where they were all sick and took them to this tree...they prayed around this Tree...the First People..."this Tree is going to help you...*the whole Tree*...the *roots*...*the bark*...*the leaves*"...so that's when we began using the cedar...because it was given to them...by the...First People ...

So...we use the cedar for purification as well as medicine...and mixing it with other things...for *salve*...and then to *tie* things on...for *traveling*...cedar *strips* are so strong...they made *baskets*...the cedar weavings from this bark....the cedar...the tips of the leaves...lay them out...strip them *off*...dry them...pound them...and put them in a bag...or cut the boughs...put them in our house...put them in...where *prayers* are offered...put them inside of the Sweat House...so when you come out...the cedar's on your *head*...to protect your *head*...to clean your *brain* and your head...your eyes...your throat....then there's the *root* to make a *tea*...you smash it up and then it is mixed to make a *blood cleansing* thing....these are the things I *still* use at home...me and my kids when we go out and collect them...and when we go collecting we take the little guys and we talk to them about it...the importance of *not destroying* the Tree...

Oh how we want to act always according to our desired outcomes. But we are reminded that we may "return to our people, but if not, if something happens..." It is indeed a journey, a journey of steps—many mine, many of others as well—the destination of which far from certain. While I didn't want to lose sight of my dream of what could be, I also felt I needed to attend to, with my best effort each day, my part of the journey. I trusted my oncologist to do her part. With proper treatment, I was told the prognosis for Hodgkin's can be good. Sitting under an IV drip for three hours, receiving a recipe of chemo drugs and knowing of their varied side effects, can be a very trusting experience. Family and friends had generously done their parts, and their prayers continued. But for my part of the journey, would each step be my best?

Rocks of the Medicine Wheel

So he did...he started fasting there...right where the Medicine...Wheel is now....he fasted there and *during the day*...where he fasted...a lot of the place is just rocky...formations of rocks...all around him....*so during the day*...he would gather...the rocks...and he started forming...a circle...representing the Lodge...the Lodge you seen nowadays that comprise...the Sundance Lodge...*he built*...that large circle...everyday he'd pile up rocks on top of...to form a circle...and at the doorway toward the rising Sun to the east....*he made it big*...and everyday he works...and the *spokes* that lead to the *center*...he piles up rocks leading to the center....what you see now on a...Sundance Lodge...it is round…with a doorway leading towards the Sun…to the east where the Sun rises.…*and he built* that according to the…to the form of a Sundance Lodge…built it according to the Sundance Lodge.…

   And…no telling how many…he must of stayed there a month or so.…and he fasted…fasted there…every day says his prayers…he has tobacco…with him…and a good supply of tobacco…and he'd fill up his pipe and offer smokes…to the Great Spirit…and he went that way on all these days of fasting.…

Every day I say my prayers. Each evening before going to bed, I would sing the Song of the Tree, the fourth song sung each morning during the sunrise ceremony of the Sundance, the song also sung in preparation of the Center Tree of the Sundance Lodge. And with that song, prayers would go out to those in my family and to others, all those in need, asking help and giving thanks. In my backyard, the Sweat rocks would be periodically heated, cedar and water placed upon them and prayers spoken in the Little Lodge, the Younger Brother of the Big Lodge, the Sundance Lodge. Each full moon my medicine bundle would be opened, its contents renewed and prayers offered.

   As I reflected on Cliff's paths of *inner healing* and *external healing*, the image of the Burnt Face's Medicine Wheel took on a new significance. Tom had often shared with me his vision that the world was like a "great wagon wheel," akin to the structure of the Sundance Lodge, the pattern of its dancers, and the Medicine Wheel itself. The spokes represent the separate paths to the center, the distinct religions and peoples of the world, each with their own ways, languages and traditions. Nevertheless each spoke is of equal importance. The wheel would fail to turn if some spokes were longer than the others, or eliminated all together; all are needed if the wheel is to turn. Yet all the spokes are linked to the same hub, the same source, the Creator, though each spoke might conceive of it and address it distinctly. During their lives, Tom was both the Sundance Chief for his people, as well as a devout Baptist, while Susie danced alongside her husband and practiced biomedicine as a registered nurse.

   It was a journey of quite awhile, and all my patience and perseverance would be needed. During that fast in 1976 for my son's health, not only had I an opportunity to fulfill a vow and help my son, but an important lesson—a berry gift—was also received and now remembered. I had been offering my prayers with tobacco, using the Eagle-feather fan, going without food and water, as Tom Yellowtail had instructed. It happened during the evening of the third night before I was to come down off the hill the next day. A tremendous uneasiness, verging on panic, overcame me. I lit a cigarette, held it out toward the east, and prayed. As the smoke ascended so, too, would my prayer. Another cigarette and then a third were lit from the fire of the previous. I prayed hard, still so unsettled. Then he appeared. Just to the south, not more than a few feet away, one of the Little People stood silent, watching. And with his appearance, a calm came over me and I felt protected. And I realized the cause of my anxiety. That evening I had acted in anticipation of desired results, confident that I alone had achieved something of importance. But, in fact, I had achieved nothing by myself, on a journey not yet completed. As in all our journeys, others do their parts. Tom had been saying his prayers, and his Medicine Fathers, and Spirit Helpers were watching over and making all this possible. Ultimately, it is not a solitary journey. After I came down from my fast, Tom and I sweated, giving prayers of thanks. And Tom asked if I would like to continue my prayers for my son, joining him later that summer in the Sundance.

Along with the days of fatigue and nights of sleepless worry, there were also days of feeling *so normal*. It was as if the weeks of chemo and their side effects were a distant memory. Especially on such occasions, I didn't want to slip into thinking *I* had made it, becoming *self*-confident. In those moments of worry or of conceit, it was the presence and watching over by so many that helped provide the patience and perseverance I would need for the long haul.

I, too, attended to a Medicine Wheel. The Crow word for sincerity is often rendered, *díakaashe*, meaning to do something with determination, with effort, literally "he/she really did it." Sincerity was the most important gift that could be given by someone in return for the health of another or, as with Burnt Face, the ultimate gift given if the Little People or other Spirit Helpers were to "adopt" you. One's sincerity, found along that path of one's inner journey, necessitates a listening with all your heart, of getting in touch with what is most essential. It's a listening to the qualities others have identified within you, or, perhaps, have charged you with becoming. Through his offering of a rock Medicine Wheel, Burnt Face sought to identify and give his best effort, his *díakaashe*, and so, too, would I.

Of particular urgency was how I would understand my cancer, laying a foundation for my Medicine Wheel. So many spoke of it as an "enemy" to be confronted and defeated, a "battle" to be won. But for me this conceptualization just didn't feel right. To do so, at some core level, felt as if I would be rendered akin to that which I confronted and adrift from what I cherished most. I would become enemy. After all, Burnt Face battled no great adversary. I certainly understood my cancer as an enormous, potentially deadly obstacle. But it was to be approached as something to be jumped over, around, and through, something to be left behind. I would seek to fill my healing path with the gifts of huckleberries that have come to embody much of what is most essential to who I am. Two of these gifts came during my early Sundancing years, and became pivotal rocks in my Medicine Wheel.

In 1977 Susie Yellowtail, Tom's wife, said that if I were to continue to "go in and use the whistle," to Sundance, I would need an Indian name. During a medicine bundle opening, held in their home, Grandpa Tom and Grandma Susie bestowed an Indian name on their newly adopted grandson, *Maakuuxshiichúilish* (Seeking to Help Others). A tremendous honor, and a huge responsibility, was conferred. It is a name I would strive to bring forth in all that I do.

While shouldering an enormous challenge and withdrawing from some of my faculty duties, I did not now want to compromise such a defining part of myself. So I continued with my full teaching load and work with my graduate students on their thesis research and end-of-semester defenses. I was up-front about my situation, periodically updating my students on my journey, though not wanting to engender on their parts any sort of sympathy. If my journey could be used by any of my students as an example of how a person can navigate a serious illness or any dire situation, then others would be helped. Reiterating Cliff's words of last fall, I told the students that each of them have and will continue to receive their own particular special gifts, filling their baskets with berries, and gifts received from a mentor, a friend, a grandparent, or a teacher—identify and cherish them. And all of them will encounter unexpected challenges along their own journeys. "It may be next year or 30 years from now that you may need to call upon your gifts, your cherished huckleberries, to get you through a tough time."

In 1978, I had received a second defining gift during my fourth Sundance, completing the cycle I had pledged for the health of my son, Matt. As I charged the Center Tree and danced back, Eagle-plumes in hand and blowing my Eagle-bone whistle in cadence to the beat of the drum, I kept my gaze on the mounted Buffalo Head, hung from the Tree, facing me. Many of the over one hundred men and women dancers were also up and dancing. Looking in from the Lodge's door stood family and friends offering their encouragement. I wore with pride the beautiful belt Lucy Real Bird had beaded for me. As I danced I remember being overwhelmed by a feeling of comfort, I felt safe, I let go and danced all the harder. After some time and recognizing what was happening, the other dancers sat down and the singers beat with increased intensity. Every charge took more of my rapidly diminishing strength.

I am not sure how much time had passed, but I do remember seeing the Dance continue without me, as my body lay there on the ground. And then I was in a deep, dark canyon, with sharp rock ridges on each side, looking up into the sky. Then I was in a thick pine forest, still searching up into the sky, with the jagged tree line on each side of me. Now I was in an open cottonwood grove, looking up, with a more subtle, flowing tree line. Then I was no longer looking up, but was up, in the clouds, rounded and white, but still striving to see something. And then I realized I would not see anything out there. I was looking through the eyes of *Bishée*, with his horns on either side of my head, viewing the clouds all around me. I was Buffalo. Then I was back again in the Lodge.

Following the Sundance, Grandpa Tom and John Trehero, a Fort Washakie Shoshone medicine man, over a hundred years of age, wanted to hear my story. It was from John that Grandpa had received his medicines. At his direction, John insisted that I never consume the meat of the buffalo, of my Medicine

Father. He also had me give a "give away" for the sponsor of the Dance, Johnny Boy Cummins, to acknowledge and thank him for helping make my gift possible. I presented the sponsor with four things of value I had with me, including the pipe I had recently made with its carved Catlenite stone bowl.

The gift of *Bishée* was something I had not been seeking; this is not supposed to happen to white guys. I would have been honored simply to have been able to give of myself in the three days of fasting and prayer for my son. But I was humbled to receive such a special gift, and knew of the great responsibility with which I had been entrusted. Grandpa instructed me in how to assemble and care for my medicine bundle. On the full moon, I should renew it with the burning of sweet grass or cedar, and offer prayers for those in need. Over the next years, at those times of indecision or challenge, I would always turn to it and seek its counsel. *Bishée* would help guide and give me strength. It was *Bishée*, along with *Akbaatatdía* (the One Who Has Made Everything), and the Creator that I addressed in my evening prayers. It is *Bishée* and *Maakuuxshiichúlish* that are essential to who I am, rocks of my Medicine Wheel offering.

They Come Out

And right by are the cliffs...*caves*...where...you hear about the Little People....*they are there*...and they're there yet today....*finally*...the Little People come out...they'd been watching him...they come out...and they...they said "Young man...you have been here for awhile...we've been watching you...you're fasting...you've said your prayers...and you've spent enough time here...and you've built this...representing a Sundance Lodge...*it is good...now we want to adopt you...we want to give you medicine...we want you to quit your fasting and you go back to your people.*...your people are at that place...your parents and the rest of them....you get back...back to your people...don't stay away from them....

We'll take those scars away from you so you'll look...look decent...so you won't be ashamed to get back into your people....and...the *medicine things* we will give you...you will have them...and...you pray for people...doctor people...when you are back home you'll have the power we are giving you...all these powers....so...you exercise...using your medicines when you get back to your people....and you will be a medicine man among your people and eventually become *a chief*...of your tribe"....

"*So*...alright...I will leave...I'll go back"....

Cliff asked if I would join him in his family's Jump Dance. His family welcomed all in the community, setting an early March date for the Dance. The Jump Dance is the Coeur d'Alene's most important annual ceremony, held over two nights, from dusk to dawn, during the height of the winter.[4] Kris, my wife, and Jennifer Gatzke, one of my graduate students, also accompanied me, having done so in the past. We planned to attend only the first night.

Kris and I greeted Cliff and his wife Lori that evening with three small gifts—a Pendleton blanket in the style I had used while Sundancing, a smaller blanket for Lori's new grandchild, and a porcupine quilled medicine wheel medallion with an Eagle Plume attached, that had been given to me many years ago by a Lakota artist. Soon the air was filled with "heart talk" and *suumesh* (medicine song). Someone would make their way onto the floor, offer heart talk of their family's joys and challenges and then sing his *suumesh*, as others would then join in *jumping,* and dancing with him in support of his family's needs and hopes.

Well into the evening Lori had me join Cliff on the dance floor, as the two of us then walked counterclockwise before the other participants, over one hundred men, women, and children. Knowing Cliff's eyesight was very poor, especially under the dimmed light, was I to have the honor of helping guide Cliff around the dance floor as he sang his *suumesh* songs? And then we stopped and Cliff spoke. Instead of his family, Cliff talked to everyone about me, my relationship with the Crow and the Sundance, what I have meant to him and the Coeur d'Alenes, and asked all to pray for my health. Then he had me give my own heart talk. Alone, I circled the floor and spoke. I don't remember much of what I said, much too nervous I guess.

When I completed my circle, standing again beside Cliff, he announced and bestowed a Coeur d'Alene Indian name on me, *Kw'lkwi'l Sqqi,* meaning "Little Red Hawk." The name is in reference to the red-tailed hawk, as Cliff said, "a patient and observant bird," who then "acts quickly and deliberately." He spoke of me as a "patient observer" who then "acts deliberately," as he "thinks and writes about," and "helps our people." As we returned to our seats, Cliff took his red bandana from around his neck and had me place it around mine, and called me "brother." On such prayerful occasions the red bandana is worn with pride by all the members of the SiJohn family. With the gift of *Kw'lkwi'l Sqqi,* I would have the opportunity to place another rock in my Medicine Wheel.

Having received this special name, I felt I needed to attend the second night and have my give away. But as we were going to our car after the Dance, Cliff and Lori approached and insisted that I spend the next evening at home, resting, and said that they had already taken care of the give away for me. When we spoke next, Cliff said the give away had gone well, and the Sundance blanket had been given to a young Coeur d'Alene girl, now also blessed. In considering the importance of an Indian name and of the rebirth that can come from receiving such a name, Cliff says:

> I never received...a name...for a very long time...and...I went to...Vietnam and when I came back...and...was in the Sweat House with my *father*...and telling him things...about what I had done...and I told him about that inci-dent...during my tour of duty...where we were surrounded by the enemy...I sang a song that *he had* taught me...a long time ago...when I was a young boy...I took the *power* of my *father* and my *T'upyes* (the grandmothers) and I placed it in

front of me...against that enemy...*the enemy didn't take* me that day...and he gave me the name *Circling Song*...we were...completely surrounded and...the song...*whirled* around me and the others that were there that we *survived*...

So my *children*...and *every one* of my grandchildren...down the line...they all have been named...they all carry their names...so to...place a significance on the names is one of the most important things...that us as Indian people carry...and we're known by that name...and it *also* says that when you get and cross the river...cross the creek to the other side...to the other big camps...to those who have died and gone on ahead of you to set up their camps...when they *see you* they will *recognize* you and they will call you by your name...

Well the question probably comes to some..."*well*...I don't *have* an Indian name"...maybe there's a reason for that...maybe when you cross over...someone will greet you...and things will work out in the next world...

I've always said we were *crippled* and *wounded*...by the coming of the fur trader...then the missionary...then the soldiers...then the immigrants...our lives were never the same...*but* when that missionary came...he *immediately* began to take our names away...and he would replace them with names *he* would decide you would carry..."from now on instead of your name being Eagle Head you're going to be called Michael...Gabriel...Mary"...and he took all those names and just threw them down..."*you'll* no longer carry the names of *animals*...that's *devil's stuff*...that's *evil*"...and they were ashamed...some of them...and they...wanting to be *good*...Indians...walked away and took that name...and we still carry that wound with us...it's *prevalent*...it's *everyday*....

I've *always*...told my family that we'll *never* do that...we'll always...keep our *names*...call each other *that* during certain ceremonies...and *never ever* give up...never be wounded....we'll always *carry* our *two* ways to the heaven trails...*one* is our ancient *beliefs*...customs...traditions...and the other way...is a *Christian way*...and *neither* is more powerful than the other...just both headed the same way...*and that's* what the Jesuit...couldn't understand or accept...that our *names* were as *important* and as *strong* as *King George* names...or as strong as...the *La France* names...that our names were...*messengers*...the messengers of the *Amotqn*...the Creator...his messengers were the Animals...his messengers were the First People...and hence we would honor those First People that the Creator placed here and carry their names...Buffalo Head...Eagle Head...Little Hawk...Poor Wolf...it's as close of a name to the Creator...as anything else....

So...we may know somebody for a long time...and that person...when they *walk*...they remind you of something...when they *talk*...when they *do* something...suddenly....as if the *sky* were to open...and a *beam*...of...*sunlight* come down...shine on that person...and then they would *call it*...*get it*...*grab it*...go like this with their finger (reaching out and pulling in with his index finger)...*name it*...and that's how that person got his name...sometimes in Dreams...sometimes in Sweat House...sometimes seeing something...go to Sweat House...think about somebody...praying..."*how* can I see this person...*what do they do* that...they could warrant...such a powerful thing as one of the First People's names?"...

You have two names...very powerful...with the people that gave them to you...gave them in sincerity...in deep sacrament....I am *sure* that...*Tom Yellowtail* thought a long time...about...the trail you walked and what you would be known in the *next* big camp by the people...as well as the people today...in the world you live...as the name he gave you....and *he'll* be *waiting for you*...and when he *sees you*...he'll raise his *hand* and he'll *holler* your name... you can holler back..."I am here"...and he'll say..."come this way ...I have a lodge for you...all set up for you right here my son...you sit here and tell me stories about...what you've been doing"...

So you have your name...that will echo in the mountains...for a long time...Little Red Hawk....when we thought of your name...it came from our *spirit*...who spoke to our hearts...to say *this is* what we will call this man...*this is* what his *name* will be...this is what it will be when...*I call him*...when I see him on the other side...this is what you will be *known as*...we'll holler your name...we'll have a *big*...*feast*...when we both get on the other side...and we'll sit down with *all our people*...and we'll tell stories....

The power of the Creator...the First People...the Animal world...that spirit *jumped* onto our spirit...into your spirit...into your heart....the power of the Creator will come through to you through that Animal spirit...the *power* to heal yourself...the power to be like the Deer who...maybe gets wounded and turns around and *licks* his wound...and take the power of *his*...*juices*...his internal *liquid*...to *close* that wound...*healing* himself from inside....that *aura* of that name surrounds you...you are reborn...again...you reborn with this touch of the power of the Creator...with this name...and that aura that *surrounds* you...and you can *use* that...to take it *internally* to heal yourself....the Creator gives you...the strength from inside...to *heal yourself*...if you *believe*...if you put your...*trust* in the Creator's power that he has given *everyone one of us*...if you open up...your heart to that spirit....*you can lay on a hillside* and you can listen to the Wind and the power of the Wind going through the *Trees* and the Trees will *sing* to you...you'll hear the Bird...*flying*...*hollering*...making his little noise...and you can say..."that is the power...that is inside of me...because of the names that were given to me...by the people who understood the power of that name"....

On the Monday following the Jump Dance, we had another look into the physical territory of my illness. I had taken a baseline Pet/CT scan in December. Because of some intense night sweats I was having, the oncologist wanted this early scan to make sure the chemo recipe was not missing some of the cancer. On Wednesday, my doctor shared the results with Kris and me. There was no indication of any abnormality. A little over two months into the six months of treatment, and there was no sign of my third-stage Hodgkin's, from my left side abdomen up through my chest and into my neck. Incredible news. I am still amazed! I immediately called and shared the news with my Mom, son, sister, uncle, then "bros," Cliff and Rob, and then Josiah and Leroy.

This by no means suggested that the journey was over. The oncologist was very pleased to be sure, but the cancer, I was told, could still exist at a microscopic level, not detectable by the scan. So the chemo continued into June, completing the 12 treatments. And with the chemo new challenges arose.

Knowing you have cancer can certainly be challenge enough, but many of the side effects of the chemotherapy, especially as they continued to manifest themselves along the way, added to the challenge. After each treatment, my white blood count was lowered, increasing my susceptibility to infections; there were days of fatigue and high blood pressure with accompanying edginess, disassociation, and sleepless nights; my testosterone levels were lowered, the cause of those intense night sweats and hot flashes; a blood clot developed in my jugular vein that would remain for months to come; my fingers and thumbs became hypersensitive to the touch, while my toes grew numb; and there was the hair loss and weight gain. In the larger scheme of things, the side effects were nothing too overwhelming. Fatigue was the biggest issue, a constant reminder to pace myself. It was a healing journey, full of all sorts of obstacles and nuisances that needed to be left behind. While my doctors addressed the more serious side effects, I kept saying my prayers and laying out the rocks of my Medicine Wheel. A third Pet/CT scan was taken on July 3, 2006, a month after my last chemo. The results restated those of March—no abnormality. I was watched over and they came out, those scars taken away.

Retelling One's Own and Hearing the Crackling of Fire

So he started back the way he came...and went to the place where the Little People had told him where he will find...your people...probably several days to travel...he's a foot...so one day...here he come into camp....he asked for the chief's camp...and they told him..."there's the chief's camp"...

The chief looked at him...he's grown up already he was a young lad when he left them...he's a young man now and he *didn't* recognize him...*so*...the young man explained to the chief..."I am the boy that got my face burned...and I stayed away from the camp...and I'm...I'm the boy...I've grown up now...I've fasted...like I wanted to...I received my medicine...and *here*...I was asked to return to my people and here I am...I've come back...my parents are here somewhere"...

So the chief said..."*okay...alright...come on in*"...and he call his announcer...a herald we call them...the man who goes around camp making announcements...the chief called the herald...to come and told him the story..."go around camp and tell the different chiefs to come to together and come to my camp...and we'll have a smoke...we have this young man who has returned to us...we will hear his story...we will ask him to tell his story to us"...*so* the herald went around camp...

And there it's a big tipi and there they come in...the chief sits here and they have the boy there....they come and take their places...*and* they...they have a ceremony...they...they filled up their pipes and smoke...make incense... prayers...and after doing that they say..."*alright...young man...we are now ready* to *hear your* story...tell us"...

So the young man...says "I am the boy...that when...quite awhile
back... when we were...moving up...from *way down there*...way down the
Missouri headed this way up the Bighorn...River...when we got to the mountain...where I left...you people...and I...I went to the mountains...and I
went on south from there...quite aways down and come to a place where I
fasted and stayed in one place....I spent all my time there...and finally the
Little People there around close by...come to me...and visit with me and talk
with me...and they advise me to leave that place and come back to...back to
my parents and all of you...and I'm a member of your group....and according
to what I received they call me Burnt Face...and I was disfigured....but those
Little People took those...took those...disfigurations off my face and make
me look different...*so here I am*...I'm the boy who left your camp"...

"Ahhh...ahhh...ahh...hay!...*that's great*"...the chief said..."*alright*...we
will...welcome you back to our camp....you will be with us now...stay with
us...we'll travel on"...so...they accepted him back...they announce...through-
out the camp..."the *young man* is back with us...he is back to his parents...he
is with us now from now on...we will depend on him...when some of you get
sick...call on him...he's been given the power to work and doctor you and
make you get well....he'll be the man we'll call on...as our doctor...among
this group"...

So...sure enough...camp went on...people respect him...anyone that get
sick they would call on him...and he'd...pray for them...doctor them and they
get well...*and they respect* him..."oh...*this man had the power*...we must respect
him...we can't make fun of him no more...no way...anymore"...so as time
went on he finally become a chief...and a great chief from that time on...and
his name was...Burnt Face...

How essential it is to be able to retell one's own, *baaéechichiwaau*, when
you have traveled a life-altering journey. In retelling your story, as *Burnt Face*
has done for me, may others be helped, inspired in some way to better face
their own challenges, and, if wounded, to begin the healing. In retelling one's
own, you renew your kinship with family and friends, with adopted "bros"
and Medicine Fathers, and come to discover the expanded horizons of that
kinship. In retelling my story, may we consider traveling the many differing
paths: the spokes that can reach the same destination, and the hub—both the
external and internal journeys—that some would have us believe are mutually exclusive. In the very act of retelling, *Burnt Face* is lifted off the pages
of this book, no longer a story, but immediate and vital, continuing to doctor the people. That which is spoken aloud, from the heart and in accord
with the ancestors, be it a story or a name, is rekindled and brought forth,
and swirls around you. Having pulled out your most cherished huckleberries
from your cedar-bark basket and laid them out as rocks of your Medicine
Wheel, in this act of retelling your story, you discover a little more of what is
most essential within, and can bring it out in all that you do. Having opened
up your heart, in your retelling, may you hear the "crackling of fire" and

"experience the healing" that comes from the inner journey, or that indivisible convergence of the spirit descending upon you—"those scars taken away," and the spirit coming through you—"reborn." For indeed, the spirit of the Creator, the Little People, the Buffalo, the Bird that is *above* is the spirit that resides *within*. And in retelling one's own, what gifts may await? Ultimately, it is up to each person to cherish his or her particular huckleberries, the special gifts bestowed, and then apply them, as rocks of his or her medicine wheel, to the challenges encountered, choosing the course of his or her journey that comes from the heart. If *Burnt Face* speaks to you, cherish this gift as yours. Surely great stories will come!

As Cliff concludes:

Sometimes I can *sit*...and...hear the crackling of fire...I can hear the humming of the old people...our beds were *all the way* around the room...and the fire and the stove...and somebody over here tells stories...somebody over here...old people...I can remember the *smell* of buckskin...of my grandma sitting there...working on *beadwork*...sometimes *cornhusk bags*...sometimes... combing her hair...she had *long* hair...and just the things that are comforting and warm to a little boy...maybe a hand on my shoulder or let me lay my head on her *lap*...but that crackling of fire...*every time I hear that*...I think of them...*I think* of that room and I'm *quickly* drawn to that room...*quickly* drawn to the things I heard in that room...the stories before *white people* came...what it was like when they were little children...

My brother [Jim] and I lived with my *grandma* for a while...my dad made us *live with* her...and his reasoning behind it was that it was part of our *education* and then he picked up where they left off....

My dad talked about the mountains...about when they would ride *their horses*...they had no transportation there was *no roads*...they rode horseback...*four days on horseback* from here up into the huckleberry mountains and the Clark Fork and the Pend Oreille Country...and he would talk about *how many people* would be going up into the mountains and of the trail...*the trails* would turn to *powder* there was *so many horses* and people going up into the mountains....and I would ask him..."you mean ten fifteen twenty horses?"... and he says..."*hundreds!*"....*people* all *moving* to go up to it...he got to see it...he got to be a part of it...he got to ride on the horses and see the *old people* and their horses with their picking baskets as they *all moved* into the mountains... that *crackling* of that fire *immediately* gives me visual pictures in my mind as he described them...of what it was like....

So that crackling of that fire...*I believe*...every person...*I believe*...has a crackling fire...if they can *just* light it....and if they *can't*...if they are *so wounded*...that the Jesuit took all of that away and their grandmothers gave it up and their grandfathers...their mothers and fathers ashamed of being what they were...and now those children are running around here *lost*...you *see it everyday*...see it everyday in *jails*...see it everyday in *drugs*...*alcohol*...and so...I think that...so many people have a crackling fire...but they *can't light it*...they haven't got the tools to light it....

And *that's where*...I believe...our *Indian names*...our...continuous *oral history*....the handing down of the *significance* of our *beliefs*...the significance of our *prayers*...what ceremonies we *do*...how we *believe so strong* in them...it's *there*...it's in the mountains...it's in the water...it's in the Sweat House...it's in the *songs* of our people...find it...listen to it...that suddenly will become a tool...to create...*enough* energy *to light a fire*....and that *aura* that *surrounds* you...will suddenly become visible...and you'll feel it touch it...taste it...and then you can experience the healing of your *spirit* and your *heart*...that crackling...that fire...that fire that puts you at *ease*...that fire that *heals you*...that fire warms your *spirit* your *heart*...that crackling of *family*...that cracking and popping of *old people*....without that fire we'll be extinguished...forever...and we'll only become a memory...in the pages of somebody's writing....

You are my friend...you are my brother...and the words that we *share*...we understand...and someday...we will sit in each other's *lodge*....and Circling Song...will embrace your *hands*...my brother...Little Red Hawk...to again...share stories...and to *share our fires* and to listen to the *crackling* of each other's fires...because the cracking goes on and on and on and on and on...and it holds us together as a people...as *brothers*...as a Tribe...as a Nation...that crackling sound...of the true spirit...of our hearts...you and me as Indian people....I still my voice on this and hope someday...someone who *reads* this...can light their fire...and hear the crackling...of you and I's fire...I still my voice on these matters today....

NOTES

A sincere *ahókaash* (Crow), *limlemtsh* (Coeur d'Alene), *qe'ci'yéw'yew* (Nez Perce), thank you, to all in the Indian community who have so generously facilitated for my "retelling one's own"—Tom and Susie Yellowtail, John Trehero in memory, Cliff and Lori SiJohn, Rob Moran and Rose Spino, Josiah Blackeagle Pinkham and D'Lisa Penney Pinkham, Phillip Barnaby, Leroy Seth, Silas Whitman, Phillip Cash-Cash, Ed Galindo, Janet and Rayburn Beck, Valerie Jackson, Diane Reynolds, Mike Penney, Sarah Penney, the Native students at the university, and so many others. My heartfelt acknowledgment and thanks to all my family, friends, colleagues, students in the non-Indian community, and especially for their tireless support and prayers—my wife, Mother, sister, uncle, and my son who was given the Indian name, *Awakúikiiaateesh*, "Little Dwarf," by Grandpa Tom, that the Little People always be a part of him. And particular thanks to Suzanne Crawford O'Brien, the "chief of this camp," for allowing me to retell my story for you.

During the second night of Cliff and Lori SiJohn's January 2007 Jump Dance, I had my "give away." With Cliff guiding my way, I spoke to the over one hundred other participants of how wonderful it is now to be able to sing and dance with them, of my healing journey, and of my tremendous gratitude to them for all their prayers. The blankets and other gifts were then distributed.

1. See Rodney Frey, *Stories That Make the World: Oral Literature of the Indian Peoples of the Inland Northwest As Told by Lawrence Aripa, Tom Yellowtail and Other Elders* (Norman: University of Oklahoma Press, 1995): 108–22.

2. See Rodney Frey, *The World of the Crow Indians: As Driftwood Lodges* (Norman: University of Oklahoma Press, 1987).

3. Joseph Epes Brown is a student of the Lakota elder, Black Elk, and author of *The Sacred Pipe: Black Elk's Account of the Seven Rites of the Oglala Sioux* (Norman: University of Oklahoma Press, 1953).

4. Rodney Frey in collaboration with the Schitsu'umsh (Coeur d'Alene), *Landscape Traveled by Coyote and Crane: The World of the Schitsu'umsh (Coeur d'Alene) Indians* (Seattle: University of Washington Press, 2001/2005).

BIBLIOGRAPHY

Brown, Joseph Epes. *The Sacred Pipe: Black Elk's Account of the Seven Rites of the Oglala Sioux*. Norman: University of Oklahoma Press, 1953.

Frey, Rodney. *The World of the Crow Indians: As Driftwood Lodges*. Norman: University of Oklahoma Press, 1987.

Frey, Rodney. *Stories That Make the World: Oral Literature of the Indian Peoples of the Inland Northwest As Told by Lawrence Aripa, Tom Yellowtail, and Other Elders*. Norman: University of Oklahoma Press, 1995.

Frey, Rodney, in collaboration with the Schitsu'umsh (Coeur d'Alene). *Landscape Traveled by Coyote and Crane: The World of the Schitsu'umsh (Coeur d'Alene) Indians*. Seattle: University of Washington Press, 2001/2005.

Frey, Rodney, in collaboration with the Schitsu'umsh (Coeur d'Alene Tribe). *Schitsu'umsh—Lifelong Learning Online*. University of Idaho, and the National Aeronautics and Space Administration, 2002. Available at: http://L3.ed.uidaho.edu/ (accessed February 12, 2008).

Frey, Rodney, in collaboration with the Nimíipuu (Nez Perce Tribe). *Nimíipuu— Lifelong Learning Online*. University of Idaho, and the National Aeronautics and Space Administration, 2002. Available at: http://L3.ed.uidaho.edu/ (accessed February 12, 2008).

Frey, Rodney, in collaboration with the Warm Springs, Wasco and Northern Paiute, Confederated Tribes of Warm Springs. *Warm Springs, Wasco, and Northern Paiute—Lifelong Learning Online*, University of Idaho, and the National Aeronautics and Space Administration, 2003. Available at: http://L3.ed.uidaho.edu/ (accessed February 12, 2008).

Frey, Rodney. "Oral Traditions." In *Companion Guide to the Anthropology of American Indians*, edited by Thomas Biolsi. Malden, MA: Blackwell Publishers, 2004.

Afterword

Thomas J. Csordas

Scholarly work on indigenous North America has changed dramatically over the past century. Concern with American Indian culture was central to the field of anthropology in the United States during its period of development in the early twentieth century. Much of anthropological theory and method was developed in the context of ethnographic and comparative studies of native North American cultures and societies. Much of the earliest work also presumed that American Indian cultures were on the verge of extinction and that ethnographic work must be done to salvage what remained. In the middle of the last century the threat of extinction seemed to have passed, but the main operative concepts included culture contact, acculturation, syncretism, and revitalization. In recent decades this important focus of research has been increasingly neglected and marginalized within anthropology, in part due to the tendency of American anthropologists to valorize ethnographic fieldwork outside of North America. Meanwhile, important scholarship has emerged in the fields of American Indian studies, ethnic studies, and history. Key concepts have become colonialization, missionization, sovereignty, and resistance.

The present volume marks an important moment in the development of scholarship on American Indian cultures, and is prime evidence of how far it has progressed. Most striking is the balance in number between Indian and non-Indian contributors. This kind of balance is the combined result of the increase in numbers of indigenous people trained with the academic skills to produce scholarly literature and cognizance on the part of non-Indian scholars to truly collaborate and share authorial credit with individuals who in a previous era may have been regarded as "assistants" and only received acknowledgement in a footnote. A second and related observation is the balance, as Suzanne Crawford O'Brien asks us to recognize in her introduction, between participatory and theoretical knowledge. This is not to be understood as participant observation in contrast to cultural theory, or as an applied approach in contrast to a theoretical approach, nor again as an indigenous in contrast to Euro-American perspective. Regardless of their ethnic or scholarly backgrounds, contributors to this volume uniformly express the value of participatory knowledge with respect to what it offers in terms of existential insight, immediacy, and engagement. In this light, the role of theoretical knowledge is to contextualize participatory knowledge such that it can be communicated to a wider audience. Third, the contributions exhibit a disciplinary balance insofar as the academic fields represented include American Indian studies, religious studies, sociology, ethnic studies, and a revitalized anthropology specifically in the form of contemporary meaning-centered medical anthropology.

Before reflecting on some of the substantive points made by the contributors, some words are in order on the subject of method. While they are all implicitly in accord methodologically, several contributors are more explicit about their formulations. Thus Jacob declares her allegiance to a Decolonized Method that determines research questions based on recognition of community needs and commitment to the principle that "communities themselves have the wisdom to solve their own problems." Nadeau and Young identify their approach as one grounded in Indigenous Knowledges, while Garoutte and Westcott raise the methodological banner of Radical Indigenism. There is in these formulations both the identification of an alternative epistemological and procedural strategy and a clear assertion of methodological legitimacy vis-à-vis social scientific and biomedical approaches in the scholarly context. There is both intellectual defiance and a profound sense of creativity, integration, and openness, and it is worth pausing to note how these are elaborated.

Indigenous Knowledges, argue Nadeau and Young, are to be distinguished from Traditional Knowledges insofar as they are not restricted to indigenous ideas but extend to anything an indigenous scholar can in good intellectual conscience usefully integrate from other sources. Thus they not only include potential fusion of traditional and western conceptualizations, but in the case of these authors the freedom to collaborate with another who in her own work fuses ecofeminism and postcolonial Christianity. Nadeau and Young reject the distinction between healed and non-healed as reminiscent of the demeaning distinction between civilized and non-civilized, such that the goal of the program they describe becomes leadership training rather than healing. To escape what they call welfare colonialism and coercive tutelage they reject the medicalization implicit in the term Post-Traumatic Stress Disorder, without rejecting the strength of academic scholarship as represented in Arthur Kleinman's concept of social suffering and Ignacio Martin-Baro's concept of psychosocial trauma. For Garoutte and Westcott, Radical Indigenism asserts equivalence in generating knowledge between biomedicine and indigenous medicine, whereas the opposed strategy of Health Literacy education connotes the one-way adoption of biomedical knowledge by community members. The contribution of indigenous data/stories is not to "reveal something beyond themselves" on a theoretical level; instead the researcher's goal is to show what they say "in a way that can be heard." In emphasizing features of orality, equality, and creativity in their method, the result is not only to transform the researcher/informant relationship into that of facilitator/interlocutor, but to assert that the interview itself is not the data, but the result, of the study.

Along with the adoption of these methodological stances, the authors generally tend to avoid the term *revitalization* associated with the academic theory of social and religious movements. Kelley borrows from music to talk about the "reprise" of identity in the sense of a "rearticulation of an earlier theme whose basic elements remained present throughout." Petrillo advocates "retraditionalization" in the sense that as healing includes the need "to find ways to come together in the renewal of identity associated with retraditionalization." She elaborates the Indian meaning of traditional as including not only material from the past, but the practice of repetition and the sense of what is proper or correct. Nadeau and Young thematize "regeneration" in the direction of a sacred vitality obtained through embodied practice and somatic metaphors deployed in song/voice and dance/movement as a remedy to a "spiritual and moral problem caused by political violence." Taken together, these attitudes toward tradition in scholarly method and in healing practice represent an important moment of identity. Is the sentence "I am a Traditional person," typed into a computer and sent as an email, somehow paradoxical, a contradiction in terms? Not only must one answer in the negative, but what is truly radical is the implicit assertion that the legitimacy of eclecticism is already pre-given in one's indigenous identity and thus one can collaborate or innovate freely.

Within this methodological milieu, Suzanne Crawford O'Brien not only frames the collection elegantly in terms of embodied experience and postcolonialism, participatory and theoretical knowledge, but also masterfully organizes and presents the chapters in a logical and compelling sequence. It is worth observing that across all the chapters we can also identify a strikingly coherent set of four problems (soul wounds) and an equally coherent set of four solutions (remedies). The authors very explicitly address the problems of diabetes, cancer, alcohol, and violence. To a certain extent these are understood as legacies of conquest and colonialism, white man's diseases. Kelley refers to alcoholism as an "opportunistic infection related to the overall disease of colonialism." Intimate violence in the domestic sphere is coterminous with the violence of colonialism and racism as Nadeau and Young describe them. Insofar as having a name is not an arbitrary fact of one's birth but a feature that substantively defines one's identity, Frey and colleagues identify a culturally specific violence in the colonial practice of renaming Indians with Anglophone names.

The notion of historical trauma now so often invoked to account for such soul wounds does not require positing the existence of a "group mind" or communal spirit, though in practice these often seem to be implied. Concrete consequences of conquest, colonization, slavery, or genocide persist in the lives of subsequent generations, relations between groups of perpetrators and victims remain colored by the violence, and critical events serve as points of reference for collective discourse. The soul wound is a spiritual and poetic concept, and as such has the capacity to be romanticized. In more mundane terms, it boils down to humiliation. This lends the traditional discourse of respect as core cultural value a particular poignancy, sometimes charged with a heightened expectation of and hyper vigilance for signs of disrespect. It lends a traditional concern with identity and self-worth the weight and urgency of a therapeutics relevant to both individual and collectivity.

Michelle Jacob discusses this in terms of W.E.B. Du Bois's concept of double consciousness. She does not quite know what to do with the apparent irony of feeling like she is rescuing traditional salmon fishermen, who are after all the practical and symbolic guarantors of a healthy traditional diet, from a long night of drinking carbonated beverages, or with the apparent irony of observing the obesity of the exercise leader whose aim is to promote a healthy lifestyle. Jacob recognizes obstacles to healing not only in the constraints imposed by structural violence but those created by complacency, and that there is at times a resistance not only to colonization, but to responsibility for one's personal well-being. With respect to diabetes, the latter is evident in the attitude observed by Jacob that "I'll eat what I want to, and I won't let the white man tell me what's healthy and what's not." Kelley observes something similar with respect to attributing drunken behavior to alcohol itself, without blame or remorse on the part of the individual drinker.

Standing equally explicitly over against these soul wounds, we find spirituality, stories, identity, and community lining up on the side of healing. To a certain extent these are understood as resistance to colonialism. Spirituality for Petrillo includes indigenous religions, Ghost Dance, Native American Church, Sundance, and Christianity. She makes a point of reinterpreting her own understanding of a story about a young boy's first Sundance as an instance of elders corroborating one another's judgment rather than as an implicit gender inequality in which female judgment must be legitimized by male authority. Crawford O'Brien folds in the Indian Shaker Church and Longhouse Spirit Dancing. The Indian Shaker Church was successful because it understood the self as relational and health as maintaining relations. As Jacob, Crawford O'Brien, and Nadeau and Young emphasize in their chapters, the healing process has to do with cultivation of embodied self, practice, and experience as much as with spirituality.

The chapters illustrating the healing power of stories add a particularly compelling dimension to this set of papers. The story of the woman who lost her husband told by Garroutte and Westcott and the story of the boy who burnt his face as told by Frey, Yellowtail, and SiJohn demonstrate how sacred narratives can be efficacious not only in the academically recognized sense of the rhetoric of ritual performance but insofar as they can be integrated into the existential fabric of a person's life in an emotionally compelling way over a long period of time. Both narratives interweave voices across generations and use personal experience without self-indulgence. Whether one is an Indian (Young) or a non-Indian (Frey), the story itself is a living being (Garroutte and Westcott), and sacred narratives become thoroughly integrated into individual narratives "not just as myth or entertainment but as how you walk this life because of the First People who come alive in the story" (Frey et al.). These include relationships with people, tribes, land, ancestors, animals, plants, stories, and with illness itself. As Crawford O'Brien observes, "Acting with generosity, respect, and kindness was, in a sense, preventive medicine." Sickness is both a failure to fulfill one's vocation as expected by the spiritual powers and the result of disrupted relations with spirits or people. Garroutte and Westcott emphasize that one listens to and learns from the "voice" of illness as in the relationship of student to teacher. This is profoundly the case in the story of the woman who went deeply into the grief of her bereavement, a therapy made possible and effective by the support of her community, and that stands as a critical alternative to medication, addiction, alcohol, or prematurely finding a new spouse. The one who is healed in turn receives a gift to be used to benefit the community, as the widow becomes a basketmaker and the burnt-faced boy becomes a healer.

Integration between indigenous healing and biomedicine is a recurring theme closely related to the integration between western scholarship and indigenous knowledge that I mentioned above. Schwarz summarizes the view of biomedicine as "potentially beneficial, but as aggressive, painful, and spiritually bereft." In a similar spirit, Garroutte and Westcott record the sentiment that "medicine doesn't see the storyline." Yet Crawford O'Brien describes the positive possibilities inherent in the contemporaneous movement among tribes to take over conventional health care from the Indian Health Service. Schwarz notes that examining indigenous understandings of the cause of disease can give clues about the moral and political landscape, in an approach that explicitly emphasizes medical pluralism in a colonial context. One might have a traditional healing ritual prior to medical treatment to affirm one's identity and protect one in a situation of risk, as well as after medical treatment in order to consolidate its effects and cover the spiritual dimension it neglects, and treatment is customized to the individual in a way that is more particular than biomedicine is perceived as doing. Kelley discusses American Indian responses to alcohol abuse in historical context and with respect to the integration of western and indigenous healing through the Longhouse tradition of Handsome Lake, the Native American Church, Alcoholics Anonymous, Wellbriety, the Red Road, and the White Bison movement. Crawford O'Brien describes the SPIPA Women and Girls' Gathering and its intensely eclectic intermingling of western and eastern, holistic and indigenous spiritualities. Not only is it striking that workshops on culturally distinct healing practice take place side by side, but that addressing the most intimate level of everyday life, medicine bags are handcrafted to serve as condom carriers. I must repeat that this innovative eclecticism on the level of healing practice is parallel to the above-mentioned methodological eclecticism on the level of scholarship. The implicit refusal to grant scholarly knowledge a status that is somehow pure and above such fusion of knowledges is, I think, part of the point.

In its emphasis on healing, this volume has its finger on the pulse of the most critical issues in contemporary American Indian life. There is much to be healed, and as the chapters of this book attest, not only with respect to the illnesses of individuals but also to the soul wounds of cultures and the identities of peoples. American Indians and other so-called "fourth world nations" territorially embedded in a dominant polity and cultural milieu have nothing to do with the popular scholarly concept of postcolonialism, since in their cases to be colonized is virtually a permanent and irreversible circumstance (a similar point is made in the chapter by Schwarz). Under such conditions the self-determination of a people is undermined when sovereignty is conflated with bureaucracy, and the territorial integrity of a people is compromised when its land can still be referred to as a reservation. Resistance can be about healing or hatred; Petrillo cites Lakota scholar Elizabeth Cook-Lynn who recognizes that hatred from others, for others, and for oneself are all potential consequences of racism and colonialism. Other indigenous peoples are not exempt, and operating at right angles to the tension between resistance to domination and integration of positive features of the dominant culture is the tension between pan-Indian solidarity and intertribal animosity (mentioned only once in this volume, by Kelley).

It must not remain unsaid that there exists an ethos of bitterness and a pragmatics of suspicion that circulate as undercurrents in contemporary American Indian life and occasionally rise to the surface in the form of counter-racist hostility. Not to bring this into the open runs counter to the collaborative spirit of this volume, and risks a perpetuation of romanticism in the relation between Indian and non-Indian. As inimical to healing and as damaging as this bitterness and suspicion may be on the interpersonal level, they can readily be understood as another consequence of colonialism. Yet when they remain unacknowledged and unanalyzed they undoubtedly create interpersonal conflicts among people who are committed to coexistence and mutual respect between cultures. The Navajo who retraces the path of the Long Walk into captivity of the 1860s as a form of pilgrimage is simultaneously commemorating their legacy and reexperiencing their soul wound, simultaneously honoring his forebears and reliving their humiliation. The challenge and risk for such a person is that of making meaning of the existential immediacy of that embodied act so that it is in fact incorporated as healing and not as trauma, as being purged of humiliation rather than poisoned by bitterness.

The most intimate moment in my career as an ethnographer in the Navajo Nation was not when I was "included" in activities as a "friend," but the moment when an eminent Native American Church road man and World War II Codetalker told me that in fact he hated white people. As a white person, I have never experienced such an explicit moment of trust and respect, knowing that it must not have been easy for him to say such a thing out loud to me. In such a moment it is clear that the legitimate expectation of human respect that comes from connecting with the wellsprings of individual and collective dignity is undermined when respect is defined as flowing unidirectionally in the present from white people to Indian people and not reciprocally between them. The dialectic of respect and racism is not a conflict that lies solely in the relation between white people and Indian people, but within the souls of each of us.

Index

About the Editor and Contributors

EDITOR

SUZANNE J. CRAWFORD O'BRIEN received her PhD in Religious Studies from the University of California–Santa Barbara in 2003. She is currently Assistant Professor of Religion and Culture and chair of the Global Studies Program at Pacific Lutheran University in Tacoma, WA. Her previous publications include *Native American Religious Traditions* (2007), and the 3 volume *American Indian Religious Traditions: An Encyclopedia* (2005), coedited with Dennis Kelley. Her work is also included in *Repatriation Reader: Who Owns Native American Remains?*, edited by Devon Mihesuah (2000), and in academic journals such as the *Journal of Ritual Studies*, and *Material Religion: A Journal of Objects, Art, and Belief.*

CONTRIBUTORS

THOMAS J. CSORDAS is Professor of Anthropology at the University of California–San Diego. His research interests include anthropological theory, comparative religion, medical and psychological anthropology, cultural phenomenology and embodiment, globalization and social change, and language and culture. He has conducted fieldwork funded by the National Institute of Mental Health on the Catholic Charismatic Renewal movement, and among Navajo Indians. He has served as coeditor (with Janis Jenkins) of Ethos: *Journal of the Society for Psychological Anthropology* (1996–2001) and as president of the Society for the Anthropology of Religion (1998–2002). Among his publications are *The Sacred Self: A Cultural Phenomenology of Charismatic Healing* (1994); (edited) *Embodiment and Experience: The Existential Ground of Culture and Self* (1994). *Language, Charisma, and Creativity: Ritual Life in the Catholic Charismatic Renewal* (1997; paperback 2002); and *Body/Meaning/Healing* (2002).

RODNEY FREY is Professor of American Indian Studies and Anthropology at the University of Idaho, having received his PhD in Cultural Anthropology from the University of Colorado in 1979. Among his primary teachers, and to whom he is indebted, are Tom and Susie Yellowtail (Crow), Lawrence Aripa (Coeur d'Alene), Cliff SiJohn (Coeur d'Alene), Alvin Howe (Crow), and Rob and Rose Moran (Turtle Mountain Chippewa and Warm Springs). His previous publications include *Landscape Traveled by Coyote and Crane: The World of the Schitsu'Umsh Coeur d'Alene Indians* (2001), *Stories That Make the World: Oral Literature of the Indian Peoples of the Inland Northwest* (1995), and *The World of the Crow Indians: As Driftwood Lodges* (1987).

EVA MARIE GARROUTTE is an enrolled citizen of the Cherokee Nation and a tenured, associate professor of sociology at Boston College. She also holds a faculty position with the Research Center for Minority Aging Research/ Native Elder Resource Center at the University of Colorado-Denver Health Sciences Center, a nationally known center for the study of Native American health. Publications include a book, *Real Indians: Identity and the Survival of Native America* (2003), and various articles in sociological and health-related journals. Current work, funded by the National Institute on Aging, examines medical communication needs among Native American older adults.

MICHELLE M. JACOB (Yakama) received her PhD in Sociology with an emphasis in human development and Women's Studies from the University of California–Santa Barbara in 2004. She is currently Assistant Professor of Ethnic Studies at the University of San Diego. She also holds an MA in Sociological Practice from California State University San Marcos. Her research is focused on her own reservation community, to better understand, treat, and prevent health problems such as obesity, diabetes, and cardiovascular disease. Additionally, she is a member of a San Diego County network aimed at creating educational environments that are more suited to indigenous peoples' needs.

DENNIS F. KELLEY (Chumash) received his PhD from the Department of Religious Studies at the University of California–Santa Barbara. He is currently an Assistant Professor with a joint appointment in Religious Studies and American Indian Studies at Iowa State University. Recent publications include the 3 volume *American Indian Religious Traditions: An Encyclopedia* (2005), coedited with Suzanne Crawford, and "The Politics of Death and Burial in Native California," in *Death and Religion in a Changing World*, edited by Kathleen Garces-Foley (2005).

DENISE NADEAU is acting director of the Interfaith Summer Institute for Justice, Peace and Social Movements at Simon Fraser University in Vancouver, Canada. She has a Doctorate of Ministry from San Francisco Theological Seminary. Her publications include *Counting Our Victories: Popular Education and Organizing* (2001), "Educating Bodies for Self-determination: A Decolonizing Strategy," *Canadian Journal of Native Education* (Vol. 29: 2006), coauthored with Alannah Young; and "Restoring Relationship: A Theology of Reparations as Gift," in *Feminist Theology with a Canadian Accent*, edited by Mary Anne Beavis (2008).

LARISSA PETRILLO received her PhD in Interdisciplinary Studies from the University of British Columbia in 2001. She is currently adjunct faculty in the English Department at the University of British Columbia, Vancouver, British Columbia, and is the author of *Being Lakota: Identity and Tradition on the Pine Ridge Reservation* (2007).

CLIFF SIJOHN is a spiritual leader of the Coeur d'Alene Tribe, born and raised on the Coeur d'Alene Indian Reservation of Idaho. His Indian name is Circling Song. A Vietnam veteran, Cliff is the Director of Cultural Affairs for his Tribe. Besides being the lead singer in his family's drum, the "Pierced Heart Singers," Cliff is also an accomplished traditional Indian flute player and storyteller.

INÉS TALAMANTEZ (Mescalero Apache) is Associate Professor of Religious Studies at the University of California–Santa Barbara. She received her PhD in Anthropology, Linguistics, and Comparative Literature from the University of California–San Diego. Dr. Talamantez is managing editor of *New Scholar: An Americanist Review*, has written two books on Native American oral traditions, and most recently coedited, *Teaching Religion and Healing* (2006). Her book *Isánáklésh Gotal: Introducing Apache Girls to the World of Spiritual and Cultural Values*, is forthcoming.

MAUREEN TRUDELLE SCHWARZ received her PhD in Anthropology from the University of Washington in 1995. She is currently Associate Professor of Anthropology in the Maxwell School of Citizenship and Public Affairs at Syracuse University. Her previous publications include *Molded in the Image of Changing Woman: Navajo Views on the Human Body and Personhood* (1997) and *Blood and Voice: Navajo Women Ceremonial Practitioners* (2003). She has published in a variety of academic journals including *American Anthropologist*, *Visual Anthropology*, *American Ethnologist*, and *Ethnohistory*.

KATHLEEN DELORES WESTCOTT was born in 1946 into the Turtle Clan of the Anishnaabe people and is enrolled at the White Earth Reservation, Mississippi Band. She is Anishnaabe/Cree and French Canadian on her mother's side and Scotch-Irish on her father's side. She received a Master's in art therapy from the University of Wisconsin–Superior. She describes her occupation as healer, teacher, and creator of handwork; she is known in her community as one who does her work in accordance with *bimaadizinwin*, the traditional spiritual principles of an Anishnaabe lifeway.

Kathleen lives in Brimson, Minnesota on several acres of heavily logged boreal forest. Her vision is to restore this land, thus providing for the return of plants that have played a key role in maintaining physical, mental, and spiritual health among the Anishnaabe people for many generations. Kathleen's two children have given her one grandson and one granddaughter, whom she engages through storytelling and song in this vision.

THOMAS YELLOWTAIL was born on the Crow Reservation of Montana in 1903. His Indian names were Medicine Rock Chief and Fire Heart. Tom was a deeply spiritual man, an *akbaalia,* "one who doctors" and "ran" the Sundances for his people. He always found a tremendous joy in sharing his oral traditions with his grandkids. Tom Yellowtail passed on "to the other side camp" in 1993.

ALANNAH EARL YOUNG is Swampy Cree (Opaskwayak) and Anishnabe (Peguis) and received her Masters of Arts in Educational Studies from University of British Columbia. She is an advisor and trainer with University of British Columbia's First Nations House of Learning. Her current work has been developing and delivering holistic programming that combines interfaith approaches to address somatic social justice with reaffirming Indigenous Leadership and Sovereignty.